**DO NOT REMOVE
CARDS FROM POCKET**

No. 1802
$19.95

THE
KAYPRO®
PLAIN & SIMPLE

BY WILLIAM HOUZE & DAVID LENFEST

TAB BOOKS Inc.
BLUE RIDGE SUMMIT, PA. 17214

KAYPRO and Suprterm are registered trademarks of KAYPRO Corporation, Inc.
Perfect Writer™, Perfect Speller™, Perfect Calc™, and Perfect Filer™ are trademarks of Perfect Software, Inc.
CP/M is a registered trademark of Digital Research, Inc.
co-POWER 88 is a registered trademark of SWP, Inc.
MicroPro, WordStar, MailMerge, and SuperSort are registered trademarks of MicroPro International Corporation. CalcStar, DataStar, and ReportStar are trademarks of MicroPro International Corporation.
The WORD Plus™ is a trademark of Oasis Systems, Inc.
dBASE II is a trademark of Ashton — Tate, Inc.
Hayes is a registered trademark of Hayes Microcomputer Products, Inc.
Profitplan and Microplan are trademarks of Chang Laboratories, Inc.
MS-DOS is a registered trademark of Microsoft Consumer Products.
Epson is a trademark of Epson America, Inc.
J-CAT is a trademark of Novation, Inc.
Signalman Mark I is a trademark of Anchor Automation Inc.

Disclaimer: the opinions in this book are strictly those of the authors, and they do not necessarily represent the views of any of the manufacturers listed in the trademark list, or any other company.

FIRST EDITION

FIRST PRINTING

Copyright © 1984 by William Houze and David Lenfest

Printed in the United States of America

Reproduction or publication of the content in any manner, without express permission of the publisher, is prohibited. No liability is assumed with respect to the use of the information herein.

Library of Congress Cataloging in Publication Data

Houze, William
The Kaypro—plain and simple.

Includes index.
1. Kaypro computers. I. Lenfest, David
II. Title.
QA76.8.K38H68   1984   001.64   84-8532
ISBN 0-8306-0802-8
ISBN 0-8306-1802-3 (pbk.)

Photography by R.S. Powers, San Diego, California.

Cover photograph courtesy of KAYPRO Corporation.

7080187

Contents

Acknowledgments

We would like to thank various people at KAYPRO, who have helped us in many ways: Andrew Kay and David Kay, Geoffrey Soule, Margaret Phanes, and Cliff Odendhal—all of whom have been gracious and cooperative in the midst of the intense and exciting growth of their corporation.

Thanks also to SWP, Inc., of Arlington, Texas, for the use of a co-POWER 88 board, and to Marti Shotwell of MBS Computers in Denver, whose staff installed it in our KAYPRO 4.

Finally, many thanks to Linda K. Woods, Geoff Houze, and to Nick Bavaro of CW Electronic Sales in Denver, for their help and good advice in the last stages of this project.

Introduction: A Plan for This Book

We are aware that buyers of computers and software, particularly first-timers, can experience extraordinary frustration in trying to operate their first system. People otherwise professionally highly competent are often reduced to tears—and other forms of impotent rage—by this expensive machine that won't work for them.

With well-tested systems like the KAYPRO and most of its bundled software, the blame usually lands on the "documentation," also known as the instructions that are supposed to tell you how to get the thing running, so you can settle down to the job you bought it to do for you. We have made the assumption that you want to get up and running as quickly as possible, with no "technobabble" creating interference between you and that job you want done. After all, you spent your money to achieve greater efficiency; our goal in this book is to get you there as quickly as possible.

As professional writers who have scribbled in a number of different arenas, and as people who have, over the years, studied writing and tried to teach others the craft, we have decided to tackle the problem of how to tell an intelligent, professional person— that's you, the buyer of a new KAYPRO—how to get the thing out of the box, how to set it up, how to drag it around the countryside, and how to run the different programs with a minimum of distraction. You don't have to learn how to program and you don't have to get an MSEE to make this tool work for you.

We have been guided partly by our commitment to the principles of document design: that the language and the shape of the book should not get in the way. The keys to good design are plain language and structured "documentation." *Plain language* was defined by Hemingway (among others) when he said, "Never use a fifty-cent word when a five-cent one will do the job." *Structured documentation* is a complex theory of documentation (what this book is up to—documenting), and three of its principles to which we subscribe are:

1) Users (that's you) are not centrally interested in facts except as they relate to achieving tasks, procedures, or the pursuit of objectives.
2) A loss of linearity—having to go from the front of the book to the back, or to another book—is a flaw in the documentation.
3) The documentation (our book in this case) is a *program* for the reader.

That means we hope we have established, through the order of this book, a program that will take you from your computer dealer to running any of the packaged software with reasonable success. Please take a look at Fig. I-1 to see an "interactive table of contents" that shows you the learning path we have described in this book. Our thought is that you need to work your way through the first seven chapters to be able to handle the KAYPRO and its operating system with reasonable success and safety. Chapter 8, "Features of the Bundled Software," works as a signpost; you may proceed to any one of the software packages from there, in any order you choose.

Our primary innovation in this book is our use of an *interactive format*. David Lenfest began to evolve this method of instruction for computer documentation from his work in designing and scripting interactive video instruction projects. That method of teaching people in video is well-developed, and David had the advantage of learning from others who had already blazed a trial in video.

The primary advantage of interactive video training is that the learner *must* become involved in the learning process. The system will not run without the responses of the learner. That is not true in print, however, and the challenge of the printed page was to create a form of dialogue that could involve the learner equally with the routines on the computer and the instructions being given in the book.

Interactive dialogue has the advantage of being direct, and of giving the learner constant feedback for every step or keystroke taken with the computer. It is too ambitious to say that it is a fail-safe method, but it appears to have the virtue of greater clarity than most forms of narrative. This written interactive method depends on an "if . . . then" kind of logic, where the reader is presented with a statement of the form "If you want to . . ." in the left column and a "then *type* or *enter*" in the right column. The first line is then answered in the left column with a "*See* . . ." echoing what the user sees on the screen. That confirmation is followed by the next action it is necessary to take to complete the routine successfully. The steps in all routines are numbered sequentially, so that the reader knows on entering a routine that it has 2, or 20, or 200 steps.

The important point here is that there is no way to get lost or to miss a critical middle step if you follow the numbers. The process of following the routines with your own actions on your own computer is reminiscent of the children's game Simon Says— except that there are no false steps or attempts to lose anyone. Indeed, the point is to keep everybody on board as they learn by doing.

We know that people do not read instructional manuals in the same way that they would read a novel or a book of nonfiction. It is also well known that technical manuals are used as reference tools. "When all else fails, read the manual" is a truism in the field of technical writing; the interactive method has the advantage of being modular, so that you can pick and choose different sections with which you need to work.

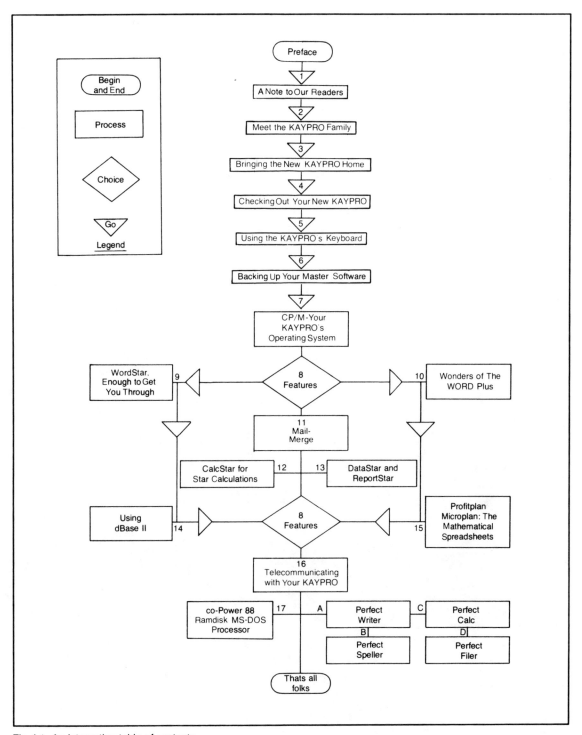

Fig. I-1. An interactive table of contents.

These are step-through procedures which we have followed ourselves, so that we *know* that they work. That's the bottom line question for us—does it work? We tell you when it doesn't. We wish you the best of luck with your KAYPRO and its bundled software. It is an impressive machine, and for the first-time user of a computer it represents an imposing and significant step into the world of personal and business computers.

Chapter 1

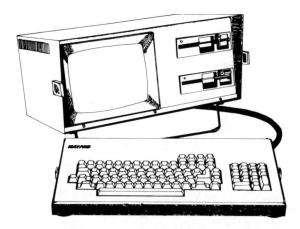

A Note to Our Readers

Our aim in writing this book has been to make using your KAYPRO and its accompanying software as easy as possible. The typical reader whom we have imagined is an intelligent person who has purchased a KAYPRO to solve a particular problem, or to answer one or more needs, and who has relatively little experience with computers. We have visualized this person as an individual with a job to be done.

A writer, for instance, might want a word processing capability that he or she can carry around. We know that the KAYPRO is popular with Hollywood screenwriters who must go out on location while a film is being shot. Another class of person would be the independent businessperson who needs the capabilities of a spreadsheet (and there are several flavors of finance management in the KAYPRO package) to keep track of a quickly growing business, and who cannot (yet) afford a bookkeeper or an accountant. The user could also be someone who has to file taxes quarterly, and who has to keep track of income and expenditures constantly to keep the IRS happy. We hope that the KAYPRO and its packaged software will make all that work easier for those people.

We have assumed that the typical buyer of a KAYPRO is new to computers, and that this person does not have a scientific or an engineering background. We feel that these people can learn to run this computer and the packaged systems easily if the instructions are presented in measured steps that are easy memory "bytes." This audience is different from the engineering community and the young "hackers" who are so fast on the tracks and in the sectors. The KAYPRO is excellent for them, too, and they need less help than the first group. It is for this second group that three kinds of BASIC (a major programming language) have been bundled with the KAYPRO. We will be talking far less to these people than we will to the first group—intelligent people who are successful in their own fields and who come to the computer for the first time.

Many of these people suffer from "computer phobia," and it is our contention that good instruction can go a long way toward dispelling that "phobia." Our primary question with each program has been, "What does our first group of readers need to know to get this program up and running at an adequate level?" We hope that our descriptions of the routines will succeed in helping to do that. After people reach that first plateau, and they want to broaden their knowledge, then they can use the bundled manuals for reference guides.

Beyond that primary question and a strong memory of our own frustrations, we have been guided by principles of document design and plain language. Following Hemingway's advice, we have used five-cent words wherever possible. And, to some extent, we have followed some of the principles of structured documentation. The first is that this book is a program for the reader. The second is that a loss of linearity is a flaw in the documentation. That means that every time you change direction to go from the front to the back, or to reread an unclear sentence, our book declines in value. We assume, further, that the first group of readers (the majority of them) is interested in facts about the KAYPRO and its programs only as they relate to the pursuit of their objectives, running the KAYPRO as effortlessly as they drive their cars.

We have paid some attention to General Murphy, the man who said, "Anything that can go wrong, will." The General has an army, and his troops are always lurking around when you least expect them. This is particularly true at the beginning of your work with the KAYPRO (or any other machine), and we hope that this book will help you to fight them off. Another of Murphy's Laws we think true is, "Assumption is the mother of all mistakes." We have tried to assume nothing about the operation of your KAYPRO and its software. If you also assume nothing, you can stay in good shape.

We welcome feedback from our readers about how we could have made the book more useful for them, or even about parts that they liked. In some cases, we have followed an "interactive" format which will take you through step-by-step procedures to the core of information you need to run a program. The "interactive" format stems from the typical question by a first-time user, "Where am I?" To answer that question our interactive sections use numbered step-through routines. In that way you can look at any one routine and know that it takes four or twenty or whatever number of steps, and you can track yourself that way. The computer is a highly procedural and (some might say) a simple-minded machine. It does what it is programmed to do, for the most part, and our interactive routines guide you through these programs as accurately as possible.

We wish you the best of luck with the KAYPRO. It's a champ of a machine, and we would like to share some of the KAYPRO's history.

The KAYPRO Family

The KAYPRO comes from a family tradition that began when Andy Kay established Non-Linear Systems, Inc., in 1953. Shortly thereafter, NLS developed and marketed the first digital voltmeter. In June of 1982, Andy Kay and his son, David Kay, brought out the first KAYPRO portable computer. By 1983, NLS had a solid reputation as the producer of highly reliable, portable electronic test equipment, and NLS was renamed KAYPRO

Computers, Inc. In the computer business that's called *hardware*, and KAYPRO Inc., is known to make very good hardware. That's why there's a bunch of it flying around every time the space shuttle *Columbia* goes up. That reputation has continued, and it has broadened with the KAYPRO computer.

The instant success of the KAYPRO II in 1982 was due largely to its combination of tough and tested hardware, bundled software, and competitive price. That combination made it a hard machine to beat—as much of the competition has discovered. As important as these three fundamentals are, and as important as marketing strategy is in a highly competitive industry, a computer catches on with the buying public because it develops a reputation for staying dependable and for growing with its users and the market. Over 100,000 KAYPRO buyers have confirmed the Kays' philosophy of designing and delivering maximum product for the dollar. We have used three of the KAYPROS (the 2, the 4, and the 10) in writing this book, and we think they are terrific. We have written about the complete product line at present: the KAYPRO 2, 4, and the 10. The Interactive Table of Contents in Fig. I-1 is a menu (in the computer sense) of the issues we have covered.

Now it's time to move on to the next chapter and the beginning of your productive experience with the KAYPRO computer family.

Chapter 2

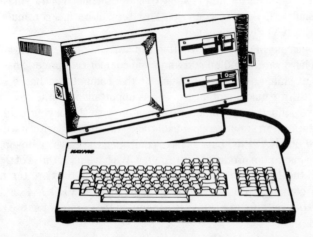

Meet the KAYPRO Family

Before we introduce you to the KAYPRO family of microcomputers, we first want to call your attention to the following bit of friendly advice:

Do not try to run your software (or even turn on your KAYPRO) until you have read this chapter and what follows in Chapters 3, 4, and 6. Following this bit of advice will ensure that you have backed up your master software properly, and that you know how to turn your KAYPRO 2, 4, and 10 on and off safely. This is especially crucial for KAYPRO 10 owners who must know how to run the SAFETY program before turning ON their KAYPRO 10; otherwise, they run the risk of physically damaging the 10's hard disk if they turn OFF the 10 without first having run the SAFETY program, and of losing the bundled software that the factory placed on the hard disk.

The KAYPRO 2, 4, and 10 are outwardly similar in most respects, but inside they differ in important ways. First, let's take a quick tour of their exterior features, getting down some of the important nomenclature as we do so.

Figures 2-1 and 2-2 depict the front and back of the KAYPRO 2 and 4. Look at the photos carefully, noting the location of the following features.

Fig. 2-1. Front of the KAYPRO 2 and 4. Photo by R.S. Powers.

- The two horizontal disk drive slots A and B, from top down as you look at the console, and their respective red indicator (drive active) lights.
- The 9-inch diagonal console or cathode ray tube (CRT).
- The red POWER ON/OFF indicator light.
- The keyboard and its umbilical cord, which connects the keyboard to the computer proper.

Fig. 2-2. Back of the KAYPRO 2 and 4. Photo by R.S. Powers.

On the back of the KAYPRO 2 and 4 (Fig. 2-2), you will find:

- The carrying handle.
- The black ON/OFF switch.
- The hardware system red Reset button.
- The console brightness control knob.
- The fuse.
- The power cord.
- The (J3) input port for the keyboard umbilical.
- Two input/output ports (J4 and J5) for serial cable connection to a modem, a telecommunications device, or to a serial printer; and an output-only port (J2) for parallel Centronics cable connection to parallel printers *only*.

Figures 2-3 and 2-4 depict the front and back of the KAYPRO 10, which has many of the same features as the 2 and 4—but some important differences as well. Note the following front-panel features:

- The single disk drive slot and its red indicator (drive active) light. This disk drive slot is called Drive C.
- The 10 MB READY red indicator light.
- The keyboard and its umbilical to the CPU.

Fig. 2-3. Front of the KAYPRO 10. Photo by R.S. Powers.

Fig. 2-4. Back of the KAYPRO 10. Photo by R.S. Powers.

And on the back:

- The carrying handle.
- The black ON/OFF switch.
- The hardware system's red Reset button.
- The fuse.
- The power cord.
- The console brightness control knob.
- The input port (J5) for the keyboard umbilical.
- The input/output port (J2) for a light pen connection.
- The input/output serial port (J3) for connecting a modem.
- The output serial port (J4) for connection to a serial printer only.
- The output Centronics port (J6), for connection to a parallel printer *only*.

So much for the physical, things-that-you-can-see-and-easily-locate external features of the 2, 4. and 10. Now let's turn our attention to Table 2-1, which shows other design and operational specifications.

You may wonder about the adjective "standard" in the title of the table. (If you did not, perhaps you should have.) In any case, let us say this right up-front: all factory shipped KAYPRO 2s, 4s, and 10s are standard in that they meet the hardware specifications indicated in Table 2-1 in mid-1984. (The KAYPRO 2 and the earlier KAYPRO 4 were bundled with different software, and they had slightly different features.) There are also options available to you now.

For a case in point, the KAYPRO 2 and 4 can now be modified at the factory, or by

Table 2-1. KAYPRO Standard Hardware.

	KAYPRO 2	KAYPRO 4	KAYPRO 10
Microprocessor	Z-80A 4.0 MHz	Z-80A 4.0 MHz	Z-80A 4.0 MHz
RAM	64K	64K	64K
Disk Drives	2 Single-Sided, Double-Density	2 Double-Sided, Double-Density	1 Double-Sided, Double-Density 1 Hard Disk
Storage Capacity (Formatted)	191K Per Disk	392K Per Disk	392K (Floppy) 8.9M (Hard Disk)
Monitor	9″, Non-Glare	9″, Non-Glare	9″, Non-Glare
Screen	25 Line × 80 Column Green Phosphor	25 Line × 80 Column Green Phosphor	25 Line × 80 Column Green Phosphor
Business Graphics	100 × 160 Resolution	100 × 160 Resolution	100 × 160 Resolution
Keyboard	Typewriter Style with Numeric Pad 18 Programmable Keys	Typewriter Style with Numeric Pad 18 Programmable Keys	Typewriter Style with Numeric Pad 18 Programmable Keys
Real Time Clock/Calendar	—	5 Year Battery Back-Up	—
Built-In Modem	—	300 Baud Auto: Dial, Answer	—
Input/Output Connections	2 RS-232C Serial 1 Centronics Parallel	2 RS-232C Serial 1 Centronics Parallel	2 RS-232C Serial 1 Centronics Parallel
Size	8½″ × 18¾″ 16⅜″	8½″ × 18¾″ 16⅜″	8½″ × 18¾″ × 16⅜″
Weight	26 Pounds	26 Pounds	31 Pounds

your dealer, to make them IBM PC format and data compatible. How? By the installation of the co-POWER 88 board. As of July, 1984, the manufacturer of the co-POWER 88 was not offering a similar modification for the 10, but check with your authorized KAYPRO dealer to see if this product is available. This means adding (at additional cost) a keyboard-controlled selection option that will make the KAYPRO operate as an 8- or 16-bit microcomputer; you can then choose from not one but *three* different operating systems. You not only get the "standard" 8-bit Z80A chip and its CP/M-operating system, but also the 16-bit 8088 chip and the CP/M-86 operating system (for still more money). Moreover, the MS/DOS operating system is also available. The advantage to you? Well, see Chapter 17 for more information.

STANDARD HARDWARE

Here are some observations of interest concerning selected line-item information from Table 2-1.

RAM Capacity and Storage/Retrieval Speed. The 64,000-bit storage capacity of the temporary memory "bin," the *random access memory* (RAM), is adequate for almost all data and text processing tasks you will undertake. The speed at which the 2 and 4 access data is quite acceptable and will meet the data and text processing needs of most users. The KAYPRO 10 is faster in its ability to store and retrieve data than are the 2 and 4. This additional speed is one of the inherent advantages of a hard disk system over those available in a "soft" or floppy disk storage/retrieval system. The hard disk in the KAYPRO 10 is simply able to locate and display, print, or telecommunicate data more quickly than the 2 and the 4.

Floppy and Hard Disk Storage Capacity. You should know that, as a rule of thumb, 2 kilobytes of data (2,048 8-bit computer "words," each representing a character) translates into roughly 2 pages of double-spaced typewritten text (standard margins). What this means is that, on both formatted disks and excluding the 64K of RAM, the KAYPRO 2 can store and access about 382,000 bytes of data, or some 191 pages of text; the 4 stores and retrieves some 764,000 characters on its two formatted disks, or some 382 pages of text. But the KAYPRO 10 has a combined hard-floppy formatted storage/retrieval capacity of some 9.3 million bytes—or some 5000 pages of text! This means the KAYPRO 10 has about 25 times the 2's and 12.5 times the 4's memory capacity.

Single- and Double-Sided Disks. A final comment about the disk drive systems is in order, especially if you wonder about the difference between "single-sided" and "double-sided" disks, and what that difference means to you.

Single-sided means what it implies, that the disk accepts data on one side only, whereas the *double-sided* disk accepts data on both sides. Why? First, the disk drive in the KAYPRO 2 has a read/write electromechanical mechanism which can only read/write on one side of a disk, *whether it says "double-sided" on the disk label or not.* (Try it and see for yourself.) Conversely, the KAYPRO 4 will only put data on one side of the disk if you put a single-sided disk into it, but it has the ability to put and get data from both sides. The same, of course, holds true for Drive C in the 10 as well.

And what is *double-density?* That merely means that the disk's surface has been prepared in such a manner that it will hold twice as many magnetically charged bits of data—0s and 1s—as a *single-density* disk will hold. As you might guess, the read/write mechanism also must be more finely tuned to lay down and pick up all those thousands of closely positioned 0s and 1s. The bits of data are put down like so many + and − charged footballs stood on end in the groove of a giant record, but all on a microscopic scale. In the double-density setup, the oxide coating on the disk simply accepts twice as many data footballs.

Business Graphics and the KAYPRO. KAYPRO has upgraded the quality of the cathode-ray tube (CRT) offered in the 2 and the 4, which means that all three computers now support graphics of the quality described as "business graphics." This means that all three 1984 models have the capability of generating pie charts, bar graphs, etc., with high resolution. That's the good news, but the bad news is that the software needed to generate such "business-level" graphics does not come bundled with the computers. If you can program in BASIC, then you can generate these graphics by using the programming software that does come bundled with the 4 and the 10, but not the 2. We do not recommend you attempt to do so, however, unless you are proficient in BASIC.

The KAYPRO's Keyboard. The keyboard for all three KAYPRO computers features the standard QWERTY layout. We find the keyboard to be very responsive, by which we mean that it has good mechanical sensitivity and tactile qualities about it. The keys are well-cupped for the finger. The layout of the keys is quite convenient, and the arrow keys are easily reached. They also have an audible echo that is built in to let you know that you have hit a key. Control (CTRL) and Escape (ESC) keys are of considerable importance and are, fortunately, well-positioned for ease of reach and speed of access. In all, your transition from an electric typewriter to the KAYPRO keyboard will not be at all difficult. Typing is a necessary skill for the successful operation of any computer; if you have not learned touch typing, we recommend that you do.

The numeric keypad also has a high sensitivity factor and layout quality. Even more important is its programmable potential. In effect, this means that the KAYPRO has a *function key* capability which many other microcomputers do not offer. You can, for example, program the keypad key to execute text processing commands when using WordStar. This means fewer command keystrokes for you to make, which means faster text processing. Please see Ezra Shapiro's article on this subject in the July/August 1983 and January, 1984 issues of *ProFiles*.

The KAYPRO's Weight and Size. Just a few sentences will do concerning the KAYPRO's weight and size. We have transported our KAYPROs back and forth from home and office with no difficulty at all. One of us has taken his KAYPRO along on several flights as well, putting the machine in the overhead rack with room to spare. Our experience, then, has been that your KAYPRO is easily transported and is no worse for wear as a result. Also, its "footprint," or the space your KAYPRO takes up on your desk or table, is acceptably small.

Input/Output Ports. Input/output (or I/O) ports have been mentioned already, but another word or two are in order. As you can see from Table 2-1, the 2, 4 and 10 all have two serial I/O ports. This means you can telecommunicate and print with a serial printer simultaneously, or you can hook up two printers, one serial and the other parallel. Or, via the serial modem input/output port, you can hook up a 2 or 4 to a KAYPRO 10 with a data transmission cable, which constitutes *networking via hardwire*. And at the same time you can hook up to a modem, thereby directing any incoming data to either or both of the printers. (More recent models of the KAYPRO 4 feature a built-in modem and two RS-232C serial ports. You should check with your KAYPRO dealer information about the latest available hardware and software, which KAYPRO upgrades frequently.) Let's take a closer look at serial and parallel, as the terms apply to printers.

SERIAL AND PARALLEL PRINTERS

A word about the difference between serial and parallel is in order here. Why one over the other? Why does KAYPRO give you the choice of using either kind of printer? Let's make it simple and short.

The KAYPRO comes with its operating system (CP/M 2.2F) configured to direct data out of the central processing unit (CPU) to a parallel printer, and *not* to a serial printer. You can reconfigure the CPU yourself with CONFIG.COM, telling it to send its output to the serial port instead of the parallel port. So, why has KAYPRO elected to configure it for parallel over serial printers at the outset?

One reason is that in most applications the printer is situated just a few feet away from the computer that drives it. Therefore, there is no data transmission loss when using the parallel I/O printer port over such a short distance. Besides, the parallel I/O port puts out and receives eight bits of data simultaneously, rather than one bit at a time, as is the case in serial data transmission. Figure 2-5 illustrates the different bit arrangements.

As in the 100-yard dash, so it is in printing: speed is the name of the game, and the sprinters often reach the tape almost simultaneously. Theory says that electrical charges do reach the tape (printer) simultaneously; therefore, 8- or 16-bit bursts of data that reach your parallel printer's internal memory at the same time are preferable to 8- or 16-bit bursts of data that reach the serial printer's internal memory one bit at a time. But

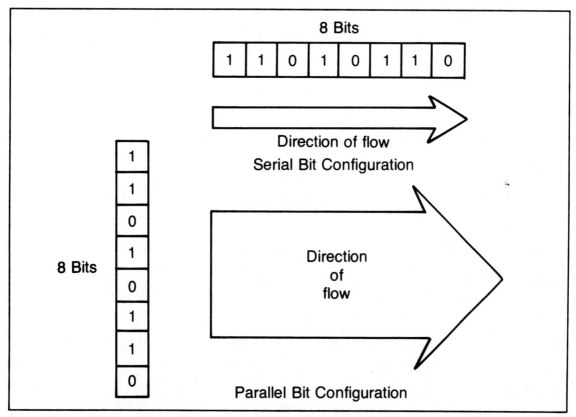

8 Bits

| 1 | 1 | 0 | 1 | 0 | 1 | 1 | 0 |

Direction of flow
Serial Bit Configuration

8 Bits

| 1 |
| 1 |
| 0 |
| 1 |
| 0 |
| 1 |
| 1 |
| 0 |

Direction
of
flow

Parallel Bit Configuration

Fig. 2-5. Serial and parallel bit arrangements.

this parallel situation is, as in track and field, good only for a short distance. That is, for accuracy you should not use a parallel printer whose interconnecting cable is more than 20 feet in length. Resistance to energy transfer from point A to B can wreak havoc with a printer expecting to receive 8 or 16 bits of data all at once. To avoid data loss, prepackaged cables run about 10 feet in length, no more.

For greater distances, the data bits are sent out one at a time, and they are sent in a coded order which tells the receiving computer or printer when each group of data bits starts and stops. In long-distance running, timing, pacing, and control of the flow of events is everything—as it is with long-distance data transmission over Ma Bell's phone lines, which are set up to accept data transmitted and received only in *serial*, or *sequential*, mode. Accuracy of transmission is thereby assured, which is always a consideration when data moves through wire over a distance of more than, say 10 feet.

So, in the interest of both printing speed and data transmission accuracy, KAYPRO preconfigures the 2, 4, and 10 to send all data to the parallel output port only, not to the serial output port. If you own an older 2 or 4, you can *only* simultaneously use a modem and printer by using a parallel printer. (Again, more recent models of the KAYPRO may let you get around such an operational restriction. Ask your KAYPRO dealer.)

Such considerations are best kept in mind when selecting a printer, or when contemplating the likelihood that you'll want to receive data via modem and print it simultaneously. While we're discussing printers, you also should know that not just any printer will produce graphics. In general, only dot-matrix, ink-jet, and laser printers will generate graphics. Printers that produce *formed characters*—which means solid letters such as your typewriter makes—are known as *letter-quality printers*. While they give you letter-quality printed text, they are slower than the other printers mentioned and normally will not be capable of generating the graphics you may want.

THE KAYPRO'S BUNDLED SOFTWARE

The phrase *bundled software* is used a lot these days, since Osborne made the idea's market advantages apparent to everyone in the microcomputer industry. This phrase means that your KAYPRO 2, 4, and 10 come with software "bundled" in a package, all ready for you to make working copies of and then learn to use and apply. In this sense, bundled software applies more literally to the 2 and 4 than to the 10, since the 10's software is put on the hard disk at the factory. Table 2-2 depicts the present software bundled with the 2, 4, and 10.

As with the hardware table, we want to say a brief word that we think you will find of value and interest about the software programs. Please see Chapter 8 for our opinions about the various programs: i.e., their utility value, ease of use, difficulty of mastering, the readability of the documentation, and so forth. A quick Cook's tour of this table results in these comments and explanations.

The Bundled Programming Software. We have not placed emphasis on the programming languages. This decision reflects our opinion that most of you (we think as many as 90 percent) will not immediately do your own programming after buying a KAYPRO. Therefore, we give the bundled BASIC and compiler programs minor play in this book. For those of you who are interested and eager to begin programming on your own, there is a vast library of books on BASIC available.

The Telecommunications Software. Both the 4 and the 10 come with

Table 2-2. KAYPRO Standard Software.

	KAYPRO 2	KAYPRO 4	KAYPRO 10
Word Processing	WordStar®	WordStar®	WordStar®
Spelling Checker	The Word Plus™	The Word Plus™	The Word Plus™
Relational Data Base Management System	—	dBASE II® with Tutorial	dBASE II® with Tutorial
Data Base Management	—	InfoStar™ *integrates*	InfoStar™ *integrates*
Data Entry	DataStar™	DataStar™ *and*	DataStar™ *and*
Sorting	SuperSort™	ReportStar™	ReportStar™
Mailing List	Mailmerge®	Mailmerge®	Mailmerge®
Electronic Spreadsheet	CalcStar™ Profitplan™	CalcStar™ Microplan™	CalcStar™ Microplan™
Programming Languages	M-Basic™	M-Basic™ C-Basic™ S-Basic™	M-Basic™ C-Basic™ S-Basic™
Modem Communications	—	Suprterm (old models) Mite™ (new models)	Suprterm (old models) Mite™ (new models)
Operating System	CP/M™2.2	CP/M™2.2	CP/M™2.2

bundled telecommunications software. Suprterm is intended to be used with the Hayes SmartModem (300 or 1200 baud models), but this program works with most modems. (We used it with three: the J-CAT, the Hayes 1200, and the battery-powered Signalman Mark I 300 baud modem.) See what we have to say in Chapter 16 about the utility value of Suprterm as a telecommunications software package. For now, though, let us just say we think you will find Suprterm easy to learn and use. (Midsummer 1984 models of the KAYPRO 4 feature a built-in modem, but it does not work with Suprterm as presently configured; KAYPRO is at work on this problem, so you might watch for tips in *Pro Files.*)

The Bundled Documentation. The bundled software you received with your KAYPRO comes with "documentation." Much of this "documentation" was developed by engineers who, as a matter of habit and training, do not pay much attention to the needs of different audiences. Some of these manuals are excellent, and some are less than useful. Here is a list of the documents you are probably going to receive with your KAYPRO microcomputer. Agreeing that a good thing is hard to beat, we are adopting the Michelin star system to rate the bill-of-fare found in the major bundled documentation. This is, in the spirit of Michelin's system, merely meant as a "guide" to what's there. You, of course, have the last word with the headwaiter.

**** = Excellent documentation, well planned and organized, with good use of examples and illustrations, written with you—the first-time user—in mind. We recommend you use it in confidence that it will help you run the program in question.

*** = Good to fair documentation, not too clearly written in a few places, but clearly more useful and instructive than not for the first-time microcomputer user.

** = Fair to average documentation containing many puzzling statements and using few (if any) good examples or illustrations, not written with the first-time micro user in mind, and containing some inaccuracies and/or misleading statements.

* = Marginal documentation, nearly useless for the first-time user; it may not be so much inaccurate as just poorly conceived, designed, and written.

= Documentation which fails to instruct in any useful manner, written above the comprehension level of the intended user audience, containing confusing statements, lacking clear organization, and not using adequate examples (in kind and number) to explain the subject matter at hand.

Here, then, are the ratings we have put together for the documentation you will probably receive with your KAYPRO.

** *The KAYPRO User's Guide,* Version 1, 1983.
** *An Introduction to KAYPRO Software,* Version 1, July 1983.
CP/M: An Introduction to CP/M Features and Facilities, Revision of January, 1978.
*** *WordStar Reference Manual for Release 3.3,* MicroPro, 1983.
*** *WordStar Training Guide,* Second Edition, February, 1983.
** *Perfect Writer.*
*** *Perfect Filer.*

***   *The WORD Plus,* 1982 (W. Holder).

**   *SUPRTERM: A User's Guide for the SUPRTERM Communications Program,* September, 1983.

**   *KAYPRO 10 User's Guide,* May, 1983.

***   *MicroPlan,* Chang Laboratories, 1983.

***   *ProfitPlan.*

**   *Perfect Calc.*

**   *Microsoft BASIC User's Guide,* 1981.

**   *CBASIC Language Reference Manual,* 2nd Edition, October, 1982.

**   *S-BASIC: A Language Facility for CP/M and Its Derivatives,* 1980.

**   *DataStar Training Guide,* for DataStar Release 1.4, 1982.

**   *DataStar Reference Manual,* for DataStar Release 1.4, Third Revision, 1982.

**   *CalcStar User's Manual,* First Issue, November 8, 1982.

**   *ReportStar User Reference Manual,* Release 1.0, 1982.

**   *ReportStar General Information Manual,* Release 1.0, 1982.

**   *ReportStar Training Guide,* Release 1.0, 1982.

**   *SuperSort,* September 30, 1981.

***   *MailMerge Reference Manual,* Release 3.3, 1983.

***   *dBASE II: Assembly Language Relational Database Management System,* Wayne Ratliff, Ratliff Software Production, Inc., Ashton-Tate, 1982.

****   *dBASE II for the First-Time User,* Alan Freedman, The Computer Language Company, Inc., Ashton-Tate, 1984. (This one would get an Oscar, if they existed for computer books.)

Well, there it is: a smorgasboard for sure. So how are you going to get over the documentation blues and make the best out of things? We have an anti-General Murphy game plan for you, and here it is:

● Read the first seven chapters of this book *before you do anything at all with the bundled software or with your KAYPRO.* Doing as we suggest may well save you needless frustration, and may even prevent your damaging your hardware or software.

● If you insist on going it alone, and you are a first-time user, then begin with WordStar or dBASE II—but only *after* you read (at a minimum) Chapters 4 and 6, "Checking Out Your New KAYPRO" and "Backing Up Your Master Software Disks." Why WordStar or dBASE II? Because their documentation is, in our opinion, clearly superior to any other bundled with your KAYPRO. WordStar's menu structure, commands, and general level of accessibility combine to make it an excellent way for you to begin interacting with CP/M, your printer if you have one, and so forth. This is also true of dBASE II, which remains transparent throughout.

● In general, then, we hope that you view this book as your starting point and general guide, venturing into the documentation where and when you need more information. The bundled documentation, with the exeception of *dBASE II for the First-Time User,* should be seen as backup or reference material, as a resource when you need more information than we have given. Our goal is to get you up and running on all the programs, and beyond that we trust your intelligence in seeking out more information.

Chapter 3

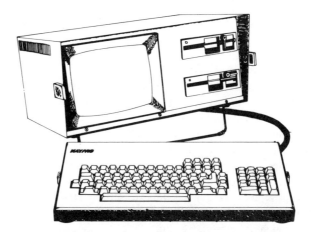

Bringing the New KAYPRO Home

W hen you carry that blue and white box containing your brand new KAYPRO out of the store, you will no doubt feel anticipation and excitement. You will probably want to get it home, or back to your office and crank it up as soon as possible. You may feel like you did when you bought your first new car. You knew how to drive that guy without a lot of instruction. Your KAYPRO is different, and this chapter is devoted to a few cautionary remarks that might save you some trouble. They're all in the spirit of checking to see if you have oil in the crankcase. If you are very experienced with computers or top-end audio or video gear, then you might know all this. On the other hand, you may find a few useful tips.

TRANSPORTING YOUR KAYPRO

Rule 1. Your KAYPRO is more delicate than your briefcase. It's heavier too, and that may remind you that it is a collection of relatively delicate and precise electronic parts that can come apart or—worse—get out of adjustment. It is to KAYPRO's great credit that they have been able to design a computer that you can carry around and plug in, and that will work. By itself, that constitutes a small miracle. Don't push it.

When you put that big box in your car, make sure that it sits flat with the UP arrows pointing UP. Don't leave it where it will slide off onto the floor when you slam on the brakes to avoid a kid on a bike or an old person straying into traffic. Brace it somehow so it won't bounce around. It's a strange thought, but if you have a VW bug or an older Audi you should remember that they hide the battery under the back seat, and it's a bad idea to leave your KAYPRO sitting on top of a battery. The disk drives have magnetic heads—

like tape recorders—and car batteries produce strong magnetic fields which could fry your heads.

If you are going to transport it regularly from home to office, or take it on trips with you, get a cover to keep the dust and moisture out of your KAYPRO. It may be worth noting that the KAYPRO fits in the overhead rack on an airliner, although it prompts comments like, "You sure do travel light, don't you?" *ProFiles*, the KAYPRO magazine, regularly lists at least three manufacturers of covers you can buy, and your KAYPRO dealer has a nifty blue padded cover made of 60-40 material.

Your KAYPRO's enemies are strong electrical and magnetic fields, dust, moisture, extreme heat, and extreme cold. Don't leave it in the trunk of your car for half a day, or even a couple of hours, when the outside temperature is pushing 90 degrees, and the inside temperature in your trunk will be well over 150. Things soften and then get brittle at that heat. Videotape recorders stop working at about 100 degrees, the tape stretches and gets gooey—and they are at least as sensitive as your KAYPRO. If the machine has been in temperatures below 50 for any length of time, let it warm up to at least 50, preferably 60 degrees, before turning it on.

OK, you've brought it home successfully. It's still there in the box, waiting to do all that neat stuff for you. Cut the tape securing the top of the box carefully so that you can reseal it with new tape. Do the same with the inside box, and save the four corner protectors that insulate the inside box from the outer one. This is an extremely good packing system; you may want to use it again, and it gives you a second, safe way to transport your computer. One author of this book carried his KAYPRO 4 from California to Colorado to Texas and back in its original carton. The box and the machine go in with the hold baggage, and they have held up well. A number of Hollywood scriptwriters use the KAYPRO, dragging the machine (carefully) out to the location of the shoot, and they all seem to survive. Save the box and the packing.

For daily transportation to and from your office, you will need a smaller, more convenient cover. With one of those, you can be reasonably assured that it won't get a lot of dust in it, that it won't get damp (if you don't stand it in a puddle), and so on. A cover will also let you carry it on the bus, or put it under your seat on the plane.

WORK STATION REQUIREMENTS

The place where you will work with your KAYPRO is called a *work station* in computer language, and it's a useful concept. You will need an area with a reasonable amount of flat space to place your KAYPRO, to house your disks, to set up your printer, and to accommodate different books, files, copy, and all the rest of the stuff that accompanies working with your machine. The key overall requirement is that it should be set up for your comfort and for spending long periods of time working with your machine. Figure 3-1 shows a typical setup. We will run through some of the basic necessities in the rest of this chapter.

Some of the considerations for traveling with your machine also apply to finding a home for it. You don't want to place it near any powerful electrical or magnetic sources like your refrigerator or your furnace. By the same token, you don't want to put it near a drafty place, like an open window, because you want to take some care to keep the dust to a minimum. And you don't want to place it directly over a radiator. This list could be endless, so use your head. Find a location that is of moderate temperature, that is

Fig. 3-1. A typical work station. Photo by R.S. Powers.

reasonably free of dust, and that is not accident-prone. (You don't want to frost it with cake batter.) When the KAYPRO is up on its stand, it can easily be pushed forward and drop 4 inches to the surface below. For a delicate piece of electronics, especially when it's running, that's a big drop. (There is a story that the Denver Broncos dropped theirs, bending the cowling over the screen so badly that they had to straighten it with pliers in order to read the screen. The machine continued to work. Like we said, it's good hardware.)

On its stand the machine is 12 inches high, 18 inches wide, and 16 inches deep. That's a fairly small space, or *footprint*. The area under the machine should be clear and uncluttered so that air currents can cool it. The 2 and the older 4 do not have built-in fans, although the new 4 and the 10 do. The vents in the bottom and sides circulate air and, fan or not, they need to be able to breathe.

The detachable keyboard is 8 inches deep and 18 inches wide. It works best when it sits on a flat, clear surface. Some people like to put the keyboard in their laps, but for long periods of work this practice is hard on the back. A clear flat space and a steno chair with a firm back are your best bets to combat fatigue.

In general, your screen should be at eye level, or at a comfortable viewing position. You should try to avoid glare on the screen from a window or other strong sources of light. Ideally, you want a balanced light condition, so that the light from your screen is matched by the light in the room. If you cannot achieve that—and it's hard to get in many offices—then you may want to invest in an anti-glare screen. *ProFiles* advertises stands for your KAYPRO that will bring it from the desktop to eye level, and they also advertise anti-glare screens. If you get headaches, or other kinds of eye strain, consider one of these solutions.

PRINTER LOCATION

All printers are noisy and stressful. Your best bet is to hide your printer in a closet, behind a solid oak door that you can close while it whines, spits, and cranks out copy. Unfortunately, printers also need to be tended to make sure the form feed paper is running correctly, for instance. You can usually get away with a 20-foot cable without losing too much signal. Beyond that, you're asking for trouble. If you can't hide it, you may want to consider a cover to muffle it. Earplugs are uncomfortable and a nuisance.

In any case, you need a very sturdy table or stand for the printer because it will shake, rattle, and roll—and it won't sound like Fats Domino or Elvis. It needs to be positioned so that you can put the box of form feed on the floor behind it. That way the printer can pull paper from the box without getting hung up. You also need to have space on the table or the floor for the paper to gather while you are printing.

POWER

Your KAYPRO uses normal 120 volt ac power—household current—but your dealer can convert it to 220 if you're traveling abroad. In either case, your biggest danger will come from the power company and sudden surges or drops in power, or (worst of all) power outages. To get ahead of ourselves a little, if you are running a program, such as WordStar or ReportStar, and the power fails—even for one second—you lose all the data that you have not saved. This can cost you time and trouble to get back to where you were when your friendly kilowatt company went "Oops." They do it all the time, and they only raise the rates.

You can protect yourself against surges (too much power) or a large drop in line voltage with a line filter plugged into your outlet between the wall receptacle and your KAYPRO. At least one of the desktop stands has a built-in line filter, and that combination could save you some grief. You need to be aware of just how erratic your particular power company or household wiring is, and take it from there. In any case, do *not* plug your new, expensive machine into an old and frayed extension cord, or into a three-way plug. Reserve a separate wall receptacle, preferably one that can use the grounded plug that comes with your KAYPRO, and buy a heavy-duty extension cord to get to that socket.

MAINTENANCE TIPS

1) Be sure to turn off ("power down") your KAYPRO when you are not using it.
2) Keep the disk drive doors closed unless you are inserting or removing a disk. If the machine is on, the drives will whirr at 400 RPM to tell you to shut the door.
3) When you are not using the machine, clip the keyboard to the main body of the machine. That helps keep dust and flying crud out of your KAYPRO.
4) Beware holding coffee, tea, or other fluids over the keyboard. It, too, is electronic, and it doesn't like liquids. A spill will cost you a ridiculous amount of money to clean up.

The next chapter will deal with setting up your machine. You might unclip the detachable keyboard and plug it into the machine with the coiled cord that connects them. Pay attention to the way the plugs fit into the two sockets. If the machine is up on its stand, you can clip the keyboard back on without crunching the cord. (You *don't* want to crunch the cord.) It is the umbilical cord between your command keyboard and your machine, so it's best to keep those communication channels as clear as possible.

Chapter 4

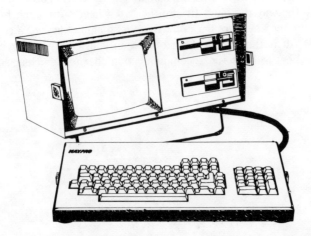

Checking Out Your New KAYPRO

In the last chapter, you got your KAYPRO home and learned a few things about where and where not to set it up for optimum operating performance. That behind us, we can now turn our attention to matters more closely related to the KAYPRO itself. Let's check it out quickly before we get to its keyboard and the actual process of backing up your software.

KEY HARDWARE FEATURES

The RS-232C serial ports on the backs of the KAYPROs present a 25-pin female plug arrangement labeled Serial Printer Output and Serial Data I/O. Then there is the single Centronics parallel I/O port, which has a female arrangement consisting of a large opening with numerous contact strips inside. (Examine the back of your KAYPRO closely, or refer to Figs. 2-2 and 2-4 in the preceding chapter.) Please note that the male Centronics and serial plugs only fit in *one* way. Look at the connectors before you fit them together. Don't jam them together. Once you do have them connected, make sure they are secure and clipped together, or screwed in.

PARALLEL AND SERIAL PRINTERS

If you do not yet have a printer, then your task is simplified because you can DO IT RIGHT from the start. By this we only mean that you can select a parallel printer, which you should do for all the reasons and advantages already mentioned and discussed in the second chapter. We take this position because of the simplicity of operation, while recognizing that many people will insist on a (much slower) serial printer.

If you do not have a printer, but plan to buy one, we advise the parallel kind. Then ask your KAYPRO dealer for the proper cable needed to connect your KAYPRO to the printer. There are now many prepackaged, ready-to-use cables on the market. Merely tell the dealer which KAYPRO you have and he'll help you select the right cable for the printer you plan to buy.

But what if you already have a serial printer? Do not despair. Consult the owner's manual for the printer, finding out which kind of cable connector arrangement is required. Taking your printer's spec sheet/owner's manual in to your KAYPRO dealer is probably your safest bet here. This advice applies to any printer, for that matter. Referring to the printer's manual is essential because, based on what you learn there about connector pin arrangements, you'll have to do three things:

1) Have the appropriate CPU/Printer cable made up if a stock, ready-made one is not available.
2. Install the cable between the KAYPRO and the printer, which you should be able to do yourself if you are at all handy with a small standard screwdriver.
3) Preconfigure your KAYPRO to drive the printer you've elected to use. You do this via the CONFIG program found on your CP/M Utilities disk. The routine for setting up a serial printer is outlined in Chapter 7 under CONFIG.

A few words are in order about the actual length of the cable you use between your KAYPRO and its printer. As previously mentioned, parallel cables should not be over 10 feet in length, whereas serial cables can be much longer before the signal in them needs to be boosted to help it along. But, printers being the sometimes cantankerous things they are, you will want your printer (of whichever kind) to be very near at hand. If you insist in having your printer farther away from your KAYPRO than what we recommend as the maximum distance (8-10 feet) than put it no more than 20 feet away if it's a parallel, and no more than 100 if serial. These distances are at the outer limits of reliability for signal transmissions.

You might be scratching your head, saying, "Not more than 25 feet away? Does that mean I can't put the printer in the attic and the KAYPRO in the den on the first floor?" Yes, that's what we mean if the distance is more than 25 feet, which in this case is likely. Besides, when that printer beeps or makes another signal indicating it needs your personal attention (to adjust paper, put more paper in it, etc.) you need to have it near the KAYPRO.

MODEMS

If you're planning to send information to other computers from your KAYPRO, or to access one or more of the informational databases that are now as close as your telephone, one essential piece of hardware you will need is a modem—short for MOdulator-DEModulator. To use one, you will have to make sure that your KAYPRO's CPU is able to communicate with other computers via the modem. This means that you will have to use your CP/M utilities disk to tell the CPU which *baud rate*—or data bit speed—you want your KAYPRO to use. Now, in fact, your KAYPRO has the capacity to send and receive data at speeds that far exceed the capacity of modems. Put simply, the compuer inside your KAYPRO is a lot faster than any of the peripherals—printers and modems—currently available. Here are the baud rates at which your KAYPRO can communicate; the * indicates the data transmission rates you will use:

MODEM BAUD RATES	BITS OF DATA PER SECOND
50	5
75	7
110	11
134.5	13
150	15
300*	30*
600	60
1200*	120*
1800	180
2000	200
2400	240
3600	360
4800	480
7200	720
9600	960
19200	1920

Selecting a Modem. Obviously, 120 bits per second is four times faster than the 30 bits per second data transmission rate; if you can afford the more expensive 1200 baud modem (a Hayes SmartModem 1200, for example) then we think you should get it, rather than a modem limited to 300 baud only. Think about it: four times as much data can be sent over the phone lines in the same amount of time! We think you should give this matter serious consideration when setting up your KAYPRO. The additional cost for a good (Hayes) 1200 baud modem, which will also run at 300 is certainly worth the investment, if you can afford to make it. The KAYPRO 4 band, built-in modem is still under development by the factory. When it is fully operational, we're sure that purchasers will be notified.

You will have to set up the correct "communications protocol" between your modem and your KAYPRO, just as you had to between your KAYPRO and your printer. Otherwise, the peripherals will not be able to "talk" to your KAYPRO in an intelligible manner, and what will result is known as "garbage." Therefore, consult your Suprterm user's manual for help in establishing the correct communications protocol. You should also read what we have to say on the subject in Chapter 16.

Modem Cables. One last word about cables, but this time about modem cables. If you've got a modem, then its cable will be an RS-232 C-type serial cable; you can buy it ready-made, have one made up for you, or—if you know how to solder and are handy at such things—you can make it up yourself. But most modems sold today come with their own serial cable, which is easily attached to the serial I/O port on the back of your KAYPRO.

YOUR KAYPRO'S DISK DRIVES

Your KAYPRO's disk drives come from the factory with cardboard drive protectors inserted in the drive mechanism. The tab of the insert will be visible because it protrudes from the drive door. This cardboard protects the porcelain drive wheels which fit into the large hole in the center of your floppies. These wheels must not be scratched, chipped, or misaligned at all. Therefore, they should never be left unprotected when you are transporting your KAYPRO from the office to home, or from/to anywhere of any distance. This may not apply to moving the KAYPRO across the room, but it would apply if you are going to take the KAYPRO upstairs, across the street, or on your next trip to Chicago's O'Hare airport.

Be sure to remove these inserts before you turn on your KAYPRO, and be sure to re-insert them before you transport your KAYPRO. If you should lose the inserts—as we have done on occasion—then either get replacements from your dealer or, in an emergency, use old, worn-out floppies instead. This advice applies, of course, to all three KAYPRO models, but with the KAYPRO 10 there are additional safety measures that must be taken when turning off the 10.

The KAYPRO 10 comes with one disk drive (logical Drive C, in the default configuration) that also must be protected. The single floppy drive should be protected the same way and for the same reasons as outlined above for the 2 and the 4. But the KAYPRO 10's hard disk must also be protected—*not just when transporting it, but before turning off the 10.*

TURNING OFF THE KAYPRO 10 SAFELY

Because the hard disk is not physically accessible to you, you must protect it from damage by running a safety program via CP/M. *Failure to run the safety program before you turn off the KAYPRO 10 may well result in severe damage to the hard disk's surface, destroying data recorded on it, and possibly destroying the disk as well if the read/write heads are allowed to come into contact with the disk surface. Failure to run the safety program will "crash the disk,"* which will cost you time and money to have it repaired/replaced.

Here is an interactive program that will step you through the safety program. We will define the condition in the left column and tell you what action to take in the right column.

CONDITION/RESULT/GOALS	ACTION TO TAKE
1) If the KAYPRO 10 is ON	Exit from the program you are in.
2) Save the data.	Enter the proper save data command for the program you are using.
3) If the logged Drive is C	Remove disk and press the red reset button (this makes side A of the hard disk the logged drive).
4) See the MASMENU.	Select the SAFETY program and press return. You will hear the disk's heads being moved and see a message telling you that it's safe to turn off the 10.
5) If the logged Drive is B	Enter A: and press Return.
6) See A> on screen	Enter SAFETY and press Return.

CONDITION/RESULT/GOALS	ACTION TO TAKE
7) See message telling you that it's safe to turn off the 10	Move the rocker switch down to OFF.

The message you will see after the SAFETY program has run reads as follows:

> The heads have been placed over the safety zone and the hard disk controller has been deselected. It is now safe for you to turn off your machine.

This message is your only means of knowing that the read/write heads have been placed over the safety zone ("deselected" in "technobabble") and that the hard disk controller has been deactivated.

Note: Remember, you can run the SAFETY program from the A sector of the hard disk only, although you need not be in User Area 0 to do so. The SAFETY program will run from a user area prompt. This means, then, that it will automatically run whether you are in User Area A0 or User Area A6 or User Area A14. The SAFETY program will not run from any User Area (0 through 15) of the C Drive (or floppy disk). Only from the A sector of the hard disk is this possible, so be sure you are, in fact, in the A sector of the hard disk by following without fail the procedure for executing the SAFETY program, as outlined above.

There is a second way to run the SAFETY program, and that means calling up the Mass Menu and then selecting the SAFETY program option from it. Here is what you must do:

CONDITION/RESULTS/GOALS	ACTION TO TAKE
1) KAYPRO 10 in Drive A	Type MASMENU ⟨Return⟩.
2) See Mass Menu	Move Selector Bar to SAFETY option.
3) Run SAFETY Program	Press ⟨Return⟩
4) See SAFETY program run automatically.	
	Now it is safe to turn off your KAYPRO.

TURNING OFF THE KAYPRO 2 AND 4

Here, the only real concern is that you not turn off the 2 or the 4 with the floppies still in their disk drives. Save your data/program, then remove the floppy disks, then turn off the 2 or the 4. See, it's just that simple.

THE RED RESET BUTTON

The red reset button enables you to clear all core memory (the 64K of RAM memory inside your CPU) and return to CP/M. You've just seen how that happens in the examples given above concerning the KAYPRO 10's safety program. One precaution: *do not push the red reset button until you have saved any data or programs to disk that you want to keep. Otherwise, you will lose whatever you have previously stored to disk.*

On the other hand, you'll find that the reset button can help you exit from situations that you can not otherwise figure out how to get out of—until, that is, you learn more about how to run the software programs. So, to put your mind at ease, know that pressing the reset button does *not* harm in any way any of the software already stored on disk. Pushing it will destroy only the data or words that you have created via the keyboard, and which have not been saved to disk as yet. The same applies, of course, to any data being received via your modem; pushing the reset button while telecommunicating will break the connection and will cause loss of data not yet saved in a file on a disk.

SETTING THE CONTRAST LEVEL

The 2, 4, and 10 have quality green-phosphor consoles, which measure 9 inches on the diagonal. The black-green contrast values may be changed to suit your individual viewing preferences and to account for changes in the ambient light surrounding your KAYPRO. You should turn on your KAYPRO, get a full screen of data, and then adjust the contrast control knob accordingly. Experiment a bit, getting a feel for the variety of contrast possible.

Well, so much for getting you off on the right foot with your KAYPRO. Now that you have it set up as you want and you know some important facts about its operational features, lets take a more in-depth look at the keyboard itself. We think you will want to know what the various function keys can do for you.

Chapter 5

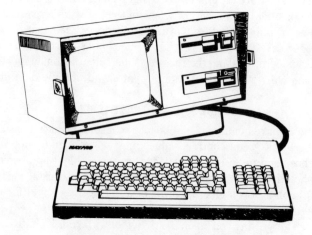

Using Your
KAYPRO's Keyboard

Your KAYPRO's keyboard is laid out in the same manner as a standard typewriter, but there are many additional keys as well. We want you to know what their functions are before you begin to back up your master software or use any of the programs themselves.

The keyboard contains all of the standard alphanumeric keys found on most typewriters today, which produce the following symbols when activated:

```
1234567890-=`!@#$%^&*()_+~qwertyuiop[]asdfghjk
l;'\zxcvbnmQWERTYUIOP{}ASDFGHJKL:"|ZXCVBNM<>?
```

These 94 symbols are properly called the *standard alphanumerics* available on the KAYPRO's "typewriter" keyboard itself. Then there are ten numerics and three symbols available to you on the number keypad to the right of the keyboard:

```
1234567890 . - ,
```

That's a total of 107 alphanumerics you can generate with the keys mentioned thus far, and their function is to produce those symbols when used strictly as alphanumeric keys in the manner shown above.

SPECIAL KEYS

There are other important keys on the keyboard which have not been demonstrated yet, and some of the same keys just demonstrated above can have more than one function when used in conjunction with special keys on the keyboard not yet mentioned. These special keys can be put into the following logical groups according to their function:

- Escape
- Control or CTRL
- Cursor movement
- Deletion
- Programmable numeric keypad keys

Now, let's quickly discuss these keys from the top down.

Escape. The Escape Key, labeled ESC on the keyboard, serves to interrupt a program routine or subroutine. This permits you to return to a higher-level menu within a CP/M-based software applications program, or to return to the CP/M operating system itself. An example of this is given in the previous chapter. It is practically impossible to generalize about the ESC key, however, because its functional use will differ from one applications program to another. Be advised, though, to use it *only* as and when told by the program in question.

Control or CTRL. Here we find the single key which probably plays into more command functions than any other key on the keyboard. This key is held down at the same time as various other keys, in order to execute various commands in nearly every program you can run on your KAYPRO. Depressing the CTRL key tells the computer that it is about to receive a command-level order from you, to be executed in one or more parts of the computer's internal logic or mathematical functional areas. Depressing the CTRL key and another character on the keyboard will sometimes display a ∧ character plus the letter pressed just after CTRL.

Cursor Movement. There are several keys which can be used to at regular move the cursor, which is that rectangular bit of phosphorescent light you see pulsating intervals on your console. But before we discuss in the next section those keys and what they do for you, let us take a few moments to explain the last two kinds of special keys.

Deletion. The Delete key <DEL> enables you to erase any or all characters to the left of it, but not to the right; it only moves the cursor backwards, or to the left across a line of alphanumeric characters. Used in this manner, the Delete key also is a cursor movement key; it also can have other program functions, depending on the software program being used in your KAYPRO.

Programmable Keypad Keys. Here we will only say that you can program these 14 keys via the CONFIG program on your CP/M disk. When you have done so, these keys will function as any character or control keys you wish them to. See Ezra Shapiro's article on this subject in the July, 1983, issue of *ProFiles*.

Now let's go back and take a closer look at the cursor and the keys that control it.

A CURSORY LOOK AT THAT RECTANGLE OF LIGHT

Imagine your computer as having inside it not a tangle of wires and other electronic marvels, but instead an enormously long roll of paper whose width you can vary according to commands you give the computer via programs you run.

For example, when using text processing programs, we can envision a paper width of no more than 8 inches for most jobs; when running electronic spreadsheet programs, the width of the paper might be considerably greater than the 80-character width of your console—perhaps as many as 250 character spaces, or maybe something less than that but more than 80.

You begin to get the idea, we're sure. The console is only a "window" that lets you see one portion of the long roll of paper inside your KAYPRO. Now, the length and width of the roll are limited only by the memory capacity of the computer and the program's established outer limits for defining "workspace parameters." This electronic paper, then, can be much longer if you have a KAYPRO 10 instead of a 4, and likewise for a 4 over the 2. This is because of the increased memory capacity available to you by way of your floppy and/or hard disks, as the case may be; all the KAYPROs have 64K of temporary or RAM memory storage space.

Now, if the console is a window that lets you look at any portion of that electronic paper rolled up there inside your KAYPRO, the *cursor* is merely a marker locating your position on that role of paper at any one place and at any one moment in time. The cursor cannot be at two different places on the paper's surface at the same time, just as you cannot be in two different places at once. So, other than marking your precise spot—a character high and wide—within the thousands and hundreds of thousands of occupied or vacant spots on the electronic paper we are imagining, what additional purpose does the cursor have?

It has several. Just as the console is your 80 × 24 character-wide-and-high window, through which you can view only that much of the electronic paper at any one time, the cursor is a one-character window all its own, but with a big additional feature of great importance: the cursor is the portal through which flows all the data that you enter by way of the keyboard or the numeric keypad. You can think of it as the tip and eraser of a pencil, all in one—if that contradiction does not pose too many problems! It is "through" the cursor that you enter your data, and it is also by use of the cursor that you remove data from the electronic paper. It is, therefore, an electronic rectangle of light through which you can, with the appropriate programs and commands, "write" on the electronic paper, erase data and text from it, define blocks of text or data that are to be erased or copied from one place in the document to another, or even copy to another place in another file.

So you see, the cursor is the point where all the action occurs: either directly beneath it or to its right or left. Since that is the case, that little pulsating blob of light is very important indeed. Time to move our cursor forward.

TAB. This key, like the one on the typewriter, moves the cursor horizontally and to the right a set number of spaces; this is useful for formatting tables and lists. Unlike the typewriter, however, you may insert those spaces *between* two alphanumerics if you wish. For example, starting with an uppercase A and an ampersand right next to one another (A&), to insert 10 spaces between them you would place the cursor on the ampersand and hit TAB twice. With the default tabulator settings, you would get:

A   &

Backspace. This key permits you to move the cursor one space at a time; depending on the software program being used, the backspace key may also permit you to delete the character(s) over which you move the cursor via the backspace key.

The Return Key. This key moves the cursor one line down on your console and returns it to the established left-hand margin. But the Return key, which equals the carriage return—or cursor return—also performs command functions, some of which you have already seen when running through the procedures described in Chapter Four. Remember: the symbols <cr> or <Return> means press the Return key *once*.

The Line Feed Key. This key moves the cursor down one line, as does the Return key, but the Line Feed key does not return the cursor to the established left-hand margin. Instead, it moves the cursor down to a point directly below where it was before the key was pressed.

The Delete Key. As discussed previously, this key moves the cursor to the left one space at a time, or continuously if the key is held down. (It is worth noting that all the keys except CTRL, ESC, and TAB will repeat themselves continuously in this manner.)

The Arrow Keys. These keys are very handy and fairly efficient when it comes to moving the cursor about the console. Because they skim over the characters, they do not move any characters about on the console at all. They simply move the cursor over the character positions the file contains. They are capable of moving the cursor up, down, left, and right throughout a file, however long it might be. When held down, they move the cursor continuously across the console in the direction indicated by the arrow on the key pressed; that is, the UP arrow key will move upwards through a file until the first line of the file is reached. You can think of a ten-page report, and then of the cursor moving from the bottom of page 10 to the very topmost line of page 1.

Conversely, the DOWN arrow key will move from line 1 of the file to the last line in it—and even beyond, if you wish. How many lines, therefore, can the UP and DOWN arrow keys move the cursor? The answer is, "As many lines as your system has memory space." For the KAYPRO 10, that would mean moving the cursor quite some distance through a given file. As handy as the cursor moving arrows are, however, they are not the most efficient way for you to move about in lengthy text documents; therefore, WordStar and other software packages have special commands which enable you to move from point A to point Z, from Z back to A, or to any number of intermediate points in a fraction of the time that the arrow keys permit such electronic travel.

It should be pointed out, however, that *the arrow keys will not move the cursor as described above when you are in the CP/M operating system mode.*

Space Bar. You can also move the cursor one space to the right by hitting the space bar one time; if you want, hold the space bar down and it will zip the cursor along to the right, but also moving before it any characters that may be to its right. Unlike the arrow keys, which simply move the cursor, using the space bar *adds characters (the space character) to your file.*

COMMAND KEY EXECUTION

A few final words about command key strokes will close out this chapter. Many people read that they are supposed to enter a program command by pressing a combination of keys, sometimes in a particular sequence, to execute the program in question. Where WordStar is concerned, most of the commands that you must use are *two-key commands* in their structure. That is, you must press the CTRL key at the same time that you press a second key. You'll get plenty of these commands in the WordStar chapter, but here are a couple of examples of what we mean by a TWO-KEY COMMAND in WordStar:

$$^K \quad ^J \quad ^P \quad ^Q \quad ^S \quad ^D$$

In each case, the symbol ^ stands for "Hit the CTRL key." While you are holding the CTRL key down, also press *once* the indicated letter key, i.e., K, J, P, Q, S, and D. (You need not press them with the Caps Lock key activated to execute these or any similar two-key commands with WordStar or other software programs.)

But what about *multiple command key sequences*? How do you do them? Take it easy, they are just as simple to execute. In the preceding example, both CTRL and the designated letter key had to be pressed at the same time. But how can you press (in Perfect Writer, for example) these keys to execute the WRITE FILE TO DISK command: CTRL X, CTRL W? The answer is that you do not try to press them all at once, but rhythmically and fluidly, almost musically.

First, press the CTRL KEY and the X simultaneously. Let them up and then, with little hesitation, press CTRL and the W key simultaneously (*and-THREE-and-FOUR*). You'll find that with a little practice you will have developed the keystroke rhythm needed to speedily execute these multiple key sequence commands. That being the case, you'll have communicated your command—save this file's contents by writing it to the surface of the currently logged disk drive—with no problem whatsoever.

So, we are saying "limber up" and don't be afraid to give that old rhythm a try. If you don't make it, don't worry; the command will not be executed and you can try again. And if you hit the wrong keys and execute the wrong command, you can always undo the command by hitting the Escape key or by another *countermanding key sequence* found in your particular program's manual.

Chapter 6

Backing Up
Your Master Software

Your software disks are an important part of the KAYPRO system, and you need to pay attention to their care, feeding, and handling. They will contain the programs you want to run and all the data that you manage with those programs. They require care in handling and storage, and it is well worth your time to be careful. First of all, we will describe briefly what computer disks are.

WHAT IS A FLOPPY?

The word sounds a little silly, and your first thought might be of a hat with a wide brim. The connotation of the word *floppy* is "unstable," and that implied meaning is more correct than not. Floppy disks are made of vinyl, like records, and they feel like a soft record. They come in three sizes, 8 inches, 5¼ inches (which is what your KAYPRO and most other micros use), and 3½ inches. Currently, most micros use double-density disks, and that means that they have twice as many tracks as single-density disks (we will get to tracks in a minute). In any case, your KAYPRO uses double-density disks. The 4 and the 10 use double-sided, double-density disks, which record information on both sides of the disk.

The whole concept of the disk is much easier to understand if you perceive the disk as a combination of a record and a tape. It is flat, like a record, but you are able to record on it and record over old information, as you can on recording tape or on videotape. The magnetic surfaces of any disk are fragile. They don't like to be bent, dented, or scratched, and your KAYPRO will not run a disk that has been absued in any of these ways.

The hard disk in the KAYPRO 10 works in much the same way, except that it is more like a conventional record in appearance and feel. You are not allowed to get at it because its relation to the read/write heads is more critical than with the floppies, and it is more sensitive to damage.

FLOPPY PARTS AND THEIR HANDLING

1) When you take the floppy out of its envelope, hold it with your thumb and forefinger *by the label. Do not touch any other part of the floppy.* Keep the label up and reading away from you. There are eight ways to hold a floppy, and only one of them is correct. (Thanks to John Bear for that one.) Find that label up-and-away position and always use it.

2) The *write protect notch*, a small square notch, will be on your left as you hold the disk by the label up. This notch can be covered to prevent someone from electronically "writing" on the disk. It will still allow the computer to read the disk, but it will prevent anyone from altering the data on the disk.

3) The *central hole* in the cover is like the hole in the center of a record. It's where the disk drive fits to spin the disk.

4) The oblong hole below it is the *read/write head access slot.* In English that means that the magnetic head reads the disk through that slot. The vinyl disk rotates inside its cover, so that the heads can read all of the disk. Again, a parallel to stereo or video equipment helps to make this clear. Just as a tape recorder has heads that read the information off the tape, or as a stylus and cartridge read the information from a record, so magnetic heads in the drive read and write information to and from the disk and send it to the CPU.

HANDLING RULES

Remember to handle only the label. *Do not touch any other part of the disk.* Use only the correct one of the eight ways. The enemies of your disk are:

1) The natural oils and moisture on your hands.
2) Moisture and dust in the atmosphere.
3) Cigarette and other kinds of smoke.
4) Magnets. Keep your disks away from magnets and vice versa, because they will scramble or erase your information.
5) Static electricity generated by walking around on most carpets. Discharge yourself by touching something metallic before you touch even your desk, let alone your KAYPRO or a disk.
6) Anything that will bend, warp, or tear the disk.

To protect against all of these environmental hazards, it is good to have a separate, closed cabinet for your disks. Your computer store stocks lots of them. Minimally, the box should be large enough to handle a number of disks, and it should have a closely fitting, hinged top so that you can open and close it easily. The general rule to protect your disks is that they should be either in your machine, in the envelope on the way to or from the storage box, or in the closed box. Note that if you leave disks in the drive when you turn the machine on or off, you run a strong risk of scrambling the information stored on them. Protect yourself and the disks by removing them before you shut your KAYPRO off or power it up. Always do a *warm boot* (with CTRL C) after inserting the disk in the drive. Following these rules will help you to minimize risks to disks.

Those are some simple rules for handling and maintaining your disks. Now, we are going to show you how to back up the master disks that were bundled with your KAYPRO.

TURNING ON YOUR KAYPRO

Remove the cardboard drive head protectors from both drives, if you have not already done so. Reach around the back and flip the rocker switch up, or ON. You will hear the drive whir, and you will see a prompt (an instruction) that says:

KAYPRO
Please Place your diskette in Drive A0>__

If you have the older II or 4, open the top drive door by pushing the top of the cover with one finger. It is spring-loaded and moves very easily. If you have the newer 2 or 4 you have a different brand of drive. Take the disk out of its envelope by grasping the label with your thumb and forefinger. Remember, keep the label up. Insert it gently into the slot in the drive. It will slide back in easily and set itself on the drive. A gentle wiggle should reassure you that it is locked into position. Then, with the older machine, shut the door gently and completely with your finger. With the new KAYPROs, once the disk is seated push the button marked "push" until the white part of the button disappears and it locks into place. With the 10, hold the disk with its label toward the screen, and push gently with your thumb until it locks firmly into place, and then close the latch.

As soon as you shut the drive door, the drive will become silent, and you will see a message that says

KAYPRO 2, 4, 63K CP/M vers 2.2F
A0>__

That's your signal that the KAYPRO is ready to work.

COPYING YOUR MASTER DISKS WITH THE 2 AND 4

Finally, you are going to put the machine to work. The first job is a housekeeping chore that will protect your valuable master software disks. They are expensive, and they are worth protecting. Please follow this procedure. We will use two columns here; the left will tell you why to do something, and the right will tell you how to do it.

1)	Turn on your computer.
2) The prompt asks for a disk in Drive A.	Insert your master CP/M disk in A and close the door.
3) See the A0>_ prompt.	Type COPY <Return>.
4) Read the instructions on the screen.	Type C.
5) See "Copy the diskette in Drive A to Drive B."	Insert a blank formatted diskette in Drive B, and press <Return>.

6) Watch the track numbers scroll on the screen.
(Disks are divided into tracks, which are like grooves on a record, and each track is subdivided into sectors.)

7) See "Writing CP/M to the diskette in Drive B."

Press <Return>. You can deal with the other options when you need them. Type E.

8) You're back to the first COPY Menu.
9) See "Warm Boot A0>_"

Take the master disk out of Drive A and store it someplace safe, like the original box your disks came in.

Now you have a working copy of CP/M, which you can use to copy your other master disks. To do that, please follow the next procedure.

1)

Put the CP/M copy in Drive A and a blank disk in Drive B. Type COPY.

2) See the COPY menu.

Remove the CP/M disk from Drive A and put a master disk in its place. Type C. Press <Return>.

3) See the tracks scroll by. When you see "Writing CP/M to disk in B"

Remove the master disk from Drive A and replace it with the CP/M disk. Type E.

4) See "Warm Boot A0>_"

Your master is copied; you can now file the master and work with the copy.

While your disks are copying you should prepare labels for them. *Never write on a label or a disk.* You will bash the tracks with your pen and trash the disk.

BDOS ERROR ON A: If you get this error message when you try to copy a master disk, you might have an incorrectly formatted disk for your machine (a single-sided disk in a 4, for example) or a bad disk. Don't panic. Turn to the chapter on CP/M, and read about the PIP program. PIP is another way to copy disks and files, and it will probably solve your problem. Remember, if COPY doesn't work, try PIP. In fact, we advise putting PIP on every disk; in that chapter you will see why.

If you want to go ahead with PIP now, you can do that. It is more dependable and selective than COPY. Here's how:

1) To put a copy of PIP on a blank formatted disk

Insert your CP/M copy disk in Drive A

2)

Insert a blank *formatted* disk in Drive B.

3) To copy PIP to the blank disk

Type PIP B:=A:PIP.COM[VO]<Return>.

34

4) See A0>_
   Warm Boot

Now you are in shape to PIP your master disks to copy disks by following the next procedure.

1) To PIP your master disk to a format-   Insert the blank with PIP on it in Drive A.
   ted disk with PIP on it.

2)   Insert your master in Drive B.

3) To start copying with PIP   Type PIP A:=B:*.*[VO]⟨Return⟩

4) PIP may or may not list the files it
   copies, but when it is through you will
   see A0>_ Warm Boot

Follow the second procedure with COPY or the PIP routine for all your master disks. For blank disks that are only going to hold data, use the B option in the COPY program. Both B and C will check your disks for error. Everyone has the experience of buying faulty disks, and the sooner you find the bad ones, the easier it is to return them. (Quality control in the disk business makes a Detroit product look like a Rolls-Royce.)

That is the basic information you need to handle your disks with success. You're dealing with an invisible electronic medium, but it is stored on comparatively fragile surfaces, and it depends on precise parts moving accurately. Take care of your equipment and it will (for the most part) take care of you.

KAYPRO 10 HARD DISK BACKUP

First of all, you must know that the entire bundled software for the KAYPRO 10 resides on the hard disk when the computer is shipped from the factory. You also need to know that the software is on the A portion of the hard disk; it also has a B portion, and each has about 5 megabytes of disk space out of the total of 10 available. (The hard disk has been previously formatted at the factory, just as you must format your floppy disks before you can put anything on them. This hard disk formatting procedure, and a few other disk logic features, consumes about 1.1 megabytes of the original 10 available.)

This means that you have a total of about 8.9 megabytes of disk storage to work with. Of that, the A and B portions have an equal share, but all of the bundled software has been put on portion A only. Nothing at all is on B when you receive your KAYPRO 10 from the dealer.

The question is "How and where do I back up the approximately 4.5 megabytes of software residing on User Areas 0 through 10 on the A portion of the disk drive?" Well, you really have two options available to you:

1) Put all the software from the hard disk on floppies. This option will require 8 double-density, double-sided formatted but otherwise blank disks.

2) Put all the software on tape.

Of the two options, we recommend you exercise only Option 1. Backing up on tape is not the best medium to put valuable data files on, let alone software worth hundreds of dollars. Tape also requires data transfer equipment that you are not likely to own.

There is another, more important reason for backing up only on floppies, and that reason has to do with the way the software is laid down on the hard disk to begin with. You see, the hard disk is a very complex electromechanical device. And, while it is true that its read/write time is far faster than that of the KAYPRO's standard double-sided disk drive for floppies, it is also true that file identification and data track spacing are extremely critical. So, one User Area must be very discretely separated by electrical boundary markers from the 15 other User Areas.

What this all adds up to is this: if you did back up all your software on tape, how in the world would you know which software should go into which User Areas when you tried to run the linear tape, fitting its contents into discrete sectors on the hard disk? You might get too much or too little into this user area or that.

For these reasons, we recommend that you not even consider tape as an option for backing up the software that comes standard on your KAYPRO 10. Go the floppy route, and even then you will have two options to consider. They are:

1) To back up the software on floppies, follow the same kind of general procedure outlined above for the 2 and 4;
2) Use a special software program, *Multi-Floppy Backup and Restore (MUFBAR) System* for CP/M and M/MP, Version 2.0, which comes bundled with your KAYPRO 10.

Either option would be OK, but we recommend the second method over the first because the MUFBAR system does many things concerning data management and file marking which you cannot do independently of the program. For example, the MUFBAR program has three interconnected programs and features.

MUFBAK. This initial backup program splits up files of up to 8 megabytes in length. This means that all files are automatically broken up into smaller ones so that they will fit on the floppies and will ensure maximum use of a floppy's available space.

MUFREST. This program is, as the name suggests, the restore program you can run to put back on hard disk all those smaller files copied to the floppies via the MUFBAK program. Each of the MUFBAK files contains its own program-supplied file head, which not only gives each file a discrete identity but ensures that files copied from the hard disk will be returned to precisely the same place from which they were copied. This feature becomes important when you wish to be certain you can transfer files from floppy back to hard disk, and to end up with files being returned to their original User Areas in a manageable and logical manner. You can see the difficulties of using tape in this regard, we're sure.

MUFLOOK. MUFLOOK is the third and final program making up the MUFBAR software package designed exclusively for hard disk file transfer to and from floppy disks. MUFLOOK permits you to inspect on your console the information that MUF-BAK has put at the head of every file transferred from the hard disk to the floppies.

Now, having given you this quick overview of the options available to you, let's get down to business. If you want to make things very simple for yourself, use the MUFBAR program that resides on portion A of the hard disk. (Yes, you'll be copying the program used to copy the program used to copy the program. But that's OK, as long as the program works, and we found it to be very easy to use.)

Here at last are the steps you must take to successfully backup the software on the hard disk:

1) Buy a box of 10 double-density, double-sided quality floppy disks.

2) Turn on your KAYPRO 10, put a blank new disk in Drive C.

3) See the Master Menu. Press ⟨ESC⟩ to exit the menu and enter CP/M.

4) See the A0> prompt. Enter FLPYFMT ⟨Return⟩.

5) Follow the program directions to format eight of the new floppies.

   Put each of the eight disks in Drive C, formatting them one at a time until all eight are formatted.

6) Exit the floppy format program and return to CP/M. See A0> Enter MASMENU ⟨Return⟩.

7) See the Master Menu on the console. Move the Selector Bar down the menu to the option: BACKING UP FILES. Enter ⟨Return⟩.

8) See the KAYPRO 10 Backup Menu. Press the DOWN ARROW to move the selector bar to the Instructions option. Enter ⟨Return⟩.

9) See the instructions on the screen. Read the instructions carefully. Then exit the Backup Menu to the Master Menu and, using the DOWN arrow, move the Selector Bar to the SAFETY program. When at safety option, enter ⟨Return⟩ to run the program. After you see the message on the console telling you the safety program has run, turn off your KAYPRO.

10) Read the MUFBAR manual in the back of your KAYPRO 10 user's guide.

11) Turn on your KAYPRO 10.

12) See the Master Menu. Again, use the DOWN arrow to move the selector bar to the BACKUP FILES option, and then enter ⟨Return⟩.

13) See the KAYPRO 10 Backup Menu on the screen. Use the DOWN arrow to move the Selector Bar to Instructions. Read them one more time, then move the selector bar to the option called RUN BACKUP PROGRAM, and then enter ⟨Return⟩.

14) See the MUFBAR program.

Read the MUFBAR program instructions on the console. Put one of the eight formatted disks in Drive C, and then proceed with the MUFBAK Program, copying all files from each of the User Areas on Drive A of the hard disk. (This will mean User Areas 0 through 10 for most versions of the KAYPRO 10, but many will have bundled software only on User Areas 0 through 7. In any case, the eight disks will hold all the files on Drive A.)

15) See the last file from Drive A copied via the MUFBAK program.

Remove the disk from Drive C and exit MUFBAR to CP/M.

16) See the A0> prompt.

Type SAFETY ⟨Return⟩. After the SAFETY program has run, turn off the KAYPRO 10.

Write the labels for your disks before you put them on the disks. You might call them "Backup Software for the KAYPRO 10," or you could label them for each of the programs they contain. *Put write-protection tabs over the write protection notches on each disk and return them to their box, storing them in a safe place.* If you were careful about following directions, you now have successfully backed up all of the software on your hard disk. Make sure that those backup copies are given the special care they deserve. This goes for *all* backup copies of *all* software for *all* models.

There, that was fairly easily done, right? Now let's find out some important things about the CP/M operating system that runs your KAYPRO computer.

Chapter 7

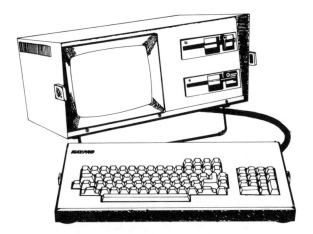

CP/M—Your
KAYPRO's Operating System

T he system that operates all three KAYPRO computers, the II or 2, the 4 and the 10. The initials, not surprisingly, stand for Control Program for Microprocessors CP/M is the fundamental organizing software for your KAYPRO. It tells the microprocessor (the brain) what peripheral devices are available, and it is the interface, or electronically logical connection, between those pieces of hardware, the software program you happen to be running, and the microprocessor.

CP/M is an ordering device that stacks different functions and activities. For instance, it connects the microprocessor with the CRT. It feeds your current software into and out of the microprocessor. It connects the software to the screen. It feeds the printer the data that has been crunched by the software. Words or numbers, it doesn't care. It's all data to CP/M.

THE FOUR PARTS OF CP/M

BIOS. CP/Ms *Basic Input/Output System,* also called CBIOS (*Customized* BIOS for your KAYPRO), M's checks for any hardware malfunction; transfers data to and from the screen, the printer and the microprocessor at speeds each unit can handle; checks the moving data for errors; finds the correct unit; and checks to see if the unit is busy; and waits until the unit is free. It is an electronic traffic cop and a cruise control all in one.

BDOS. The *Basic Disk Operating System* controls the filing and storage of data on your disk. A disk is said to have numerous files that can range from a size of one page (256 bytes) to the whole disk. Each file is composed of records having the same potential for variation in size. BDOS assigns data to records, and it also maintains the file assignment of each record.

CCP. The *Command Control Processor* is your direct connection through CP/M to the screen. The CCP reads the commands and the data you type on the keyboard, and it feeds that information to CP/M. The CCP contains built-in commands that we will review later in this chapter.

TPA. The term *Transient Program Area* refers to a storage area that contains both the software program you are running and the data that program is managing. That information is kept in a file on a disk. The name of that particular file, also known as ⟨filename⟩ in "technobabble," is the command that you use to load that program and file into the microprocessor and from there to the screen or the printer.

You will notice that your KAYPRO tells you that you are running CP/M version 2.2F. Older KAYPROs will show Version 2.2. Version refers to the evolving sophistication of CP/M since its invention. If you want a history of this evolution we recommend a longer discussion of the whole system.

HOW IT WORKS, OR CP/M ARCHITECTURE

You can see from Fig. 7-1 that TPA is much larger than the rest of the sections of CP/M. In fact, TPA equals the size of your main memory minus the areas taken up by CCP, BDOS, and BIOS. Now, let's look at the process your KAYPRO follows every time you turn it on.

When you *boot* the system you tell CP/M where to find the beginning of CCP, and you load it into RAM. It needs to know the precise location of CCP, which can vary according to the size of TPA. That's the beginning, and you will find yourself booting quite often to restore the system, or to return to GO. No fines, no jails, just start at the beginning.

In Chapter three you used COPY or PIP to copy your working disks and you saw how boot worked then. Now that you know a little more about what CP/M is, let's try a "cold" boot and a "warm" boot. Turn your KAYPRO on, and observe the request to put a disk in Drive A. Remembering to handle only the label of the disk, insert the working copy of your CP/M disk in Drive A and close the drive door, or push the button marked PUSH. Your screen will show you:

KAYPRO II (or 2 or 4 or 10) 63K CP/M vers 2.2F A0>

That was a *cold boot* because you started with the power off, turned it on, and booted the system. On the back of your KAYPRO there is a red button you can push to get a *warm boot,* which means booting the system with the power on. Try pushing the red button. You will see the display flash back to the original message and then redisplay the A0> prompt. You can also warm boot from the keyboard by pressing CTRL and C at the same time. We will talk more about control characters in that section.

When you booted your KAYPRO the boot program read the entire CP/M system into main memory. Control then moved to CBIOS, which then moved to CCP, and you were ready to go when the A> prompt came up on your screen. That prompt is the computer's way of telling you it is ready to respond to commands from the keyboard. The A0> prompt also tells you that you are at command level. You are at program level when you enter a program.

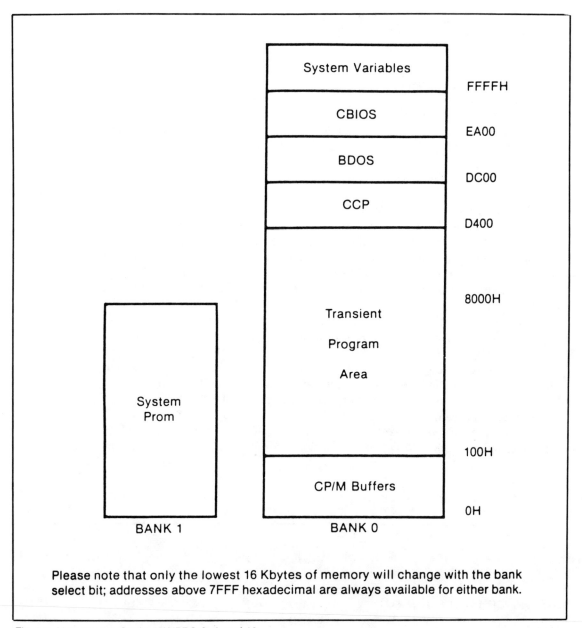

	System Variables	
		FFFFH
	CBIOS	
		EA00
	BDOS	
		DC00
	CCP	
		D400
		8000H
System Prom	Transient Program Area	
		100H
	CP/M Buffers	
		0H
BANK 1	BANK 0	

Please note that only the lowest 16 Kbytes of memory will change with the bank select bit; addresses above 7FFF hexadecimal are always available for either bank.

Fig. 7-1. Memory map for the KAYPRO 2, 4, and 10.

BUILT-IN COMMANDS

CP/M has a long list of built-in commands that all function at the command level and that are part of the CCP. You will find some of these commands very useful in working with your KAYPRO. In this book we are going to present the most common and the simplest of these built-in commands.

DIR. This stands for DIRECTORY, and it will give you a list of files contained on your disk. Try it by typing DIR and Return. You should get something like Fig. 7-2 which shows a DIR listing for the files that make up CP/M. Return, by the way, is generally the signal to the microprocessor to execute the command you have typed. That produces what computer language calls a *menu*.

Directory entries contain the name of the file, a.k.a. ⟨filename⟩, and the other is to ask for all files of a particular ⟨filetype⟩. For instance, you might have files called ⟨TRY.ONE⟩, ⟨DONE.ONE⟩, and ⟨ZORT.ONE⟩. To see all the files of the type ⟨.ONE⟩ enter DIR *.ONE and DIRectory will list them for you. For the present, enter DIR *.COM to see a list of all the COMmand files on your CP/M disk. As you name more files and filetypes and your disks become crowded with information, you will find this function to be very useful.

DIRectory will work for each drive in your machine. If you are in Drive A and want to see what is on that disk, type DIR and Return. Simple enough, you have already done that. If you also have a disk in Drive B, then type B: and Return; wait for the B> prompt, and then type DIR to discover what is on Drive B. If you want to stay in A drive, you can also type DIR B: ⟨Return⟩ to see the files in Drive B. If you have a KAYPRO 10, DIRectory can be used to display all files in any of the 15 user groups on Drives A and B of the hard disk, as well as the floppy disk Drive C.

DIRectory is a function of CP/M that automatically lists all your files and creates an automatic index of your information. *TYPE* provides you with the next level of searching through your files. Both DIR and TYPE have to do with retrieving and reviewing information that you have stored. TYPE allows you to review a file on the screen without printing it. This feature may be very useful if you are carrying your KAYPRO from one place to another, and you don't want to carry the printer as well. TYPE gives you instant recall of data you have on a disk.

When you are at command level, that is, when you see the A> or B> prompt and the flashing cursor (for the KAYPRO that is a flashing underscore, as you have noticed by now), enter

A> TYPE ⟨filename⟩ ⟨Return⟩

```
                        CP/M Directory


A:  MOVCPM    COM : PIP      COM : SUBMIT   COM : XSUB      COM
A:  ED        COM : ASM      COM : DDT      COM : STAT      COM
A:  SYSGEN    COM : DUMP     COM : COPY     COM : SSCOPY    COM
A:  TERM      COM : SBASIC   COM : OVERLAYB COM : BASICLIB  REL
A:  USERLIB   REL : FAC      BAS : XAMN     BAS : DPLAY     BAS
A:  CONFIG    COM : LOAD     COM : DUMP     COM : BAUD      COM
A>
```

Fig. 7-2. CP/M directory.

Remember that ⟨filename⟩ is a generic term, and that to make this command work you need a specific ⟨filename⟩.

Here are two tips about using type. First, the file you want to look at must contain printable characters. These include textual material, source coding, or character data. COM files are generally not printable, and you will see a lot of unintelligible garbage on your screen if you TYPE a COM file. Second, if you have more than one screen of information in a file, it will all scroll past you and look like a speed-reading test. That may not be convenient, or even useful. So, if you want to stop the scroll at any time to read the file, type CTRL S. Once you have read that material press any *single* key to continue. CTRL S is another control character that is part of CP/M.

USERS. Version 2.0 and later enhancements of CP/M enable you to assign files to any one, or all, of 16 different user numbers from 0 through 15. This capability has a number of possible applications. Owners of the 10 will need to be able to alternate between different user numbers to access all of their software and to be able to PIP files to and from their floppy discs.

For owners of the other KAYPROs, user numbers are more a matter of convenience. For instance, if you and your spouse and any number of your children are using the KAYPRO, everyone can be assigned a User number to keep the different people's work separate. This practice would also apply to small offices where a number of people were entering data, or where you wanted to separate different accounts. (Once you have amassed enough information on one disk, you may want to go to a separate disk for each person, or account.) Thinking of each disk as a separate file drawer is a useful way to conceive of an organizing scheme. At least, with USER you have the potential to create different and separate sets of files on the same disk.

The possibility of secrecy pops up here. If you know about the 16 possible user numbers, and other people working the system don't know about them, then you can hide confidential information under a random user number. Another person could only find that information by calling all 16 user numbers separately and asking for a DIRectory under each, to see if there were any information stored under that number. It's not very secure, but it's still a possibility.

CP/M assumes USER #0 unless it is told differently. To create a separate USER number, type USER *n* (where *n* is any number from 1 through 15) and Return. The screen will reply with the A> or B> prompt and all information that you enter under that number is exclusive to that number. To move from that user number, enter the next user number that you want to work in. CP/M recognizes only the active user number, which is the one most recently specified. With the KAYPRO 10 you might move from USER A0 to USER 15 by entering USER 15 at the A0 prompt.

Note: if you cold boot a KAYPRO 10 with SYSGEN in Drive C, the drives will reorder themselves. Drive C becomes the logged disk drive (or Drive A), Drive A becomes Drive B, and Drive B becomes Drive C.

ERA. This stands for ERAse, and it allows you to erase any file on the disk. If you have specified different user numbers, remember that you have to be in the user number that the file resides in to erase it.

REN. This command allows you to REName any existing file. You can't rename a file that isn't there, or one that belongs to another user number. Also, CP/M does not allow you to use the same name twice. If you had a file named BLURT, and you wanted to call a second file BLURT, CP/M would come back with a NOT FOUND message. When renaming files it is a good idea to have the directory on the screen. The command format for REN is:

A> REN ⟨newname⟩=⟨oldname⟩ ⟨Return⟩

For example:

A> REN BLURT=MOVCPM ⟨Return⟩

You probably won't want to call the MOVCPM file BLURT, but anything is possible.

CONTROL CHARACTERS

Control characters are created by pressing the control key (CTRL) and an upper-case letter at the same time. The CTRL function parallels the difference in action between upper- and lowercase letters on a typewriter, and it adds a third dimension to your KAYPRO keyboard. When the instructions indicates CTRL + letter key, that means press CTRL and the other key at the same time. Pressing the CTRL key by itself causes nothing to happen, just like hitting the shift key by itself.

Control characters are reserved for special functions at command level and at program level. For instance, at command level CTRL C will reboot the system, while in WordStar CTRL C scrolls the cursor down the screen. The following list of functions applies to CP/M command level; those functions may or may not be valid at program level. Each program handles CTRL somewhat differently.

CTRL C. Entering CTRL C will abort whatever program you are in (most of the time), and it will warm boot the system. We have already discussed booting the system, and this third way to boot is more convenient than reaching around to the back of the computer.

CTRL S. To halt the scroll of any information on your screen, type CTRL S. Particularly when you use TYPE to review data you will need to stop it from time to time. You may continue your scroll by typing any single letter.

CTRL P. Entering a CTRL P sequence turns on and off your line printer. You would start to print data with a CTRL P, and if you wanted to interrupt the run—to correct the paper feed, for instance—you would type CTRL P again. CTRL P is called a *toggle* in computer language because it acts rather like an on-off switch.

CTRL U. CTRL U will delete a current command line from memory. Once deleted, your line will be followed by a number sign (#) called a *pound sign* in computer talk. For instance, if you typed ERRAR when you meant ERROR you would type CTRL U; the screen would then show you ERRAR#.

CTRL H or DELete. CTRL H will backspace the cursor one space and delete the letter or number in that space. DELete will perform the same function.

CTRL X. This CTRL command will backspace the cursor to the beginning of the line.

TRANSIENT PROGRAMS

Transient programs are loaded into main memory by CP/M, and they are used to get information about your disks, to create files, to assemble new programs, and to perform common operations, PIP, which stands for *Peripheral Interchange Program*, is probably the most useful of these commands, and we'll start with it.

PIP

PIP allows you to copy individual files and groups of files from one disk to another and to any peripheral device such as a printer. PIP copies, combines, loads, and prints files. It also allows you to copy files from one USER number to another. In general, it is worth the space to put PIP on every disk, even if you don't copy the whole CP/M menu. Here's how:

> Put your CP/M disk in Drive A.
> Put a newly formatted disk in Drive B.
> A> PIP B:=A:PIP.COM[V0]

PIPing a file does not change its original status—even though you may build in changes to the copied version—because PIP copies an *image* of the original file to random access memory and then sends that copy to the destination file or disk. That means you can't hurt your data when you PIP it. That's a good reason to use PIP.

PIP and the Disk Drives. Drive names (A: or B:) can be used, or they can be left out of PIP commands. If the drive name is left out, the active drive is assumed. Further, you can PIP a file on one disk to another on the same disk.

PIP Command Format. The generic command format for PIP is:

> A> PIP ⟨destinationfile⟩=⟨sourcefile⟩[parameters]⟨Return⟩

Warning: if the destination file already exists and it has the same name, then executing the PIP command will replace the data in the old file with the data in the new file.

PIPing on the Same Drive. Let's say you want to copy one file, TEXT.ONE, into a new file, TEXT.TWO, on the same disk, and that disk already has the PIP program. Here's how:

> A> PIP TEXT.TWO=TEXT.ONE ⟨Return⟩

PIPing from One Drive to Another. Let's say you want to copy TEXT.ONE from Drive A to Drive B to store it, so that you can free up space on Drive A. Here we go:

> A> PIP B:TEXT.ONE=A: TEXT.ONE ⟨Return⟩

PIPing General Files. Files have two kinds of names: the specific filename which comes before the period, and the more general filetype, or *extent*, which comes after the period. So far, we have shown you how to PIP specific files, but let's suppose that you have a group of files that all have the generic filetype PAM, and you want to copy all Pam's files from a disk in your A drive to one in your B drive.

> A> PIP B:=*.PAM ⟨Return⟩

The star, or asterisk, tells CP/M that you want all files of the type PAM copied on your disk in the B drive. You could also perform this same maneuver by substituting a ? for the asterisk. (Using the * or the ? in place of an explicit file specification is known in the computer business as using a *wild card.*)

PIPing User Numbers. If you want to transfer files from a USER number other than 0 on one disk to a different USER number on a different disk, follow this format. Here's PAM again:

A0>G3 ⟨Return⟩

PIP A:[GB]=B:*PAM [V0]⟨Return⟩

That means copy all of PAM's files in USER area 3 on Drive B to USER area 0 in the A drive. PIP is a pip. On the KAYPRO 10 it would look like this:

A15> PIP
A:=C:.PAM[G3V] Return

That means move all the Pam's files from USER area 3 on Drive C to USER area 15 on Drive A of the hard disk.

PIPing Several Files at Once. PIP allows you to combine several source files into one destination file. Let's say that Pam had three separate files on Disk A, and you decide it would be more useful to have all of Pam's files combined into one. Here's how.

A> PIP B:NEW.PAM=ONE.PAM,TWO.PAM,THREE.PAM ⟨Return⟩

In technobabble this kind of combination is called *concatenating* the files, and the advantage of using this format instead of the *.PAM method is that the files will be copied in the order you specify. To copy those same files to a different disk remember to add the destination disk drive.

A> PIP B:NEW.PAM=A:ONE.PAM,TWO.PAM,THREE.PAM   RETURN

Note: you cannot concatenate .COM files like PIP, STAT, OR SYSGEN.

PIPing from Other Disk Formats. Pip allows you to copy files from a single-sided disk to a machine that uses double-sided disks. That's very useful when you have disks from a KAYPRO II that you want to run on a 4. It will also copy files from a Xerox 820, or an Otrona, but it is *not* clear that these foreign files will run in your KAYPRO. You may, however, try the Multi-Format program if you have the newer CP/M 2.2F disk. According to the KAYPRO documentation, this program allows you to copy KAYPRO single- and double-density disks to each other's formats, and to copy disks formatted on Osbornes, Xerox 820s, TRS-80s, IBM PCs, TI, Morrow, Zenith, and NEC.

Parameters and PIP. Adding *parameters* to your PIP command adds different and simultaneous functions. Here is a short list of possibilities. Remember that the parameter is specified with brackets, [parameter], and that it follows the list of source files. You have already seen a couple of them—[V0], [Gn], for instance.

[E]   [E] stands for echo, and you would add this parameter if you wanted the data to be displayed on your screen as it was copied. Using echo slows down your operation, but at the same time it gives you a chance to verify your data.

[G*n*] This parameter allows you to PIP from one user number to another. In this case, *n* refers to a user number between 0 and 15. As is usual with PIP, the destination file is locked into your current user number. If you are USER #0 and your cohort, Pam, is USER #3, try this to get a copy of Pam's work:

A> PIP ME=∗••∗[G3] ⟨Return⟩

Again, if you own a 10, you would enter this command to PIP Pam's work ONLY from user #3 of Drive B of the hard disk to user number 0 of the floppy in Drive C:

B3>USER 0 ⟨Return⟩
BO>PIP
∗PIP ME=∗.PAM[G3V] RETURN
∗C:=B:∗.PAM[V0] RETURN

Something new! ∗.∗ means every file under USER 3. You could also have said, for the 2 and the 4:

A> PIP ME=∗.PAM[G3]

[VO] This parameter tells CP/M to *verify* all the files that it is transferring. Adding this parameter will double the time needed to make the transfer, and it will *verify* that all the data have been transferred to the new file before returning to CP/M. If we take the previous operation on Pam's files and decide that we want to verify it, add a V0 after the 3 but before the closing bracket.

A> PIP ME=∗.PAM[G3V0] RETURN

PIP and your Printer. You can us PIP to send information to your printer with LST or PRN. The difference between the two is that PRN will add line numbers to your printed data. PRN will also indent every tab 8 spaces and it will make eveyr page 60 lines long. There are ways to change those automatic parameters, called *defaults* in computer language. First let's look at LST. Let's say you want to print PAM's files.

A> PIP LST:=∗.PAM   RETURN

Don't add a [VO] because the printer cannot verify its output, and your system will hang up.

If you use PRN and you want to specify parameters for the page, here are a series of parameters that you can add in your brackets.

P*n*   This specifies that your page is to have *n* lines and tells the printer to feed another page when it has printed that number of lines.

T*n*   This allows you to change the tab indentation of your data to *n* spaces.

N   This allows you to add line numbers at the beginning of each line, in the same way that LST does.

Here is a command to print PAM's files.

A> PIP PRN=*.PAM[NT5P50] ⟨Return⟩

You have told the printer to number the lines, to maintain a 5-space tab indentation, and to print a 50-line page. You can add those changes to LST as well.

Error Messages. The PIP program sends back two common error messages. One is BDOS ERROR, and the other is a filetype that ends with three dollar signs, $$$. BDOS ERROR probably means that you have been trying to write to a *read-only* file. If this has been the case, you need to return to CP/M and reboot the drive in which that particular disk currently resides.

The $$$ filetype marks a place on the disk where CP/M tried unsuccessfully to make a new copy. That may mean that your disk is too full to take a new file, or it may indicate another problem. To get rid of the $$$ file at command level, type ERA *.$$$ ⟨Return⟩, and it will disappear. If you think there might be a space problem, check your disk with STAT (coming up next).

STAT

STAT will display the space remaining on a disk, the active USER numbers, and the read/write status of the disk. CP/M allows you to specify a disk as *read-only* (RO) or *read/write* (R/W). *Read only* is a protective device that prohibits a user from writing information on a disk and, consequently, from altering the information on that disk. For most purposes, STAT's primary function is to display the amount of available space left on a disk and the space being occupied by individual users and files. This function is particularly valuable because it can save you from overloading a disk and thereby losing all the data you entered after the disk was full.

STAT by itself (or, as they say in technobabble, with no *operands*) will display the read/write (R/W) status and the amount of space available on a disk. For example:

A> STAT ⟨Return⟩
A> R/W, Space: 194K

tells you that the disk has a read/write status and that there are 194K bytes left on the diskette.

STAT A: or B: STAT with the drive specifications A: or B: will tell you how many bytes are left on the drive you specify.

STAT ⟨filename⟩, ⟨filetype⟩. This command will display the status of a file. Try STAT PIP.COM, and you will see:

```
Recs Bytes Ext Acc
 58   8K    1 R/W A:PIP.COM
Bytes remaining on A:  194K
```

STAT *.⟨**filetype**⟩. Using STAT with a wild card filename and an explicit filetype will tell you the status of every file that has the same filetype. Try STAT *.COM to see all the command files on your CP/M disk.

```
A> STAT *.COM ⟨Return⟩
```

STAT USR: STAT USR: will tell you the USERs and their file space on your disk. This command can be followed by a DIR after the USER number to see a menu of all the nonsystem files on the disk.

STAT A:DSK: STAT A:DSK: (or B:DSK:) will give you the capacity of your disk. On the KAYPRO 4 it looks like this.

A:	Drive Characteristics	
3152: 128	Byte Record Capacity	Means that the disk can handle 3,152 records of 128 bytes each.
394:	Kilobyte Drive Capacity	Means 394K.
64: 32	Byte Directory Entries	Means 64 DIR entries of 32 bytes each.
64:	Checked Directory Entries	Means your system will check 64 entries.
256:	Records/Extent	Means 256 entries are possible for each filetype.
16:	Records/Block	Means 16 records per block.
40:	Sectors/Track	Means 40 sectors per disk track.
1:	Reserved Track	Means one track is reserved, for CP/M in this case.

Note: when you check a data disk from which you intend to print, many people advise leaving 25K blank to ensure that you do not overrun any material. This choice will be between you and your printer. On the KAYPRO 10 the command presents the following information: STAT A: (or B: or C:).

STAT has other functions that you may want to consider, and we recommend seeking out a more extensive discussion of CP/M to examine them.

Configuring for a Serial Printer

Serial printers work differently than parallel ones, as we have commented before. If you get a serial printer, here is what you need to do to run it from your KAYPRO.

1) To set up to run a serial printer   Insert your CP/M copy disk in Drive A,

2) See a menu that says KAYPRO 2, 4, or 10 CONFIGURATION PROGRAM

your WordStar copy disc in Drive B, and type CONFIG ⟨Return⟩.

Type an uppercase I ⟨Return⟩. (Lowercase i will give you a help message).

3) See the IOBYTE menu.

Press ⟨Line Feed⟩ until LST=TTY is in reverse video. Press ⟨Return⟩ and uppercase X (in that order).

4) See the CONFIG menu.

Press Cap.

5) See baud rate menu.

Type in your printer's baud rate and ⟨Return⟩.

6) See a confirming prompt.

Type 0 ⟨Return⟩.

7) See the CONFIG menu.

Type X ⟨Return⟩.

8) See the A0> prompt.

Hit the red reset button once.

9) Now, you need to SYSGEN your WordStar copy disk.

Type SYSGEN and follow the prompts to SYSGEN the disk in Drive B.

10) You should be ready to go.

D.COM

D.COM is a great little wrinkle that is part of CP/M for the 10 (and now for the 4). If you have a 2 or an older 4, you can get a copy from a friend with a 10. It alphabetizes your files, tells you how much space they occupy, and how much space you have left. It is a variation of STAT, and it is much easier to read. We recommend it.

We have noticed, however, that D.COM does not always provide an accurate reading of the amount of space left on a disk. Its behavior in this respect is erratic, and it appears—sometimes—to report the last total figure from a previous screen instead of the current one. For example, if you checked a disk that reported 18K of space left, then went back to a file, deleted 70K of information, and checked the disk again with D.COM, you might find the sum to still read as 18K instead of the 88K you had created. This peculiarity works in the opposite mathematical direction. At this writing we have no solution to this oddity, but be careful, you might burn a file. Check D.COM's addition and subtraction. D.COM seems erratic under CP/M version 2.2, while under 2.2F we have experienced no trouble with it. Figure 7-3 shows the D.COM screen.

Name	Ext	Bytes	Name	Ext	Bytes	Name	Ext	Bytes	Name	Ext	Bytes
ACK	KAY	2K	! CHAP12	KAY	56K	! LTR1	TAB	4K	! TITLE	BAK	2K
CAPTIONSBAK		4K	! CHAP15	BAK	32K	! LTR2	BAK	2K	! TITLE	KAY	2K
CAPTIONSMSS		4K	! CHAP15	KAY	32K	! LTR2	TAB	2K	! TOC	BAK	2K
CHAP11	BAK	20K	! CHAP16	BAK	8K	! PIP	COM	8K	! TOC	KAY	2K
CHAP11	KAY	20K	! CHAP16	KAY	8K	! STAT	COM	6K			
CHAP12	BAK	56K	! D	COM	4K	! SYSGEN	COM	2K			

22 File(s), occupying 278K of 390K total capacity
40 directory entries and 112K bytes remain on B:

Fig. 7-3. D.COM screen.

This chapter has been a brief review of the CP/M functions that we feel are vital to establish your comfort and flexibility with the KAYPRO. If you start to program and to work with code, rather than the software packages available to you, then a more extensive knowledge of CP/M will be required.

Chapter 8

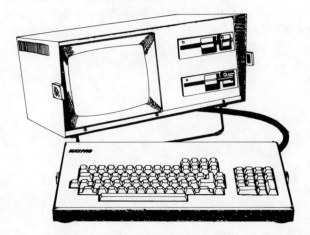

Features of the Bundled Software

This chapter is designed to act as a signpost to help you find which software packages you want to work with. After this chapter you can skip to any appropriate later chapter to help you to get up and running on the software package of your choice.

A survey of KAYPRO's bundled software currently available falls into three broad categories: word processing programs, serious data manipulation applications, programming languages and compilers, plus a subset of the last group, games. The first area of the software from KAYPRO follows the traditional supply and demand axiom, which says that wherever there is a serious demand for a product, there will soon be a supplier on the scene attempting to meet that demand.

Business processes lots of paper, and text processors were created to meet that need. This is also the case with spreadsheet financial analysis programs, database management programs, and telecommunications programs. Words, numbers, electronic storage and retrieval, and communications via the computer are the basic needs; literally hundreds of competing programs have appeared, all claiming to be superior at meeting the needs of the business community. Some of the successful survivors of these competitions have been bundled with your computer.

For reasons already discussed, we are not going to discuss the variations of BASIC and the compiler languages that have also been bundled with your KAYPRO. If serious programming is your immediate need, then we recommend you check the bookshelves. There is a vast array of material out there to help you.

KAYPRO bundles a good assortment of games in OBASIC and MBASIC. They include StarTrek, Chase, BlackJack, Wump, Rocket, Taxman, Ladder, Catchum, and Aliens. A generic biorhythm chart is also included, and in our opinion reading that one is like reading the horoscope in your daily newspaper—fun but not too reliable. While they may be fun for some people, it is our judgement that the serious business or professional person will not want to spend a lot of time with them.

While playing games on the KAYPRO is one way for you to begin to use your computer, it is not the kind of hands-on application work we think most important at this stage of your introduction. Most of the games are difficult to play and the frustration levels generated can be counterproductive, slowing your progress with doing the real work. In fact, many of them employ abusive and hostile language that reprimands you for not being quick enough. We did not find their attitude to be positive or supportive in any way. For your kids that may be a different story. Many games were invented as working relief for programmers. StarTrek, for instance, originally was a memory map checker for IBM; while the programmers have a good time with them, their value to those who are not computer professionals is questionable.

The software application packages that come bundled with your KAYPRO permit you to do some fancy footwork in the worlds of text processing, database management, spreadsheet financial analysis, and telecommunications. We want to introduce briefly each of these applications programs to you, giving you in turn some idea of what each of them can do for you. Once you have seen the overview you may then choose the ones that will do the most work for you.

Text Processing Programs. This is an extremely critical component of any software package. Without a good text processor, you are handicapped when using the KAYPRO in business and the professions. Fortunately, KAYPRO presently offers a very usable pair of programs in WordStar and MailMerge.

Without a doubt, the single most impressive feature of WordStar is the fact that *you get what you see* on the screen! That is, you get everything but the special text editing characters which don't print out—like ∧S before and after a word, which tells the printer to underline that particular word.

WordStar has another excellent feature, and that is the relative ease of using WordStar's voluminous stylistic, help, copying, deleting, and printing command structure. The range of text processing commands available through WordStar, plus their power when used to manipulate text and files, is more impressive than what you get in many other text processing programs.

WordStar is a very "friendly" word processing program, particularly for writers accustomed to a typewriter, because of its close correspondence between the screen and the printed copy. We happen to like WordStar because of its overall sophistication as a processing tool, and because the bundled manual is (in our opinion) better than most others on the market today. Even though WordStar does not have a lessons disk, its internal help menus and its external documentation go a long way toward compensating for the lack of one. Futher, once you learn the contents of the seven different menus in WordStar, you can suppress them and don't have to look at them.

MailMerge allows you to turn your Rolodex into a mailing list that can address a form letter you have written in WordStar to hundreds or thousands of customers. With this program you can also create a command file that will address mailing labels and your envelopes. Command files can also be created to print a series of files such as chapters in a book in a row without you having to invoke the print commands for each file.

Spelling Programs. Staying with text processing a while longer, you will be glad to know that your KAYPRO comes with an excellent spelling program. SPELL from The WORD Plus. Here is a quick Cook's tour of that electronic dictionary and our opinion of its usefulness.

KAYPRO has made a good choice in selecting SPELL, by Oasis Systems, which runs interactively with WordStar and other CP/M-based text processor programs. SPELL has 45,000 words in its dictionary, which is adequate for most routine office correspondence. You can also supplement SPELL by creating your own special file of words (correctly spelled at the time you enter them!), thereby adding your private working vocabulary to the larger one already offered by SPELL.

SPELL does have another advantage, though, and that is that it will show you any misspelled word or typo *in context* and *right now*. That means that you run the program to isolate all words not recognized by SPELL as legitimate, and then you have the option to see that word in context right away—which permits you to add the word to a special dictionary that holds your working vocabulary, or to correct it then, or to mark it for correction later. We like SPELL and think you will, too. We think you'll find it easy to use because it is immediate; we recommend that you give it a try when you use WordStar.

Other Useful Language Tools. Oasis Systems' overall program, is called The WORD Plus, and it contains eight programs. We will discuss them briefly.

- TW (The WORD) initiates the SPELL program.
- REVIEW lets you see words in context.
- MARKFIX marks misspelled words in the file.
- HYPHEN automatically hyphenates words.
- FIND looks up words or phrases in a long text.
- ANAGRAM produces anagrams.
- SPELL checks spelling.
- LOOKUP produces an array of similar words.
- WC (Word Count) counts words in a file, and that is very handy for authors who need to tell their agents and publishers how long the latest best seller is.
- WORDFREQ counts how often a particular word shows up in a file. This is also a very useful tool for writers, particularly for people who get attached to a particular word.

We think you will agree from this quick rundown that The WORD Plus offers you a nifty package of language-related tools. We are confident that you will find many uses for these programs; moreover, they are extremely easy to use. Now, let's look at what you get in the way of database management programs.

Database Management. With dBASE II, DataStar (and its interactive companion programs, CalcStar and ReportStar), and Profit/Microplan, KAYPRO offers you three distinct data processing packages. These powerful database programs are useful because they allow you to create your own database structures designed for your particular business, move selected data from one file to another, and enter data into two database records to suit your own needs.

One primary difference among these programs should be noted. dBASE II is a *relational database management system*, while the others are *file handlers* or *spreadsheets*. Operationally, the difference means that with dBASE II you can build separate file structures, reorder them without destroying the data, and relate them to each other without having to build a whole new database. This relational ability saves you an immense amount of work once you begin to accumulate a lot of data. The others do not have this relational ability, but they are perfectly useful in doing more limited tasks.

With any of them, you can turn your current physical filing system, like a Rolodex or a filing cabinet, into an electronic filing system, label-generating mill, etc. This means getting the word out to your clients in Syracuse who buy your ski wax applicators, which they also use to open beer bottles and as rescue signal mirrors in the back country. You can also do this with WordStar and MailMerge; dBASE II and the Star products will read some WordStar files.

You can also use DataStar/ReportStar or dBASE II to set up your inventory and all those part numbers and other specs into a database which is easily maintained, added to, deleted from, and printed to specification. This can also work with invoices, and the possibilities are up to you. Here is where dBASE II outshines the Star products: it allows you to set up more than one file, (for example, an inventory file and a billing file) and it will update your inventory from your billing file.

Spreadsheets. In this area of applications software you strike it rich, because you get three different mathematical spreadsheet analytic systems with your KAYPRO. Profitplan and Microplan share nearly identical menus, while Microplan allows for more programming functions and higher mathematical and statistical work. In any case, they both allow you to do fairly advanced financial analysis and planning. You could even set up a tax program with them. They are also excellent for doing financial projections, budgeting, and other business related calculations. (dBASE II will also perform all these functions more reliably with less trouble.)

The third spreadsheet is CalcStar and it offers several important and interesting spreadsheet features. For example, with CalcStar you can balance checkbooks, estimate job costs, depreciate assets, forecast business trends, prepare income statements, and control your inventory for golf balls, white swans, or your store's tapes and records of Fletcher Henderson classics. (Again, dBASE II will do all these tasks easily.) Now let's look at the telecommunications program that comes with your KAYPRO.

Telecommunications. Suprterm is a full-fledged telecommunications program that KAYPRO designed for use primarily with the Hayes Smartmodem. Even so, the program is supposed to work with any RS-232C-compatible 300 or 1200 baud modem. Suprterm is bundled with the 10 and 4 and is an option with the 2. The 4 is the only machine of the three to come with a modem installed. It is limited to 300 baud, however, and (unfortunately) it is not fully operational at this writing. Suprterm is fully automatic in its command structure only when it works with the Hayes Smartmodem; otherwise, you need to respond to its many prompts to make it work.

What can Suprterm do for you? Well, you can "access the infosphere," that's what. Put simply, you can communicate with someone at the other end of a wire who also has a computer of practically any shape. It allows you to send data and text files over the phone lines, microwave networks, satellites, and other means of receiving data and text from other entities out there. You can access very large (and very small) databases, you can store that good stuff that you get from them directly on the hard disk in your 10 (or on a floppy in your 2 or 4), and then you can print it out from there. We used Suprterm extensively with a Hayes 1200 modem and our KAYPRO 10, both sending and receiving data and text files with no difficulty whatsoever.

Suprterm is your access to the world of electronic information—plus a credit card to pay the access fees to the different databases. It may well be worth it. You can get the Dow-Jones directly for managing your stocks, for instance.

The Perfect Appendixes. Perfect software was bundled with older models of the KAYPRO; in the interests of people who have Perfect Filer, Perfect Writer, Perfect Speller, and Perfect Calc, we have included short introductions to their programs in the appendixes at the back of this book.

Well, you are now entering a world of choices in the software you want to use, and we wish you good luck with it.

Chapter 9

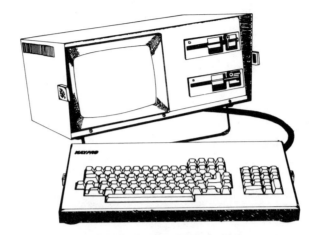

WordStar—
Enough to Get You Going

First things first. Be certain you have made a work copy of your WordStar master disk. If not, do this now before you go any deeper into WordStar. The following applies only to the KAYPRO 2 and 4 having two disk drives, A and B. Be patient, KAYPRO 10 users; a word of advice follows below for you as well.

Turn on your KAYPRO. When you see the CP/M command prompt A0> on your console, put your *write-protected* master copy of WordStar into Drive B. Then into Drive A put a formatted disk on which you have already copied PIP.COM, D, or STAT. Then use this command form to copy the master WordStar disk to the disk in Drive A:

PIP A:=B:*.*[V0]

When you see the A0> on your console, you will know PIP has transferred all WordStar files from Drive B to the disk in Drive A. Remove both disks and put the master disk in a safe place. Label the working copy.

If you have a KAYPRO 10, your WordStar software appears on the hard disk in User Area A1 and, depending on when your 10 was manufactured, on A4 and A5 as well. Each of these user areas contains the complete WordStar text editing program. Even so, you cannot afford to risk losing valuable software should the hard disk fail—or, in computerese, *crash*. Therefore, you must back up all software on the hard disk first. You may have already done so by using the MUFBAR (Multiple User File Backup and Retrieval Program) backup utility program on User Area A0 of the hard disk. See Chapter 6 for specific instructions on backing up all of the software on the hard disk. End of lecture!

WORDSTAR'S MAJOR FEATURES

WordStar prints what you see on your console screen, minus print and other program control symbols. This means you format your text on your console as you create your text, data tables, and other document contents. You know *before* you print your text what it will look like, because it will print text you have formatted on your console *exactly* as you have entered it.

Seven menus help you use WordStar right away. These are:

- Opening Menu
- Main Menu
- Onscreen Menu
- Print Menu
- Block Menu
- Help Menu
- Quick Menu

WordStar's seven menus help you, among other things, to create, name, rename, edit, save, delete, copy, transfer, search, replace, review onscreen, and print copies of your word and data files. The menus also show you how to use some of WordStar's other powerful features, such as moving, inserting, and deleting blocks of text; reforming paragraphs; and adding "headers" and "footers" to your documents. WordStar permits you to scroll in either direction through your text files, at any one of nine speeds you specify.

Depending on your preference, WordStar enables you to print your text's right-hand margin either *right-justified* or *ragged*, as you prefer. The choice is yours, as it should be. WordStar also enables you to set, change, or delete fixed and variable tab stops.

Finally, you can use WordStar and MailMerge together to generate multiple form letters and mailing labels.

These are just some of the main features of WordStar. There are many others as well, and you should consult your bundled WordStar manual(s) for additional details concerning WordStar's many useful text processing features and other formatting options.

So much for the highlights of WordStar. Now let's get acquainted with each program in turn by looking at the menus and the key commands for each program. Lists of commands and printed facsimilies of menus are not very helpful for beginners, however. To overcome that one, several short sample texts follow, each of which clearly shows you what you get when you execute a given command. Presenting the material in this manner establishes for you the link between the text as end product, the commands that are used, and the most important link in the chain of all, *you*. Let's look at WordStar in greater detail.

LEARNING WORDSTAR

WordStar *can* be learned quickly merely by relying on the menus and doing a little experimenting. The Opening Menu will be brought up on your console after you run through these steps:

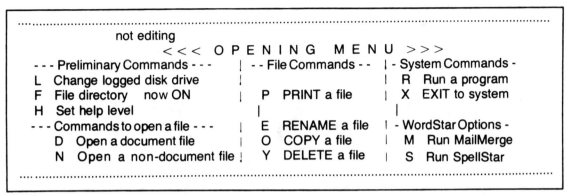

```
............................................................................................
            not editing
                    < < < O P E N I N G   M E N U  > > >
 - - - Preliminary Commands - - -  | - - File Commands - -  | - System Commands -
 L   Change logged disk drive      |                        | R   Run a program
 F   File directory    now ON      | P   PRINT a file       | X   EXIT to system
 H   Set help level                |                        |
 - - - Commands to open a file - - -| E   RENAME a file      | - WordStar Options -
     D   Open a document file      | O   COPY a file        | M   Run MailMerge
     N   Open a non-document file ! Y   DELETE a file       | S   Run SpellStar
............................................................................................
```

Fig. 9-1. WordStar Opening Menu.

1) Turn on your KAYPRO.
2) Load the CP/M operating system in Drive A.
3) If you have a KAYPRO 2 or 4, you will soon see A0>. When you do, your console is telling you that CP/M is waiting for your next command. If you have the KAYPRO 10, you get the Master Menu after turning on the computer. In that case, you merely hit the DOWN arrow once, thereby selecting "Text Processing," hit the carriage return once, and presto! You're in User Group A1, which brings up WordStar's Opening Menu in short order.
4) Put your working copy of WordStar in Drive A, and then type: WS ⟨Return⟩. After a few brief preliminary messages from MicroPro, the menu shown in Fig. 9-1 will appear on your console.

If you have a 2 or 4, now is the time to put a formatted disk into Drive B. By the way, it is extremely useful to have copied earlier at least PIP.COM and STAT.COM onto all of your formatted and otherwise empty disks. Why? Because doing so makes it easy to transfer files of text/data from one disk to another. You will not have to use your CP/M utilities disk each time you want to move files about. It is also helpful to have D.COM, a different form of file directory command, on the disks you write to and read from as well. They tell you quite a bit, which really helps you avoid "disk spillover," and related file copy space problems.

Why put the formatted disk containing PIP, STAT, or D in Drive B at all? Well, it is wise to keep WordStar in Drive A and in Drive B the disk on which you will create and edit your text and data files. This general setup applies to most programs you will be working with, whether it is WordStar or dBASE II.

OK, back to the Opening Menu. Here is what you should do to begin using WordStar. Notice the first "Preliminary Command." That's right, "L" for "Change logged disk drive." Go ahead and press the letter L in order to switch from Drive A to Drive B, in which you have already placed a disk that is formatted and which also contains PIP.COM, STAT.COM, or D.COM.

After pressing L you will be asked to specify the drive name to which you want to switch. In this case, since you are already logged on Drive A, and since you want to use the disk in Drive B, you must tell WordStar that you wish the logged drive to be changed from A to B. Type B: ⟨Return⟩. How will you know that you have switched from Drive A to B? Simple. The red light on your console will light up at Drive B and beneath the Opening Menu on your screen you will see

Directory of Disk B: PIP.COM (or STAT.COM or D.COM)

You now know that you have changed your logged disk drive from A to B and that the disk in B is readable. In case you wondered how or where WordStar is, the answer to that is simple. WordStar is "in" three places at once: on the write-protected working disk in Drive A, in your KAYPRO's random access memory buffer, and a portion of WordStar (its Opening Menu) is showing on your screen. You can now use WordStar's many commands and six other menus to help you create, edit, save, or print text and data you enter on the disk in Drive B. When that disk gets nearly full, you can replace it with another formatted and empty one. Frequently invoking the STAT and D programs will enable you to monitor just how full the Drive B disk is getting.

What about the other commands shown on the "Opening Menu"? Well, here is a brief explanation of what each does for you.

F File Directory. This command turns the file directory on and off; all you have to do is press F and you see your disk directory line below the opening menu disappear and reappear. You can try pushing F a few times. When through, leave the directory listing *on*.

H Set Help Level. Another preliminary command, this one permits you to dictate how much of the Help Prompt Menu will show at the top of the console while you are using WordStar to edit a file. The help level is already set at its maximum, 3, but you should push the H to see what the lesser help levels (2, 1, and 0) will show you on the screen. For now, better leave the help level at its maximum setting.

D Open a Document File. This is the command you *must* use to tell WordStar you want to begin creating a text file on the currently logged disk drive, which you already have established as B. This D command is your gateway to whatever you want to put—via WordStar—on the disk in Drive B. It is also the only way you can tell WordStar to open up an already existing file residing on the disk in Drive B, so that you can edit that previously created and stored file.

N Open a Non-Document File. You might be asking yourself the question, "What in the world is a non-document file?" If so, that's a good question to ask. What WordStar treats as "non-document" files are simply lists of data, not the words you so carefully place one after another when writing your boss or business acquaintance a letter. All of the text processing commands normally available to you when you are writing a letter with WordStar are not available when you are preparing a special non-document data file in the non-document mode of WordStar. In this case, what is a data file? Well, how about a list of names and addresses of your relatives or friends or clients? Such lists could be put together in either the document or the non-document mode, but any sizable database is best created in the non-document mode. Basic text processing commands help you create them.

P Print a File. This command tells WordStar that you want to print a file (whether document or non-document). Various print options are made available to you when you tell WordStar that you have saved your file and are ready to print it.

60

E Rename a File. Occasionally you may wish to rename a file. This command permits you to do so, but caution is advised. You must be certain you give your files names that are descriptive or their contents. Otherwise, without looking at the files' contents you will have no certain idea what they contain.

O Copy a File: It is convenient to copy a file from one place to another on the same disk, or to a different disk, or to copy one file over another (which is called *over-writing* a file). Again, caution must be exercised when over-writing a given file of the same name, because you will erase the original when you over-write it. The PIP program can be used to copy files as well, but with this advantage: PIP can be made to *verify* the accuracy of the copy transactions—something WordStar's copy command does not do.

Y Delete a File. This command is used to accomplish just what it says: remove a file from the disk. Once text is deleted in WordStar, it is gone forever—unless you have a backup copy on another floppy. True, WordStar does create a backup copy of any existing file that is edited and then closed again; that's the .BAK, which is your file *before* you edited it. Of all the action commands available to you through WordStar, the D command must be used with *extreme caution*.

R Run a Program. Typing R will enable you to run any file whose extender is .COM. One example is using D or STAT to find out how much space you have left on your B disk. You can also run The WORD Plus's programs, or run MailMerge.

X Exit to System. Using this command will take you out of WordStar and put you into the CP/M operating system.

M MailMerge. Because MailMerge is a part of the bundled software program, the M command will tell WordStar to run the MailMerge program—provided you've set up your non-document files first and you've transferred a working copy of MailMerge to your WordStar disk. With WordStar in Drive A and your WordStar-generated non-document file disk in Drive B, you would be all set to run 20 letters, each identical except for the variables that you merge into them.

S SpellStar. At this time, KAYPRO does not bundle SpellStar. If you've got a copy, you would use it interactively with your document text files, much in the manner that you use SPELL interactively with WordStar.

So much for the Opening Menu. You should experiment with the commands just to see what comes up on your console. Knowing what the four different help levels are all about is particularly useful at this stage of your acquaintance with WordStar.

Now to begin opening (or creating) your first document file. Just a few reminders first, though. Is WordStar in Drive A? Is a formatted disk in Drive B? Is the Opening Menu on your console? Have you already switched the logged disk drive from A to B? Does the disk in Drive B contain PIP, STAT, or D? If your answers are *yes* to the foregoing, then you are ready to open your first document file in WordStar. Do the following:

1) Get the A0> on your console; then enter WS⟨Return⟩.
2 At the Opening Menu, Type L B:, then D ⟨Return⟩.
3) At the prompt "Name of File to Edit?" answer as follows: B:FORMLTR.MSS ⟨Return⟩.

The next thing you see on your console will be the MAIN MENU, which will look

```
........................................................................................
          B:FORMLTR.MSS   PAGE 1 LINE 1 COL 1        INSERT ON
                <<<  M A I N   M E N U  >>>
  - - Cursor Movement - -   | - Delete -  |  - Miscellaneous -   |   - Other Menus -
↑S char left ↑D char right  |↑G char      |↑↑I  Tab    ↑B Reform  | (from Main only)
↑A word left ↑F word right  | DEL chr lf  |↑↑V  INSERT ON/OFF     |↑J Help  ↑K Block
↑E line up   ↑X line down   |↑↑T word rt  |↑↑L  Find/Replce again |↑Q Quick↑P Print
        - - Scrolling - -   |↑↑Y line     | RETURN End paragraph  |↑O Onscreen
↑W  up line  ↑Z down line   |             |↑↑N  Insert a Return   |
↑R  up screen↑C down screen |             |↑↑U  Stop a command    |

  L - - - - ! - - - - ! - - - - ! - - - - ! - - - - ! - - - - ! - - - - ! - - - - ! - - - - ! - - - - ! - - - - - - - R

........................................................................................
```

Fig. 9-2. WordStar main menu.

like the one shown in Fig. 9-2.

What you see on your console is WordStar's Main Menu, the one you'll use as your home base when operating WordStar. From this menu alone you will be able to *access* (or call up) five other menus: Help, Block, Quick, Print, and Onscreen. Each of these five menus has a number of commands and explanatory material of interest and importance. You should access each of them in turn now, looking them over very carefully. You may exit each and return to the Main Menu merely by hitting your space bar once, or by using the CTRL U and ESC keys. To look at the menus press:

CTRL J   to see the Help Menu for the other four help-level settings.
CTRL K   to see the Block Menu to move blocks of text about the file.
CTRL Q   to see the Quick Menu to move the cursor about quickly.
CTRL P   to see the Print Menu to look at print options.
CTRL O   to see the Onscreen Menu to look at editing commands.

```
........................................................................................
          B:FORMLTR.MSS PAGE 1 LINE 1 COL 1        INSERT ON
               <<<  H E L P   M E N U  >>>
                            |               |     - - Other Menus - -
H Display set the help level |               |        (from Main only)
B Paragraph reform(CONTROL-B)| S Status line |  ↑J Help   ↑K Block
F Flags in right-most column | R Ruler line  |  ↑Q Quick  ↑P Print
D Dot commands, print controls| M Margins Tabs|  ↑O Onscreen
I Index of commands          | P Place markers|  Space bar returns
                             | V Moving text  |  you to Main Menu.
                             |               |

  L - - - - ! - - - - ! - - - - ! - - - - ! - - - - ! - - - - ! - - - - ! - - - - ! - - - - ! - - - - ! - - - - - - - R

........................................................................................
```

Fig. 9-3. WordStar help menu.

```
..................................................................................
            B:FORMLTR.MSS PAGE 1 LINE 1 COL 1        INSERT ON
                    < < <  Q U I C K   M E N U  > > >
   - - - Cursor Movement - - -   |  - Delete - |  - - Miscellaneous - -  |   - - Other Menus - -
  S  left side      D  right side  |  Y  line rt  |  F  Find text in file  |    (from Main only)
  E  top scrn       X  bottom scrn |  DEL lin lf | A  Find Replace      | ↑ J  Help    ↑ K  Block
  R  top file       C  end file    |            | L  Find Misspelling   | ↑ Q  Quick ↑ P  Print
  B  top block      K  end block   |            | Q  Repeat command or | ↑ O  Onscreen
  0-9 marker        W  up  Z down  |            |    key until space    | Space bar returns
  P  previous       V  last Find or Block |      |    bar or other key   |    you to Main Menu.

  L - - - - ! - - - - ! - - - - ! - - - - ! - - - - ! - - - - ! - - - - ! - - - - ! - - - - ! - - - - - - - R

..................................................................................
```

Fig. 9-4. WordStar quick menu.

After you look at the five menus you will be much better prepared to handle what follows. By the way, if at any time you think you need help, merely access the menu which contains the commands and explanations you need.

Figures 9-3 through 9-7 reproduce the first "page" of each menu to help you recognize them when they appear on your screen.

Now it is time to get back to your file which you have already named FORMLTR.MSS. In this instance you used only seven of the available eight spaces to create the filename, the main file identifier, and you used all three character spaces for the suffix, or *extension* as it is referred to in your CP/M and WordStar reference manuals.

Here are four simple rules governing the construction of filenames:

- Do not use any name already in use on that disk.
- Do not use ?, *, or any other special characters such as =, +, >, <, }, [, etc. when constructing your filenames.
- Do not use upper- and lowercase letters intermixed (WoRDStAr.kAy) to create a filename.
- Do not create a file with the extension .BAK.

```
..................................................................................
            B:FORMLTR.MSS PAGE 1 LINE 1 COL 1        INSERT ON
                    < < <  O N S C R E E N   M E N U  > > >
  - Margins   Tabs -  |   - Line Functions -  |    - More Toggles -     |   - Other Menus -
  L  Set left margin  | C  Center text        | J  Justify    now ON   |  (from Main only)
  R  Set right margin | S  Set line spacing   | V  Vari-tabs now ON    | ↑J  Help    ↑K  Block
  X  Release margins | |                       | H  Hyph-help now ON    | ↑Q  Quick ↑P  Print
  I  Set  N Clear tab |   - - - Toggles - - -  | E  Soft hyph now OFF   | ↑O  Onscreen
  G  Paragraph tab   | W  Wrd wrap now ON    | D  Prnt disp now ON    | Space bar returns
  F  Ruler from line  | T  Rlr line  now ON    | P  Pge break now ON    | you to Main Menu.

  L - - - - ! - - - - ! - - - - ! - - - - ! - - - - ! - - - - ! - - - - ! - - - - ! - - - - ! - - - - - - - R

..................................................................................
```

Fig. 9-5. WordStar onscreen menu.

```
.....................................................................................
:   B:FORMLTR.MSS PAGE 1 LINE 1 COL 1          INSERT ON       :
:            < < <  B L O C K   M E N U  > > >                 :
:  - Saving Files -  I  - Block Operations -  I  - File Operations -  I  - Other Menus -  :
: S Save - resume   I  B Begin   K End     I  R Read    P Print   I  (from Main only)     :
: D Save--done      I  H Hide/Display      I  O Copy    E Rename  I ↑J Help    ↑K Block   :
: X Save - exit     I  C Copy    Y Delete  I  J Delete           I ↑Q Quick   ↑P Print   :
: Q Abandon file    I  V Move    W Write   I  -Disk Operations-  I ↑O Onscreen           :
:  - Place Markers -  I  N Column   now OFF  I  L Change logged disk I Space bar returns  :
: 0-9 set/hide 0-9  I                        I  F Directory now OFF  I you to Main Menu.   :
: L - - - - ! - - - - ! - - - - ! - - - - ! - - - - ! - - - - ! - - - - ! - - - - ! - - - - ! - - - - - - - - R :
.....................................................................................
```

Fig. 9-6. WordStar block menu.

Here are some valid filenames:

> A:JONES.MSS
> CHAPTER1.KAY
> CHAP10.ELH
> C:LETTER.AAA (C: is valid only on the KAYPRO 10)

Although not very useful, numerical-only suffixes such as .123 are also valid, as is the omission of the suffix. Such filenames, however, only invite operator and/or computer confusion down the road.

Now let's use WordStar to create a short document. Please read the letter shown in Fig. 9-8 and look at the specified commands before you try to enter the text on your own. Remember: the ∧ symbol indicates that the CTRL key has been depressed along with one or more other keys to execute the command in question. For example, the command form ∧P ∧B means that you are to press simultaneously the CTRL key and then, in rapid succession, the letters P and B. What you see on your screen is ∧B, which is not printed but which tells your printer to boldface a character, word, blocks of text, or—if you wish—an entire file.

```
.....................................................................................
:   B:FORMLTR.MSS PAGE 1 LINE 1 COL 1          INSERT ON       :
:            < < <  P R I N T   M E N U  > > >                 :
:  - - - - - - Special Effects - - - - - - -  I  - Printing Changes -  I  - Other Menus -  :
: (begin and end) I  (on time each)   I  A Alternate pitch   I  (from Main only)   :
: B Bold D Double I  H Overprint char I  N Standard Pitch    I ↑J Help    ↑K Block :
: S Underscore    I  O Non-break space I  C Printing Pause    I ↑Q Quick   ↑P Print :
: X Strikeout     I  F Phantom space   I  Y Other ribbon color I ↑O Onscreen        :
: V Subscript     I  G Phantom rubout  I  - - User Patches - -  I Space bar returns :
: T Superscript   I  RET Overprint line I  Q(1) W(2) E(3) R(4)  I you to Main Menu  :
: L - - - - ! - - - - ! - - - - ! - - - - ! - - - - ! - - - - ! - - - - ! - - - - ! - - - - ! - - - - - - - - R :
.....................................................................................
```

Fig. 9-7. WordStar print menu.

```
L----!----!----!----!----!----!----!----!----!----!----!----!---R
.HE ^PBDraft One of Marketing Letter^PB
.FO ^PSHarris File^PS <cr>
^OJ; ^OL <margin lft:0> <cr>; ^OR <margin rt:65> <cr>
<cr>
March 17, 1984 <cr>
<cr>
<cr>
E. Harris, Sr. VP, Finance<cr>
<cr>
<cr>
Those of us in the Marketing Department would like to propose
a change in the way we do things in the advertising department. <cr>
<cr>
Here is what we have in mind:<cr>
<cr>
1. By the end of the next quarter, replace all existing electric
typewriters with Kaypros. They will enable us to be much more
productive and efficient, and this applies both to ad copy
generation and profitable product-mix forecasting.<cr>
<cr>
2. Replace the IBM typewriters with six Kaypro 2s, two Kaypro 4s, and
two Kaypro 10s.
<cr>
3. Conduct after-hours instruction in using the Kaypros (here, we
recommend you order ten copies of^PS The Kaypro - Plain and Simple,^PS
to help us make the transition fast and easily.<cr>
<cr>
We are sure that the results will more than off-set the short-
term costs involved. Our productivity curve will shoot up
dramatically, and that translates into many benefits for the
firm.<cr>
<cr>
Attached to this memo are the cost-benefit ratios worked out in
support of this recommendation. They clearly indicate that the
Kaypro is the smart way to go for our firm. <cr>
<cr>
You may not know it, but our biggest competitor in Los Angeles
recently installed^PB twenty Kaypro's^PB throughout their accounting,
advertising, and marketing departments, and that was done a
little more than a month ago. ^PS Dollar for dollar, the Kaypro
offers us exactly what we need to compete in today's business
climate.^PS <cr>
<cr>
I look forward to your positive response to this
recommendation.<cr>
<cr>
<cr>
J. T. Moore<cr>
V. P. Operations<cr>
<cr>
cc: Ms. S. Johnson, Manager, Marketing Department<cr>
^KD <cr>
```

Fig. 9-8. Sample marketing letter produced using WordStar.

Now that you have read the letter through and looked at the commands given, enter the text yourself, following and executing the commands in the order presented. If you need help executing any of the commands, check the appropriate material in your WordStar manual.

Make sure the cursor is positioned at Line 0,, Column 0, and then enter the letter text, treating all ⌃ as indicators of a command key sequence which you should execute. Remember: you are being given only a few KEY WordStar commands. There are, in all, some 145 commands available to you through the WordStar program alone. Many other commands exist for MailMerge and SpellStar.

Did you enter the last command: ⌃KD? You need to do so to save the letter. This Block command saves your text and puts you back into WordStar. After your text is saved and you see the B>, go ahead and check to see how lengthy that letter actually is by entering a single D after the B>. You'll see how long the file FORMLTR.MSS is—and the length of PIP, STAT, and D as well.

You must be wondering what all those commands will do to the text of your letter. We don't want to keep you in the dark, so here is a list of the commands you were asked to enter when you put the letter's text onto your disk in Drive B. Following each command are section/page references to your WordStar documentation. Look them up to learn more about what such commands can do for you.

⟨cr⟩	A carriage return, meaning press the Return key once.
.HE	A header command: 7-29.
⌃PB	Command to boldface text: 7-10.
.FO	A footer command: 7-30.
⌃PS	Command to underline text: 7-8.
⌃OJ	Command to turn right-hand margin justification on/off: 6-4.
⌃OR	Command to set right-hand margin: 6-8.
⌃OL	Command to set left-hand margin: 6-7.
⌃KD	Command to save file and return to WordStar. 9-4.

Next you should type a ⌃P to view the print options. Read them carefully and answer according to your printer setup. (Be sure the printer is on and you have paper in it.) Print the letter you entered on the disk. After you have printed your letter, give the system a warm boot by entering CTRL C. When the B> appears, enter A: and then Return. You will be back on Drive A. Again boot the system by entering CTRLC. At the A> enter WS. When you get the Opening Menu for WordStar back on your console, log into Drive B again by pressing L, and then B: when asked which drive you wish to be the logged (or default) drive.

Next, you will see the Main Menu, and beneath is several files listed as being on the disk in Drive B: PIP, STAT, or D, and FORMLTR.MSS. Delete the FORMLTR.MSS file by entering ⌃K to get the Block Menu. Then select J and enter FORMLTR.MSS as the "Name of file to delete?"

This has been a brief introduction to WordStar. There is obviously a lot more to learn, and we can testify that it is worth your trouble. It's a great program.

Chapter 10

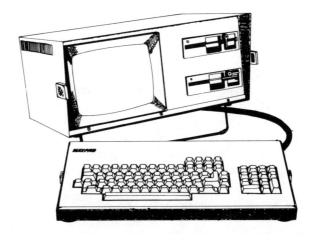

The Wonders of The WORD Plus

L et's take a closer look at some of the major features of The WORD Plus, one of the
snappiest programs we've ever used.

THE WORD PLUS

The WORD Plus offers you a very fine spelling checker. The basic dictionary file
itself contains 45,000 English words. You can quickly check the spelling of entire files,
and you can add to special supplemental word files the working vocabulary common to
your profession or business. The program is as easy to use as it is useful.

The WORD Plus also offers these fine features for the writer who wants
"wordpower" at his/her fingertips:

- The SPELL program checks the spelling of the file of text you tell it to check.
- The MARKFIX program, used with the SPELL program, marks all misspelled
words in your text; then it either corrects them at your command, or merely marks them
and lets you do the correcting.
- The ANAGRAM program permits you to find one or more word choices for a
given anagram.
- The HYPHEN program automatically hyphenates words in your document files;
it can also tell you how to hyphenate a given word when used in an *online mode*. That is,
you can find out how to hyphenate a given word independently of any automatic file
hyphenating activity.
- The LOOKUP program enables you to find the correct spelling of a word of

whose exact spelling you are unsure of; it looks up a match, or near-match of the word you give it.

● FIND is a program which helps you find the correct spelling of a word—even when you are not sure which letters the word begins or ends with. Tell FIND you want to see all words that start with "x" and end in "y," (enter X∗Y) and it will list them for you. FIND also locates rhyming words for busy poets. FIND uses ∗ and ? as wild cards.

● WC is a program that counts the number of words in any specified file.

● HOMONYM HELPER is used in conjunction with MARKFIX to mark in a file all homonyms, such as *too* and *two*, or *horse* and *hoarse*. Then you scroll through the file, checking to see that the correct homonyms have been used.

● DICTSORT is a handy program which sorts all words in a file already checked for spelling. The file contents are sorted into alphabetical order; these "dictionary-sorted" files can then be used to add words to special dictionary files.

● WORDFREQ is another handy program. It permits you to see how many times each word appears in a given file.

In all, using The WORD Plus in conjunction with WordStar offers you an impressive array of sophisticated and powerful text processing tools. It is a cluster of checking, marking, finding, counting, spelling, and up dating programs. Using The WORD Plus is quite easy once you understand the purpose of each of the modules which make up the package. Moreover, you can use it quite readily with your bundled WordStar software (or the previously bundled program, Perfect Writer). Or you can use many of the programs offered beneath The WORD Plus umbrella outside of WordStar. We have in mind WC, WORDFREQ, ANAGRAM, and others.

In our opinion, the Wayne Holder user's guide for The WORD Plus is quite readable and easily understood. In that manual you will find very clear directions for using any or all of the programs offered. So, what follows is a brief overview of the hardware requirements and major commands used to run the various programs.

Before reading our discussion of the hardware requirements and the program commands, be sure you have copied your Master WORD Plus disks and are using the work copies, which should *not* be write-protected. If you have not copied your master disks, do so now. Do not use the CP/M COPY program to make backup copies; rather, use PIP to *verify* the transfer of The WORD Plus files on three working disks.

First, be sure the blank disks have been formatted. Next, PIP from the Master WORD Plus disks to the working disks these WORD Plus files, grouped as follows:

Working Disk 1	TW.COM, SPELL.COM, REVIEW.COM, MARKFIX.COM, MAINDICT.CMP
Working Disk 2	LOOKUP.COM, FIND.COM, ANAGRAM.COM, HYPHEN.COM, HYEXCEPT.TXT, MAINDICT.CMP
Working Disk 3	MARKFIX.COM, HOMONYMS.TXT, WC.COM, DICTSORT.COM, MAINDICT.CMP

This completes the backup process.

By the way, if you have a KAYPRO 10, your WORD Plus programs will already be on the A portion of your hard disk. Use DIR or D at the A1> prompt to see The WORD

Plus files contained on User Area A1 of the hard disk. Of course, you already should have backed up all of your hard disk's bundled software by using the Multi-Floppy Backup and Restore System (MUFBAR) for CP/M and MP/M. See Chapter 6 for more information.

Now a word about hardware requirements, which are readily met by KAYPRO models 2, 4, and 10. The WORD Plus is CP/M-based and works on either the 1.4 or 2.2 versions of CP/M. Minimum memory required is 32 kilobytes, which presents no problem because your KAYPRO has 64K of RAM memory space. However, SPELL, LOOKUP, DICTSORT, and WORDFREQ require lots of memory, because they are the programs which create long lists of words that must reside in RAM when being used. Consequently, you should break any files longer than 30K into two or three shorter files when using these powerful programs.

Here is a quick overview of the program commands and an explanation of each.

The Word (TW). To use TW, which automatically initiates the running of SPELL, REVIEW, and MARKFIX—or any WORD Plus program—you must first have named and saved, via WordStar, your document file. Then you must have the disk containing the document file in Drive B (or on A1 or in Drive C if you have a KAYPRO 10). Then, at the A0> prompt (A1> for the KAYPRO 10), enter this command:

A0>TW B:⟨filename⟩.⟨ext⟩

Of course, you would enter your file's actual name after B:

The first module of The WORD Plus's spelling program is then put into operation. Its format will appear on your console, and it looks like this:

SPELL+ ver x.x
Copyright 1981 — Oasis Systems
Compiling Word List
n unique words
Checking Main Dictionary
Listing unmatched words
n unmatched words

The number of "unmatched words" are those words in your file for which SPELL can find no exact match in the 45,000—word dictionary file, MAINDICT.CMP. The number of unique words are merely those which appear only once in your file. Those words could also be identified by using WORDFREQ.

When SPELL has checked all the words in your file against its main dictionary, you will then have to decide what action to take in light of SPELL's findings. After SPELL is finished running, the REVIEW program automatically comes up on your console next. It will look like this:

REVIEW+ Version x.x Copyright 1981 Oasis Systems

Add word to:	Other Options:
U>pdate Dictionary	P>revious word
S>pec. Dict. "SPECIALS.CMP"	N>ext Word
M>ark word	R>esume review

D>ISCARD WORD   L>ook up word
C>orrect word   V>iew context

--> ZEROX -

You would then select the appropriate options and continue with the SPELL program until the file was completely checked, marked, fixed, hyphenated, homonyms checked, and so forth. (By the way, we want to point out that the "D>iscard" option which appears in the REVIEW program does *not* do away with your word. For some strange reason, Oasis Systems has used *discard* when they really mean *ignore*, or "preserve word as is and move on to the next one on the list." All of the other options in the REVIEW Program mean what they imply and will do what they say.

There are a number of *option switches*, or additional commands you can use in conjunction with SPELL, all taking the form $+character. For example, $P sends a list of your file's misspelled words to your printer. Regardless of which switch you use, it is always placed *after* the basic command form, as in A> SPELL B:FILENAME.TXT $P. Here are a few of The WORD Plus option switches:

$P   sends the misspelled words to the printer.
$L   lists misspelled words on your console only.
$PL   lists the misspelled words on console and printer.
$F   writes all the misspelled words to a special file.
$FB   designates Drive B as the special file destination.
$S   tells SPELL to ignore WordStar "dot" commands in a file.
$C   has SPELL recall misspelled word context.
$B   tells SPELL to ignore specified backslash commands.
$I   tells SPELL to ignore all words in all capital letters.

Other WORD Plus Commands. Here, in short order fashion, are the remaining commands needed to use WORD Plus programs other than SPELL.

To use:	Enter this command form:
MARKFIX	A>MARKFIX B:FILENAME.TXT (marks with *)
MARKFIX	A>MARKFIX B:FILENAME.TXT $M@ (marks with@)
HYPHEN	A> enter the word you want to hyphenate
HYPHEN	A>HYPHEN B:FILENAME.TXT (words up to 14 letters)
HYPHEN	A>HYPHEN B:FILENAME.TXT $14 (words longer than 14 letters)
LOOKUP	A>LOOKUP EXITING (for correct spelling)
LOOKUP	A>LOOKUP ISOTROP $L (long list search mode)
FIND	A>FIND XEROG*Y (for example)
ANAGRAM	A>ANAGRAM MARGANA (unscramble anagram)
ANAGRAM	A>ANAGRAM ?ee (all three-letter words ending in *ee*)
WC	A>WC B:FILENAME.TXT (how many words in file)
DICTSORT	A>DICTSORT B:FILENAME.TXT (alphabetizes file)
WORDFREQ	A>WORDFREQ B:FILENAME.TXT. (word frequency count)
WORDFREQ	A>WORDFREQ B:FILENAME.TXT$A (alphabetize count)

REVIEW   A>REVIEW B:FILENAME.TXT. (SPELL list review)

Well, those are the hightlights of The WORD Plus. This brief look at the program's features, commands, and options is not intended to replace your own work with the program's routines and options. First-hand use of the program will take care of that in no time at all.

To help you get up and moving with The WORD Plus, we want to show you how to run a WORD Plus program for the KAYPRO 4 and 10. The machines can run The WORD Plus's programs interactively with WordStar, but KAYPRO 2 owners cannot do so because of floppy disk memory limitations—unless they upgrade their machines to double-sided, double-density.

RUNNING THE WORD PLUS WITH WORDSTAR

We assume that you are working with a copy of your master disk. To run Word Count (or any other WORD Plus program) in a truly interactive fashion with WordStar, you need a KAYPRO 4 or 10 to do so. Why? Because only the 4 and 10 permit you to put all of the backup WordStar and The WORD Plus software on one disk.

The KAYPRO 4 owners should back up their WordStar and WORD Plus programs according to the instructions in Chapter 6. Having done that, 4 owners should PIP all The WORD Plus programs to their backup WordStar disk. Then, they can proceed with the sample interactive program given below.

Here is the same short and easy routine you can run if you have a KAYPRO 4 or a 10. You should follow the same general routine to run any of The WORD Plus programs interactively through WordStar's Opening Menu. The left-hand column contains conditions/goals, and the right-hand column contains action to take.

1) To run WC (Word Count) with WordStar

Insert your WordStar and WORD Plus copy in A and text disk in B. Type WS ⟨Return⟩.

2) To run both disks

At the Main Menu, Type L B:⟨Return⟩.

3) We will assume that you have a text file in your B Drive, perhaps the sample letter from the WordStar chapter. If not, you need to write and save one to run WC. You are now at the Main Menu with a saved text file on your B Drive.

Type R for *Run a Program.*

4) See a prompt for "Name of Program?"

Type WC and the name of the file you want to count and then ⟨Return⟩.

5) See your terminal pause while it counts, and then show you the number of words in your file.

So much for the nice things you can do with Word Count. Try your hand at using some of the other WORD Plus programs. You'll find them all very easy to run.

Chapter 11

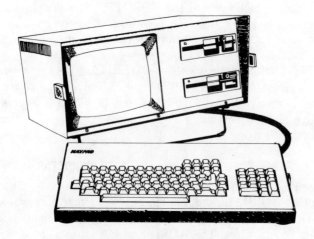

MailMerge

MailMerge is an extremely useful addition to the KAYPRO bundle of document processors. By July of 1984 it was included with the software package for all three KAYPRO computers. For people who purchased their computers earlier, it may be obtained at extra cost from a dealer and added to your WordStar copy disk. It exists as a file called MAIL MRGE.OVR that attaches to WordStar, and it needs three other WordStar files to function: WS.COM, WSMSGS.OVR, and WSOLY1.OVR.

In our discussion of MailMerge we will assume that you are already familiar with WordStar and with the use of dot commands. If you have not used dot commands yet we suggest that you check out the MicroPro manuals on dot commands before you start using MailMerge. If you want to go ahead with MailMerge and use those books as reference tools, here are just a few tips about using dot commands that we think are essential.

The two inflexible rules about dot commands are that *they must start in column one* and *they must be followed by a hard carriage return.* The dot, or period, by itself will provoke a ? in the right margin which will go away when you add letters. Some dot commands, .DF for instance, must go at the head of the file, while others can be inserted in the body of the file at appropriate places.

Dot commands that are specific to MailMerge (which we will define next) will yield the letter M in the right margin to remind you that they belong to MailMerge and not WordStar. Beyond the first two inflexible rules about dot commands, they can be inserted in your text files and your data files to achieve whatever printing goals you desire, or they can be used in MailMerge command files.

MailMerge will do three primary jobs for you. Combined with WordStar, it allows you to create personalized form letters with a separate address file that will reprint the letter for each address in the file. It also has the ability to change data within the letter. Those two functions will allow people with small businesses to handle their mailing lists with great efficiency. Finally, it can join files for you, either in sequence so that you could print all the chapters in a book, or it will allow you to *nest* files, meaning to insert one file within another. It will also access tables of data that have been created in InfoStar, DataStar, or ReportStar.

MailMerge has a fourth function, "Conditional Printing," which will only run on a Z8080 system; so, unfortunately, it will not work with KAYPRO's Z80A operating system. The first three options, however, provide you with a lot of work- and timesaving possibilities. Let's see what we can do with them.

DOT COMMANDS

MailMerge works with dot commands inserted within WordStar files or in Mail-Merge command files. Before we show you how to use them, we will give you brief definitions of each one of the dot commands in MailMerge, with the exception of the commands that control conditional printing.

.DF (Define File). This command is always followed by the filename that will supply variable data, and that combination is *always* followed by the .RV command. If you wish to change disks (to go to a DataStar disk to add a table, for instance), then add CHANGE after the filename. The format for a .DF command is .DF ⟨filename⟩CHANGE, with change being optional.

Note: if you plan to be swapping disks to add information, you will not be able to keep the WORD Plus on the same disk with WordStar. MicroPro (the manufacturer of WordStar, MailMerge, InfoStar, DataStar, and ReportStar) recommends keeping the following files on one drive, while you leave the second drive free for different disks.

WS.COM
WSMSGS.OVR
WSOVLY1.OVR
MAILMRGE.OVR
The master document
The disk output file
All data files and inserted document files not on different disks.

If you follow this scheme, you will leave Drive B open for different data disks. To follow MicroPro's suggestion means setting up a separate WordStar and MailMerge disk to handle each form letter.

As an alternative way to handle the space problem, you may want to leave your WordStar and utility disk alone, simply adding the necessary files from other disks to your text disk with PIP so you don't have to switch disks around. This scheme looks to be the simpler of the two methods. The choice is yours for maximum efficiency in the use of your disks and time, and for simplicity in the printing operation.

.RV (Read Variables). This command instructs MailMerge to examine the file named in the preceding .DF command. The .RV command must contain the generic names that will be replaced in each form letter. For instance, Name, Street, City, State,

Zipcode are all *generics* that would change with each letter. You will have to build in an answering code in the form letter by surrounding each generic with ampersands (&) in exactly the same form as they appear in the .RV command. You may use as many .RV commands as are necessary. An .RV command would look like this:

.RV M,NAME,STREET,CITY,STATE

.AV (Ask for Variables). This command differs from .RV in that it asks the operator to supply variables at printing time, rather than pulling them from another file. If you use a generic term such as *phone number*, that term will show up on the screen as a prompt to be answered. As an additional feature, you may limit the number of characters that can be entered. For example, if your .AV command reads .AV ZIPCODE, then the operator can enter any number of characters in response to the prompt, but if your command reads .AV ZIPCODE, 5 then you would be assured of a five-digit zipcode—but not necessarily of the right five digits. One cautionary note about this command is in order. If you use .AV without .RV, you will have to restart MailMerge at the end of each document.

.SV (Set Variables). This command allows you to insert variable information in the master document. For example, .SV PERSON1, LORI SMITH would insert Smith's name every time &PERSON1& occurred in the text. This command would be very useful in creating a contract that was to be reused continually. The master form, or contract, would remain the same and only the .SV command would have to change before printing.

.FI (File Insert). This command can be used to set up files for chain printing, as in printing the chapters of a book in sequence. In this case there is no limit to the number of .FI commands you may enter. If you intend to change disks in your chain printing procedure, you will need to add CHANGE after the last file in a disk. (This procedure assumes that WordStar and MailMerge are on one drive and that your text files are on another). The command would be written in the following format:

.FI B:CHAP5.KAY CHANGE

When you had finished printing Chapter 5, you would see a prompt asking you to insert the new disk.

The other use for .FI is to insert files in a master document for *nested printing*. Only seven files may be nested within any single file being printed. This command can be very useful when you are adding data files from InfoStar to a master document, or when you want to add standard "boilerplate" paragraphs to a report.

.RP (Repeat). This command causes MailMerge to continue printing a file that is merging variable data into a master file identified with a .DF command. It is always used with an .RV command, and it should be placed near the beginning of the file. It will continue to print until all the data are printed. If you follow .RP with a number n, the merged file will be printed n times.

.PF (Print time line Forming). In English, that means that with this command you can tell MailMerge to reform pages as files are being merged. The net effect of this command is the same as using CTRL B in WordStar. You may find that sometimes this command does not always yield the printed page you want. All of the problems that result from MicroPro's preoccupation with "soft hyphens," "hard hyphens," and line breaks come into play here. In the Onscreen Menu (CTRL O) we advise turning off Hyphen Help and Soft Hyphen and using your dictionary if you want to break a word. More simply, don't break words at the end of the line. If you follow that practice, you will save yourself a lot of grief.

.PF must be followed by one of these three commands: .PF DIS, .PF OFF, or .PF ON. DIS means DISCRETION, and when it is added to .PF it will reform a paragraph when it sees a generic name in the text. It will stop reforming when it sees a hard carriage return. DIS is the standard, or default position for MailMerge. .PF OFF will turn off the reforming function after you have started it, and you would use it to print lists of data in non-document files or from InfoStar that you do not want reformed. .PF ON turns .PF back on. You would use this command to turn .PF back on after the data files had been inserted.

.OJ (Output Justification). In English, this command is a toggle switch that controls a justified or a ragged-right margin. It must be used with .PF, and like .PF it has three optional positions. .OJ DIS is the standard or default position, which will reform text according to the format of the original document. .OJ ON will justify your right margins, whether they have been justified in the original text file or not. .OJ OFF will form ragged-right margins in your printed copy, even if you have justified the right margins in your original.

.IJ (Input Justification). This command appears to have the same functions in controlling your right margins as .OJ. It has the same three options (DIS, ON, or OFF), which work in the same way.

.DM (Display Message). This command tells MailMerge to show the text on the screen when it prints your master document, and it can be followed by a message. .DM can be helpful when you need to instruct the operator. It is also very useful when combined with the .AV.

.CS (Clear Screen). This command will clear the screen when MailMerge is printing. It, too, can be followed by a message.

CREATING AND PRINTING A FORM LETTER

We are going to show you the basic steps necessary to crank out a form letter. Like most of the rest of the population, we are never overjoyed when we get those "Dear Occupant" letters. We understand, however, that mass correspondence is essential to all business, great or small, so we're going to show you how to add to the flood of mail that hits the Post Office every day. You will pardon us if we are a little silly in our example. The topic of creating form letters is not one that has much inherent humor, so we're going to try to inject some into our examples.

There are three parts or steps to generating a form letter:

1. Creating a data file in the non-document mode in WordStar or in InfoStar, ReportStar, or DataStar.
2. Writing your basic letter, or boilerplate in the document mode in WordStar.
3. Printing your letters and envelopes.

Building a Data File

Data files are written in WordStar's non-document mode or in InfoStar, ReportStar, or DataStar. Non-document mode operates differently from the document mode, and here is a list of do's and don'ts that apply to non-document files.

1. Word wrap does not function.
2. Tabs are fixed, and you may forget them.
3. CTRL B, or paragraph reforming, does not work.
4. Each line is called a *record,* and each record must end in a hard carriage return.
5. Every record has a practical limit of 240 columns, although you may extend to the next line.
6. Each item of data in a record (line) is called a *field.*
7. All fields must be separated by commas, with no hard carriage returns.
8. If a field contains a comma or is preceded or followed by a space, it must have quotation marks on either side of it.
9. You must have the same number of fields in each record, even if some of them are blank spaces surrounded by commas.
10. The order of the fields must be the same in all records in a data file.

We're going to create a list of addresses that can be used for your letters and your envelopes, and the list will have the following fields; M (for Mr., Ms., etc.), NAME, STREET or PO BOX, CITY, and STATE AND ZIPCODE. That means we will have five fields per record.

1) To begin a data file in WordStar from the Opening Menu	Type N ⟨Return⟩.
2) See "Name of file to edit?"	Type ADDRESS.LST ⟨Return⟩.
3) See "NEW FILE"	Type Ms.,Esther Flugle, 3923 Cherry Lane, "Wombat,",NJ 12345.
4)	Type ⟨Return⟩.
5) See your first record.	Type Mr., Henry Dingbat,32 Elm St., "San Leandro,",CA 54321
6)	Type ⟨Return⟩.
7) See your second record.	Type Dr.,David Horn,56 Bark St., "Pocatello,",ID 32145
8)	Type ⟨Return⟩

9) See your third record.	TYPE Mr.,John Drum,575000 Gratiot,"Detroit,"MI 23145
10)	Type ⟨Return⟩.
11) See your fourth record.	Type Ms.,Hermione Quick, ,"Lone Tree,",NE 41235
12)	Type ⟨Return⟩.

13) See your fifth record.

That is the beginning of a mailing list. Each one of those people will receive a copy of the form letter we are going to generate next. As you can easily tell by now, you may enlarge or modify your mailing list at any time without affecting your form letter.

Generating a Form Letter

The form letter will need a number of dot commands inserted in it, and the other major oddity will be the use of the ampersand. The & symbol is used to "frame" each field as it is entered in the form letter, and it is MailMerge's signal to pull new data from the data file. Because we are assuming you are already fam>ilar with WordStar, we are going to present you with a model letter with each command explained, rather than run you through an interactive routine you probably don't need at this point.

From the Opening Menu in WordStar, type D, and you might call the sample FORM.LTR. Later, you will work out a number of other creative filenames. At this point you should see a status line that looks like this, and then you can copy our sample letter (Fig. 11-1) to give you a hands-on feel for how to do it. The ⟨ character (left angle bracket) indicates a "hard" carriage return, and M means MailMerge.

Now that the first two major preparation steps are finished, it's time to print out old one-shot's letters.

Printing your Form Letters

When it comes to printing lots of letters and envelopes, it is very useful to have your company letterhead on form-feed paper. Otherwise, you or your clerk(s) are going to spend a lot of time feeding single sheets of paper into the printer. Labels also come on form-feed stock, and MailMerge can accommodate those needs, too. We will start with printing your letters as single sheets.

1) To print form letters from the Opening Menu in WordStar	Type M.
2) See "Name of file to MailMerge?"	Type FORM.LTR⟨Return⟩.
3) See the standard WordStar printing menu of questions, but with one difference:	

"Number of Copies (RETURN for 1)?"

Type ⟨Return⟩ for all questions except "form feeds" and "pause for paper change." Type Y for those questions.

4) Assuming your printer is on and loaded with its first sheet of paper

Type ⟨Return⟩.

5) See "MAILMERGE printing B:FORM.LTR"
"P= Stop PRINT"
"ENTER TODAY'S DATE"

Type JULY 4, 1884 ⟨Return⟩.

6) See your first letter printed.

Insert your next sheet of paper and type P.

7) See "PRESS SPACE after reading screen."

Press the space bar and type P.

8) Your second letter will start to print and ask you to enter the date again.

Follow steps 5-7 for each letter.

9) You are MailMerging your letters.

```
            B:FORM.LTR  PAGE 1 LINE 1 COL 01          INSERT ON


.OP (means OMIT PAGE NUMBER)                              < (=Hard CR)
.DF ADDRESS.LST (means define the file named ADDRESS.LST)  M (=MailMerge)
.RV M,NAME,STREET,CITY,STATE (means read variables)        M
                                                           <
                                                           <
            ONE - SHOT POWDER + AMMUNITION COMPANY, INC.   <
                    HOLE IN THE WALL, WYOMING              <
                                                           <
.AV "ENTER TODAY'S DATE", DATE (means enter date)     &DATE& <

&M& &NAME&                                                 <
&STREET&                                                   <
&CITY& &STATE&                                             <

DEAR &NAME&                                                <

        At the One-Shot Powder + Ammunition Company, Inc.  <
we know that you have purchased thousands of rounds of our <
reliable product. We know that all those rounds have taken <
care of the varmints that plague your area.               <
        Because of our heroic General Custer's bad luck    <
with that Crazy Horse, we have an over-supply of           <
30 caliber rounds that we are offering at 20% below our    <
normal catalogue price. Orders of over 1,000 rounds will   <
receive an additonal 5% discount.                          <
                                                           <
        Stock up now while there's time.                   <
                                                           <
Sincerely yours,                                           <
                                                           <
                                                           <
George 'One-Shot' Hardcase, III                            <
President                                                  <
                                                           <
.PA                                                        <
```

Fig. 11-1. Sample form letter produced using WordStar and MailMerge.

Printing your Envelopes

You may address your envelopes by creating another data file formatted for stickers, or you can create a D (document) file with .DF ADDRESS.LST, .RV M,NAME,STREET, CITY, STATE, and the &NAME& setup in the address section of your letter. The choice is yours.

MailMerge is very useful as you can see, and if you need more information about it please check MicroPro's bundled manual.

Chapter 12

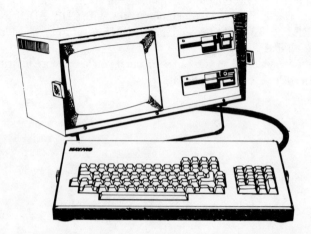

CalcStar for Star Calculators

CalcStar is produced by MicroPro, and it is one of three spreadsheets bundled with your KAYPRO. It is not notably better or worse than Profit/MicroPlan, and it may be slightly easier to learn.

Let's start by explaining just exactly what these things called spreadsheets really are. A *spreadsheet* is an old accounting term. It means to have all of your data spread out on a sheet of paper in order to make a forecast, see a trend, or simply derive an answer. Today, the spreadsheet is used in much the same way in the computer. With it, we set up what are called *models*. A model is an hypothetical situation, based on a few known, real-life facts. We take these few facts and add more data, usually guessed at, to project the probable outcome.

For a classic example of how a spreadsheet can help a business, let's look in on Mr. Russ Tiernan, but some months after he had purchased DataStar and a KAYPRO 10. Russ was promoted to Regional Manager soon after computerizing his spring supply division. Now Russ has bottom-line responsibility for four spring divisions and regional sales as well.

Russ had 25 salespeople, and five really stood out. But the spring business was not always on firm ground. Raw materials were sometimes short, and his major customer base, the transportation industry, was often cyclic in demand. But, all in all, sales were "somewhat" predictable.

One afternoon, his secretary handed him a manila envelope. Opening it, he saw it was from the Head Office. Inside was a computer printout, containing sales performance figures of two of the best-selling springs in the inventory. Current advertising costs for the two were also indicated. The accompanying letter from his manager, Smithers, was blunt: Russ's task was to analyze District 12 sales for this quarter. He was not only to come up with projected sales figures, but he needed advertising figures to reach those sales goals. Some task, all right, especially in light of the rumor that some division managers had been called to Smithers' carpet for having their sales/advertising forecasts out of line. Russ wanted none or that!

Russ started to reach for the phone. Johnson, in accounting, could help on this one. But, phone to his ear, he paused. The idea came to him that this would be a perfect opportunity to use his CalcStar program. Why, he could devise a forecasting model and set it up on the KAYPRO. Not only would he learn how to use the program, but he would assure himself that the figures were realistic.

The first task was to get the KAYPRO started and see just what it had in the way of a spreadsheet. He remembered that CalcStar came with all three KAYPRO models, so his 10 was sure to have it. If CalcStar was anything like the WordStar program (which he and all his secretaries used) or like DataStar (which improved efficiency so much in his old position that he got this raise), he knew it must be simple to use and powerful. The first thing he had to do was to start the CalcStar program. This is what he did.

COPYING CALCSTAR

Note: buyers of the 2 receive only CalcStar. Buyers of the 4 will experience a problem in dividing up the files on the distribution disk provided by KAYPRO. As it comes from KAYPRO all three programs occupy 390K of an available 390K on the disk. It is possible for owners of the 4 to copy all those files to one disk by using PIP and the following routine. It seems less troublesome for the operation of these programs to divide them up into two disks. We will show you how to do that, too, but first how to put them all on one disk.

Here's how to copy CalcStar, DataStar, and ReportStar on one 390K disk.

1) To copy all of the CalcStar, DataStar, and ReportStar files onto one 390K disk — Insert a disk with PIP on it in Drive A and a blank formatted disk in Drive B.

2) — Type CTRL C.

3) See the A0> prompt. — Type PIP ⟨Return⟩.

4) See an asterisk. — Remove the disk from Drive A and insert the CalcStar, DataStar, ReportStar master in A.

5) See PIP
   *
   on your screen. — Type B:=A:*.*[V0] ⟨Return⟩.

6) See an asterisk as the last item on the list of files. — Press ⟨Return⟩.

This copy disk will work *most* of the time, and *some* of the time it will hang up on you. It may be safer to divide the master disk into two copy disks. One would hold DataStar and CalcStar, and the other would hold ReportStar. As you gain experience with this system you may want to consider a different division of files.

The following is an opening way to divide the files into two disks. Use your regular PIP routine to copy the following files to a blank formatted disk that has PIP and D on it to put CalcStar and DataStar on one disk. You will also need some files from ReportStar.

ACCOUNTS.BAK	2K	D.COM	4K
ACCOUNTS.DEF	2K	DATASTAR.COM	26K
ACCOUNTS.DTA	2K	DEMO.CSD	4K
ACCOUNTS.NDX	OK	FORMGEN.COM	34K
BATCH.OVR	2K	OKSTATES.DTA	2K
CS.COM	2K	OKSTATES.NDX	2K
CS.OV1	16K	PIP.COM	8K
CS.OV2	18K	PRODUCTS.DTA	2K
CS.OVR	30K	PRODUCTS.NDX	2K
CSDUMP.COM	2K	REDIT.COM	28K
CSDUMP.OVR	4K	REPORT.COM	32K
CSMASK.MSK	8K	RGEN.COM	18K
CUSTOMER.DTA	2K	RINSTALL.COM	30K
CUSTOMER.NDX	2K		

The last four files on the list actually belong to ReportStar, and they replace the Install programs native to DataStar and CalcStar. Please see the RINSTALL routine in our DataStar and ReportStar chapter for the installation procedures. Assuming that you have installed the program for your KAYPRO, here is a routine to run the program.

1) On the KAYPRO 10	Choose Spreadsheets from the Master Menu with the arrow key, press ⟨Return⟩.
2) To choose CalcStar	Move the highlighter down with the DOWN arrow key to CalcStar and press ⟨Return⟩. Owners of the 2 or 4: Insert either of your copy disks and type CS ⟨Return⟩.
3) See ID # and Version #.	Hit the space bar to clear the screen of the ID # and Version#.
4) Examine CalcStar screen, also shown in Fig. 12-1.	

Note: as you can see, the screen can be divided into three parts, top, middle, and bottom. The top of the screen is subdivided into three sections as well: Cursor Movement, Commands, and Misc.

CURSOR MOVEMENT

This section contains an abbreviated listing of the cursor controls. The cursor in this program is not really called a cursor, though. In this spreadsheet, they call it a *window*, because we look at our data one small section at a time. Because most people

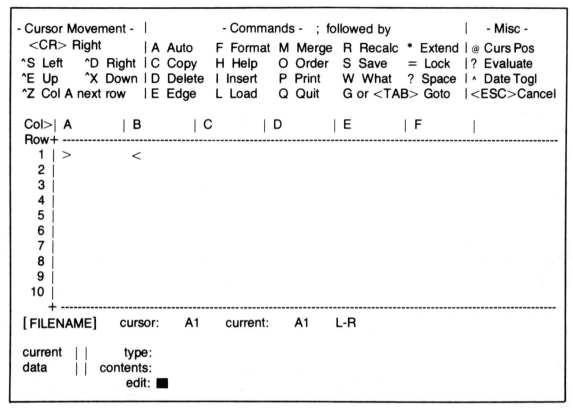

```
- Cursor Movement - |            - Commands -   ; followed by          |   - Misc -
  <CR> Right        | A Auto    F Format M Merge R Recalc  * Extend | @ Curs Pos
^S Left    ^D Right | C Copy    H Help   O Order  S Save   = Lock   | ? Evaluate
^E Up      ^X Down  | D Delete  I Insert P Print   W What   ? Space  | ^ Date Togl
^Z Col A next row   | E Edge    L Load   Q Quit    G or <TAB> Goto  | <ESC>Cancel


Col>| A         | B        | C        | D        | E        | F        |
Row+ ----------------------------------------------------------------------------
  1 | >            <
  2 |
  3 |
  4 |
  5 |
  6 |
  7 |
  8 |
  9 |
 10 |
  + ----------------------------------------------------------------------------
[ FILENAME]     cursor:    A1    current:    A1    L-R

current  | |     type:
data     | |     contents:
                 edit: ■
```

Fig. 12-1. CalcStar screen.

are familiar with "cursor," we will continue to call it that. The small section that the cursor is in is called a *cell,* and each cell is separate from all the other cells within the spreadsheet. So, the window, or cursor, allows you to see, add, or delete the contents within *any one cell at a time.* Moving the cursor around the screen—or from cell to cell, to be more accurate—is done by using these controls.

You should note that the ^ symbol means the CTRL key is pressed and, while you hold it down, you also press the appropriate letter. For example, ^Z means, you hold down the CTRL key and press the letter Z. The letter you press does not have to be in the uppercase mode, so, ^z is the same thing. You can press the Return key and the cursor (window) will move one cell to the right.

COMMAND KEYS

You can press the Return key and the cursor (window) will move one cell to the right. There are also specific commands that will perform a variety of functions. For example, by pressing the ; (semicolon) key, you tell CalcStar you want to enter a command, and the prompt Command> will appear at the bottom of the screen. Now press the H or h key, and the automatic help screen will appear. You may leave the program using ;Q. Data are printed by using :P. You can load another spreadsheet (one that you have already created) by using the ;L and entering the filename (e.g., DEMO), or you can copy the contents of one cell to another—and save lots of time—by using the

;C command. And typing ;? will have CalcStar tell you how much memory is available for entries.

THE CALCSTAR SCREEN

Now look at the center of the screen. This is also called a *window*, but this window is much larger. Instead of showing you just one cell, it shows about 60 cells. Since the spreadsheet can be hundreds of cells wide or long (or both), this is how you get to see a large group at one time. As you move the cursor beyond the F column, for instance, the window will scroll to the right to follow you and allow you to see the next 60 cells. Also, you will see any text (yes, you can actually write on CalcStar's spreadsheet) you may use for descriptions, all of your data/numeric entries, and the results of your calculations.

The cells within the window are each given a *position coordinate*. You can tell what coordinate you are in by looking at the Current Cursor Position indicator (in the next description), or by simply looking at its position on the screen. The top of the window, in the left corner has:

COL> |A |B |C |D |E |F

This is the COLumn row, read from left to right. Below the word "COL> |" is

ROW+- - - -
              1
              2

You read the ROW column going down, 1,2,3,4,5,6,7,etc. So, the upper left corner is COL A, ROW 1, or, using the shorthand in CalcStar, A1. Below that would be A2. To the right one cell of A1 is B1, and one cell below B1 is B2.

There are 255 rows to use, and the column has A to DW (that is, you will go through all of the alphabet, then go through it again using AA, AB, AC, etc., until you go through it three more times and end with DW. That is quite a few columns!

You will notice the >   < that is in cell A1. This is your cursor. The difference between this cursor and the one used in WordStar is that when you enter data, it doesn't immediately appear within this window. It first appears below at the bottom of the screen in the "edit:" portion, where a more familiar cursor can be found. Once you have entered your dta (text or numeric), you press Return or Enter (if you are working with the keypad) and the data will appear in the cell that the cursor <   > is in.

Finally, look at the bottom of the screen. This is called the *current data area*. Program prompts, messages and all of your data entries will be displayed here, along with the status and contents of each cell. It also shows the current position of the cursor (B4, H19, etc.).

Now that you have a basic understanding of what the screen will show, and how to move around on it, let's continue by entering some data. The present cursor position should be A1.

5) Change width and enter
    first text.   Type ;F.

6) Look at the bottom left of the screen. See Precision, Width, Form

Press W for Width.

7) Choose from 3 to 63 spaces for this cell.

Type 25 ⟨Return⟩.

8) See the cell enlarge.

Use the ⌃X key to move the cursor down three cells to position A4.

9)

Type District.12 1st Qtr Sales ⟨Return⟩.

10) To right-justify the text

Type /R ⟨Return⟩.

11) To move cursor to B1

Type ⌃D. and use up arrow.

12) To enter abbreviation for January

Type "Jan" ⟨Return⟩.

13) To right-justify the text

Type /R ⟨Return⟩.

14) Enter abbreviations for February and March.

Type "Feb" and "Mar" in positions C1 and D1.

15) Justify each entry after you enter it.

Type /R ⟨Return⟩.

16) Finish at position D1.

17) To move the cursor to B1

Type ⌃S twice.

18) To move the cursor to B2

Type ⌃X.

19) Enter the number 1 below January.

Type 1 ⟨Return⟩.

20) The screen reads 1.00, but it has to read 1.

21) We can eliminate the .00 by changing the precision of our entry.

22) See Command> at the bottom of the screen.

Press ;F

Press P for precision and type 0 for no precision. Press ⟨Return⟩.

23) Add remaining numbers.

Enter a 2 under Feb in C2, a 3 under Mar in D2. Don't forget to change the precision of each entry with the ;F control. The precision should be 0.

Type ⌃Z.

24) Move to position A3.

Type /== ⟨Return⟩.

25) Set up dividers

26) You have told CalcStar to enter the = symbol, and fill the entire cell with it. We now want to fill the rest of the cells under the remaining months.

Use the Copy Command and save time again!

27) Copy data from Jan to March.

Type ;C.

28) See "From Coord?". (This is the coordinate you're going to copy *from*.)

Type A3 ⟨Return⟩.

29) See "To Coord?"

Type B3>D3 (This means copy it in cells B3 through D3.) ⟨Return⟩.

30) Enter data in A5.

Use ⌃X and move the cursor to position A5. Type "Large Truck Springs" ⟨Return⟩. Type /R ⟨Return⟩.

31) Enter data in A6.

Use ^X and move cursor to A6. Type "Auto Coil Springs" ⟨Return⟩. Type /R ⟨Return⟩.

32) Enter data in A8.

Use ^X and move to position A8. Type "Total Advertising $$" ⟨Return⟩. Type /R ⟨Return⟩.

33) Enter data in B5. We now want to enter the dollar amount sold in the months of January through March. January's will go in position B5, so move to B5 now.

Use arrows to move to B5;
Type 6000 ⟨Return⟩.

Note: we don't enter $ signs or # symbols when entering numeric data. CalcStar will give you an error message if you do. That's why your descriptions or headings should explain just what these numbers are.

34) Enter the rest of data.

Again, using the arrows, move the cursor along the B row and enter 8000 for February; 2000 for March.

35) Enter coil data.

Type ^Z and move to A6. Move to B6, under the 6000; enter 5500 for January, 9500 for February, and 4500 for March. Move to B8.

36) Enter advertising data

37) Enter the amount spent each month for advertising.

Enter 1500 for January, 2500 for February, and 500 for March.

38) To find out the average sales per month, and to help us in further computations, we will call up the Regression Function, which uses other data entered to arrive at its conclusions.

Move the cursor to position G5. Type ;F and again change the width to 25 ⟨Return⟩. Type "Average Monthly Sales =" ⟨return⟩. Righ-justify /R ⟨Return⟩. Use^X and either retype the same as above, or use the copy command from G5 to G6.

39) Enter data.

Move to H5 and Type +REGR (B2>D2,B5) ⟨Return⟩.

40) Calculate regression.

41) See the answer in the cursor: 5333.33. See also the formula appear in the "contents" portion of the bottom of your screen.

Note: although regression, slope, or projection functions are difficult to understand at first, let's give it a try. +REGR is the command for Range, first coordinate; it returns the average of the second coordinate. So, (B2>D2, is the range, and B5 is the second coordinate. The answer is the average.

42) Find average sales of auto coil springs.

Use ^X and move down one cell. Type +REGR (B2>D2,B6) ⟨Return⟩. The answer should be 6500.00.

43) Enter advertising / sales calculation.

Move to Position G8. Type Advert./Trk. Sales = ⟨Return⟩. Type /R ⟨Return⟩.

44) Enter advertising calculation.

Move to H8 and type +REGR(B8>D8,B5) ⟨Return⟩.

45) See 5333.33, the same answer we got above! Why? Because that is how many ad dollars it took to make that average a month for the first quarter.

46) Enter advertising ratio for coil springs sales.

Move down to Position G9. Type Advert./Auto Coils S1s = ⟨Return⟩. Type /R ⟨Return⟩.

47) Enter advertising Calculation

Move to H9 and type +REGR(B8>D8,B6) ⟨Return⟩.

48) See 6500.00.

49) Increase width at I5 and enter new heading.

Move to I5 and increase the width to 25 again using ;F, W, and 25 as your inputs. Now Type Projected Sales-2nd Qtr. ⟨Return⟩. Type /R ⟨Return⟩.

50) Copy entry.

Use the ;C to copy the contents of I5 to I6.

51) Enter calculation on J6.

Move to J6 and type +PROJ(6) ⟨Return⟩.

52) See 4500.00.

Enter ;R and A (for *All*) to be sure. ⟨Return⟩. See 2765.

Note: we are performing a PROJection now. We are asking CalcStar to give the best estimate, based on the past three months (the first quarter) of what the monthly sales will be at the end of 6 months in June (the end of the second quarter).

53) Repeat projection for J5.

Type +PROJ(5) ⟨Return⟩ at position J5. See 2762.5. Then type ;R and A, just to be sure about its accuracy.

54) See −666.66.

55) Calculate ad $$ to increase monthly sales to average of 5333.33.

Move to position I8 and type "Ad $$ to make $5333/mth" ⟨Return⟩. This will tell us how much, on the average, we would have to spend in advertising to have sales of $5333 a month. We have already set up a relationship of sales to ad dollars spent, so this will take it one step further. Into the future!

56) Enter next requirement.	Press ∧X and enter the same thing—only this time it's $6500/mth.
57) Enter function.	Move to J9 and type +DEPD(6500) ⟨Return⟩. The estimated number of ad dollars to reach sales of $6500 a month is 1500. This is a monthly average of ad dollars to be spent.
58) Enter function again.	Use∧E and enter the formula again: +DEPD(5333.33) ⟨Return⟩. The average monthly ad cost would be 1033.33. This is not peanuts, but clearly something in the way of increased ad spending needs to be done, because there seems to be a strong correlation going that way. No wonder the spring business isn't for the weak at heart!

PRINTING A SPREADSHEET

Now let's print your spreadsheet. At the bottom of your console, you will have to answer some questions. Is your printer ready? Does it have paper in it? Although you don't have to have one, a 132-column printer is really what you need to print out spreadsheets. If you have only an 80-column printer (one that only takes 8½ × 11 or 8½ × 14 sheets) then you will get most of your printouts in segments. Here is one way to answer the printing questions:

59) To Print your Spreadsheet	Enter ;P.
60) See To which File? PRINTER.	Press ⟨Return⟩.
61) See "Top Left Corner A1?"	It is on ours, so press ⟨Return⟩.
62) See "Bottom Right Corner J9?"	It is, so press ⟨Return⟩ again.

Note: We have now told CalcStar the boundaries of our window i.e., our work is between A1 and J9, the two extreme corners.

| 63) See "Form Length CONTINUOUS" | This is the 66-line page default, so press ⟨Return⟩. |
| 64) See "Output Width 132?" | Try typing 80 ⟨Return⟩ and see what happens. |

The screen should now say "Printing in segments: Title?:" You may type a title to the report, or just press Return. If you decide to type a title, press Return after typing it, and it will be immediately printed. You will be asked again if there is another title. If so, type it. This will continue until you press Return and nothing else at the Title?: prompt. At this time your spreadsheet will be printed. After printing, press the space bar to return to the CalcStar window.

Now you should save your finished spreadsheet, which should look like Fig. 12-2.

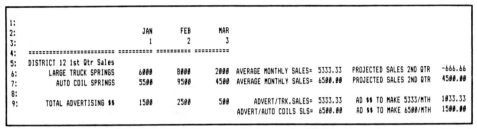

```
1:
2:                                 JAN      FEB      MAR
3:                                  1        2        3
4:    ========================= ========= ========= =========
5:   DISTRICT 12 1st Qtr Sales
6:       LARGE TRUCK SPRINGS      6000     8000     2000  AVERAGE MONTHLY SALES= 5333.33   PROJECTED SALES 2ND QTR    -666.66
7:       AUTO COIL SPRINGS        5500     9500     4500  AVERAGE MONTHLY SALES= 6500.00   PROJECTED SALES 2ND QTR    4500.00
8:
9:       TOTAL ADVERTISING $$     1500     2500      500      ADVERT/TRK.SALES= 5333.33   AD $$ TO MAKE 5333/MTH     1033.33
                                                          ADVERT/AUTO COILS SLS= 6500.00   AD $$ TO MAKE 6500/MTH     1500.00
```

Fig. 12-2. Spring sales calculation, or, advertising pays. This is the way a 132-column spreadsheet printout would look.

65) Invoke "SAVE" command.	Type ;S for save.
66) See a prompt asking for a filename.	Type PRACTICE
67) See a prompt asking for a password.	Type ⟨Return⟩ for none.
68) See a prompt asking for a partial or a complete save.	Type A for all and ⟨Return⟩.
69) To leave CalcStar	Type ;Q for quit.
70) See a prompt asking you to verify that you want to quit.	Type Y.
71) See a warm boot.	

CalcStar is evidently more reliable on the 10 than it is on the 4. We strongly advise using dBASE II for complex and interrelated programs (because it is designed as a relational database), or that you use Profitplan or Microplan for simpler spreadsheet operations.

Chapter 13

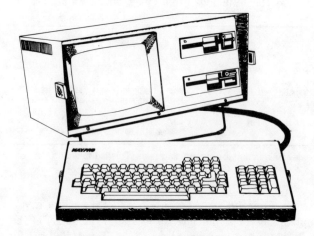

DataStar and ReportStar

DataStar is a database management system that will allow you to organize your work and utilize the stored information reasonably efficiently. If you are up to speed with WordStar, then DataStar will be somewhat easier for you to use because it shares many of the same cursor movement commands. What follows is one example of what DataStar can do for you and your business.

A TYPICAL DATASTAR SCENARIO

Mr. Russ Tiernan, whom we met when he tried out CalcStar, manages a small spring supply division of a large international firm. He has two plant managers and approximately 150 employees. Russ needed a database management system that would quickly and accurately store and produce customer lists, how much and what they had ordered, their payment history, and a complete sales staff record.

Previously, Russ had kept a record of all customer information (names, addresses, and purchasing officers) on a 3 × 5 Rolodex system. A paper filing system containing hundreds of invoices was his way of finding out which customer had bought what, and when. Russ's secretary spent a lot of time going through that five-drawer file cabinet. Sometimes Russ did, too.

In a smaller file cabinet Russ kept a record of those companies that had not placed an order in the past year. And in yet another five-drawer cabinet, Russ kept his monthly inventory. The 60- and 90-day past-due accounts were tagged and then moved from the current invoice cabinet to a special basket on his desk.

All but the past customer files had to be compiled on a weekly basis, photocopied, and sent by express mail to the head office, where they would be loaded into the large mainframe computer for accurate record keeping.

While payroll and employee records were kept in the mainframe at the head office, Russ had to send his time cards in with his weekly business reports. He was given the option of having a set of his own employee files and wage listings, but he felt he didn't have room to store them or time to keep them in order. After all, his secretaries were always busy typing correspondence and business invoices on two electric typewriters.

For some time, this paper database system worked well enough and Russ could usually find everything—most of the time. But as time passed, Russ began to suspect that he needed a simpler way to accomplish the same tasks. That's when he discovered DataStar and KAYPRO computers.

So, he asked the head office for the funds to purchase one. They agreed on a small microcomputer system, on a trial basis. Russ was elated, and so was the local KAYPRO dealer when Russ came with a check for a KAYPRO 10!

FEATURES AND BENEFITS OF DATASTAR

Russ skimmed the DataStar training and reference manuals to find out what DataStar had to offer him. In short, he discovered that with DataStar he would be able to:

- Perform accurate calculations to fourteen digits.
- Reduce the number of errors made when entering data, by either checking it against another file's data, or by visually checking the data before storing it.
- Handle large data entry jobs through the Batch File process.
- Organize his data by any means he chose: name, address, customer number, order number, dates, invoice number, totals, etc.
- Use the same design that his current forms use, from 1 to 3 pages wide and several pages long.
- Retrieve his information by scanning the entire field or by recalling one specific record, or by locating several records by a specifying common factor (i.e., all customers who have outstanding debts over 90 days).
- Use DataStar as his data entry file for his accounting, personnel, or parts inventory programs.
- Refer to many useful help screens if he encountered a command question, or to a variety of help messages for procedural problems.
- Have a problem or error explained by the many help prompts.
- Use up to 79 columns across and 17 lines down on his KAYPRO 10's console (when no help screens are present).
- Support most CP/M programming languages for total interface with other programs. Russ could use DataStar as an internal data entry/retrieval system when writing "specific purpose" application programs. Languages such as COBOL, BASIC, and FORTRAN are just some of the languages that interface with DataStar.
- Use DataStar interactively with WordStar to create unique, personalized correspondence.
- Use MicroPro's SuperSort to accomplish all types of sorting applications.

PLANNING A SAMPLE FORM

Russ knew he wanted to first set up a file containing all of his customers. This would include both past and present customers. He first decided just what information he used most and would like to have at hand most quickly. For this, he went through each paper file he had on one of his customers and found what information was common and unique to each file.

His Rolodex files contained the name, address, and telephone number for each of hundreds of purchasing agents. Next, he looked through his current invoice files. They showed what item and how many of that item had been purchased. These files also contained any special shipping information, along with the method of payment, and a very brief credit history. From all of these scattered sources, Russ made some sample headings of what he might name these separate items.

Russ knew that by using DataStar he could arrange these headings on his KAYPRO 10's console until the format met his needs. Moreover, he would no longer need three separate places to store basically the same information. He could, if he wished, make a separate data disk for his delinquent accounts, another for his current ones, and still another for the old, inactive accounts.

After some preliminary planning and thought, Russ was ready to transform his old "paper database" into an electronic one. The more thought he gave to the idea of changing to an electronic database (and not just a filing system), the more he started to realize the following advantages over his old systems:

- He could locate a customer's file or invoice in a fraction of the time it had once required.
- He could continuously add, delete or just update any portion of any customer's file.
- He could use WordStar along with the DataStar program to create specific form letters, invoices, billings, or update notices.
- He now had an easy method of creating a mailing list for himself and the head office.
- He had eliminated the need for cross-checking his facts with regard to inventory or credit availability for a particular customer.
- He could process any customer's order, old or new, in less time and keep a closer watch on all phases of his business—from accounts receivable to tax on inventory.
- He could send reports daily to the head office by telephone modem and receive information the same way. This would allow him and the head office to avert any possible inventory, supply, or billing problems.

KEY PAPER-TO-DATABASE RELATIONSHIPS

Here is a quick rundown of terms that mean the same thing, but are used somewhat interchangeably. Russ gave these some real thought during the planning stages of converting his old paper system over to an electronically-based DataStar system.

A Customer's File	= A Record
A Customer's Name, Address	= A Data Field
A Customer's Account Number	= A Data Field

Many Customer's Account Numbers	=	A Related Data Field
All Customer's in San Antonio	=	A Related Data Field
Bob's Spring Mart, Houston	=	A Specific Record
Bob's Spring Mart's Account Number	=	A Specific Data Field Record

SETTING UP A DATASTAR DATABASE

Russ noticed in his user's manual that DataStar consists of two distinct parts. The FORMGEN part is what he must use to design his blank forms. The DataStar portion of the program will allow him to enter, retrieve, and manipulate his data. In fact, Russ could design his forms and then have one of his support staff key in all of the old and new data.

Russ knew from looking over all of his various files that he would need a "universal" record system that could be used for all his customers, no matter how large or small the order. He needed a customer listing that would replace his Rolodex and his past-due accounts bin (both on his desk). In this way, whenever a customer wanted to place an order, Russ or his office manager could quickly check to see if the customer would pay C.O.D. or on credit (and if on credit, how long to extend it). After some necessary housekeeping chores, we'll show you what Russ did to create his first record.

Note: buyers of the 2 receive only CalcStar. Purchasers of the 4 will experience a problem in dividing up the files on the distribution disk provided by KAYPRO. As it comes from KAYPRO, all three programs occupy 390K of an available 390K on the disk. It is possible for owners of the 4 to copy all those files to one disk by using PIP and the following routine. However, it seems less troublesome for the operation of these programs to divide them up into two disks (and we will show you how to do that, too), but first here is how to put them all on one disk.

1) To copy all of the CalcStar, DataStar, and ReportStar files onto one 390K disk.	Insert a disk with PIP on it in Drive A and a blank formatted disk in Drive B.
2)	Type CTRL C.
3) See the A0> prompt	Type PIP ⟨Return⟩.
4) See an asterisk.	Remove the disk from Drive A and insert the CalcStar, DataStar, and ReportStar master in A.
5) See PIP *on your screen	Type B:=A:*.*[VO]⟨Return⟩.
6) See * as the last item on the list of files.	Press ⟨Return⟩.

This copy disk will work *most* of the time—and SOME of the time it will hang up on you. It may be safer to divide the master disk into two copy disks. One would hold DataStar and CalcStar and the other would hold ReportStar. As you gain experience with this system, you may want to consider a different division of files.

The following list is a beginning way to divide the files into two disks. To put

CalcStar and DataStar on one disk, use your regular PIP routine to copy the following files to a blank formatted disk that has PIP and D on it. You will also need some files from ReportStar.

ACCOUNTS.BAK	2K	D.COM	4K
ACCOUNTS.DEF	2K	DATASTAR.COM	26K
ACCOUNTS.DTA	2K	DEMO.CSD	4K
ACCOUNTS.NDX	0K	FORMGEN.COM	34K
BATCH.OVR	2K	OKSTATES.DTA	2K
CS.COM	2K	OKSTATES.NDX	2K
CS.OV1	16K	PIP.COM	8K
CS.OV2	18K	PRODUCTS.DTA	2K
CS.OVR	30K	PRODUCTS.NDX	2K
CSDUMP.COM	2K	REDIT.COM	28K
CSDUMP.OVR	4K	REPORT.COM	32K
CSMASK.MSK	8K	RGEN.COM	18K
CUSTOMER.DTA	2K	RINSTALL.COM	30K
CUSTOMER.NDX	2K		

The last four files on the list actually belong to ReportStar, and they replace the Install programs native to DataStar and CalcStar that are not provided on the single distribution disk. Please see the RINSTALL routine for the installation procedures.

Unlike owners of the 10, owners of the 2 or the 4 will have to run RINSTALL to be sure that these programs are set correctly for their KAYPROs and their printers. Here's how.

1) To run RINSTALL   Type RINSTALL ⟨Return⟩.

2) See "INSTALL version 4.48 for ReportStar Release 1.03" and the printer menu. There are two lists, and you need to see which printer description fits your printer.   Type that letter.

3) See a lot of narrative about printers, and   Type Y if all that fits.

4) See the Communications Protocol Menu.   Choose N if you have a parallel printer, or X for X-ON/X-OFF if you have a serial printer.

5) See "OK (Y/N):"   Type Y.

6) See "Driver Menu"   For a parallel printer Choose L; for a serial printer, choose T.

7) See a prompt.   Type Y.

8) See a prompt for nonstandard options.   Type Y.

9) See "Are you running under MP/M? (Y/N):"	Type N unless you are running linked to other computers.
10) See a prompt about help levels.	Choose 4 at this stage.
11) See a prompt about the location of the system disk drive.	Type A.
12) See a prompt about writing reports to disk or to the printer.	Type U for a choice of either.
13) See a prompt about reporting errors.	Type S for flexibility.
14) See a prompt to check your choices.	Type Y.
15) See another checking prompt.	Type Y.
16) See Warm Boot A0>	

Note: from this point on, we will abbreviate the CTRL key with the same abbreviation used in the DataStar program. When you see a ∧ symbol with a letter or letters next to it, this means to hold down the CTRL key and press the appropriate letter(s). For example, to execute ∧ CB, hold down the CTRL key and first press C; then, still holding down the CTRL key, press the letter B.

RUNNING DATASTAR

1) To access DataStar on the 10	Use the DOWN arrow to select DataStar. Press ⟨Return⟩.
1A) To access DataStar on the 4	Type FORMGEN ⟨Return⟩.
2A) To start a file	Type ACCOUNTS ⟨Return⟩.
3A) To access DataStar	Type C D
3) See "Enter Name of Form Definition File or/Press RETURN.	Press ⟨Return⟩.
4) See "If you have not yet designed a Form, chose a name for the Form - Enter it here."	Type ACCOUNTS ⟨Return⟩.
5) Only on the 10 see ACCOUNTS.	
6) See Help Screen 4.	Read Help Screen 4.
7) Go to Help Screen 1.	Hold down CTRL and press J. Repeat this until you read the Help Screen 1 in the right upper corner of your console.

This routine will continue after our explanation of the help screens.

Using the Help Screens

Pressing ∧ J is called *rotating the Help Screens*. There are four Help Screens in all. You want to stay with Help Screen 2 when first using the program by yourself. It contains all of the cursor control commands you'll need to start. Later, after you have memorized the commands, you'll want to use Help Screen 1. It only contains a minimum of information and allows you the maximum room you can use. We will be using Help Screen 1 in our practice examples. We will, of course, "walk" you through this.

Remember, you have 17 lines on the console to work with when you are using Help Screen 1, but only 7 lines down when using Help Screen 2 or 3. You'll need that screen room, so practice with Help Screen 2, memorize the commands, then abandon it for Help Screen 1.

At this point, we should look at the screen we will be working with. At the top of the blank screen we find, LIN=000 COL=000. This is called the *Status Line*. Here's what it tells you: LIN tells you at what part of the screen you are, from top (000) to bottom (017). With Help Screen 1 in the right upper corner showing, that means it will show our cursor position all the way to the last line, line 17 (LIN=017). The COL stands for column. Each time you move the cursor one space to the right or to the left, it will tell your position in increments of one. Right now the LIN should equal 000 and the COL should equal 000. Again, you should have Help Screen 1 in the upper right corner.

8) Enter first Field.	Type ACCOUNT #: ⟨Return⟩.

Note: each Field item (i.e., ACCOUNT #) must end with a colon. If you make a mistake, use your DELete key or use the ∧G to delete one space to the right.

9)	Press the space bar once. Now, Press the Shift key and press the _ (underline) key eight (8) times. The first underline started at LIN=000 COL=11.
10) At the end of eight underlines, the Status Line should read: LIN=000 COL=019; with the cursor at the COL=019 position, the last underline is at COL=018.	
11) Add the Data Entry.	FROM LIN=000 COL=019, press the space bar 5 times. Now type DATE (M/D/Y): _ _/_ _/_ _.
12) The status line should now read LIN=000 COL=046 with the cursor on COL=046.	Now press ⟨Return⟩.
13) Bring the cursor just below the A in Accounts, or have the status line read: LIN=001 COL=000	Press ⟨Return⟩.
14) See the cursor at COL=000.	
15) Add Billing Name.	Type BILL TO:, a space, and then hold down shift and make 15 underlines.
16) See status line read; LIN=001 COL=024	

17) Add Shipping Name.	Press the space bar 5 times. Type SHIP TO: and make 15 underlines here also.
18) See SHIP TO: ____	

Note: there is *always* a space placed after the : and before the first _! The status line should read COL=53.

19)	Press ⟨Return⟩.
20) See LIN=002 COL=000 and the cursor directly below the B in BILL.	
21) Add Address line.	Type ADDRESS:, leave a space, then make 15 underlines.
22) The status line should now read LIN=002 COL=024.	
23) Add Shipping Address line.	With the cursor at LIN=002 COL=024, press the space bar 5 times. Type ADDRESS:, leave a space, then add 15 underlines.
24) The status line should now read: LIN=002 COL=053.	Press ⟨Return⟩.
25) See LIN=003 COL=000. The cursor should be under the A in ADDRESS.	

This routine will continue after this brief discussion.

Note: You should be able to complete the form at this point. Figure 13-1 shows what the form looked like when we finished it; yours doesn't have to be an exact duplicate, but if you can get yours to at least resemble ours, then you have caught on. If you need help

```
ACCOUNT #: _____    DATE (M/D/Y): __/__/__
BILL TO: _____      SHIP TO: _____
ADDRESS: _____      ADDRESS: _____
CITY: _____         CITY: _____
STATE: __  ZIP: _____  STATE: __  ZIP: _____
P.O. #: _____
SHIP VIA: _____     TERMS: _____
DESCRIPTION: _____
UNIT COST: _____    TOTAL COST: _____
SALES TAX: _____    TOTAL DUE: _____
```

Fig. 13-1. Completed blank form.

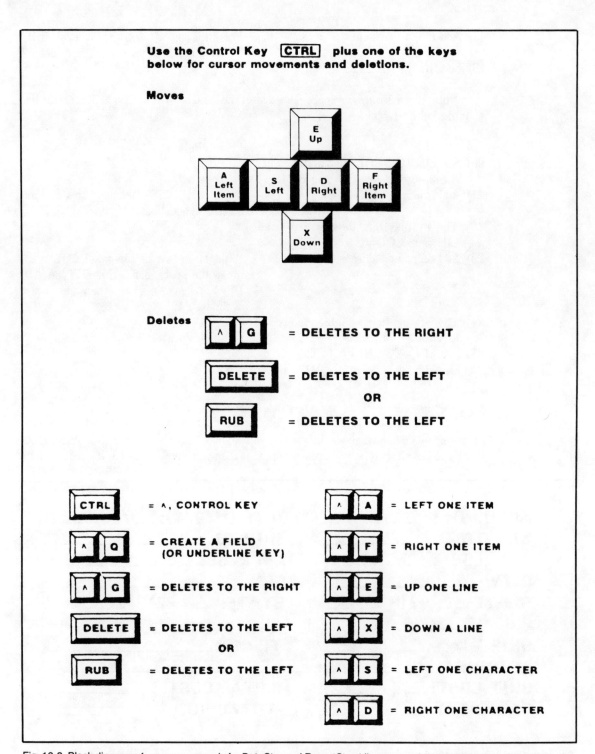

Fig. 13-2. Block diagram of cursor commands for DataStar and ReportStar (diagram as shown in MicroPro's User Manual).

with a command, just use ^J until you see Help Screen 2 or 3. Or, look at Fig. 13-2 and 13-3 for a complete listing of all the cursor commands. Then, once you have the command, return to Help Screen 1 by using the ^J command. So finish the form and then we'll move on.

After you have completed the rest of the form, move your cursor by using ^E and other cursor commands in Fig. 13-2 (or, if you have a 10, by using the UP arrow key—which doesn't work on the 4) to the first underline in the data field of "ACCOUNT #: ." It is at this point that we want to make a *key field*. This means, whenever we wish to retrieve, delete, or add to this or any record that uses this form, we will refer to it, and retrieve it, by way of this "ACCOUNT #:".

Every form, no matter what you have designed it to do, or what information it will contain, must have a key field. If can be the "Employee #: ", or the "Social Security # ", or "Client Name: ", or "P.O. #: " or anything that you feel is a *unique identifier.* You need only one key field per form. However, sometimes you might wish to have more than one, especially if the way you need to find a record isn't always the same. If you usually look for a record (or file) by account number, then it obviously must be the number 1 key field. But, if you sometimes wish to retrieve a record by the purchase order number, then you may also assign that as a key field. It will, however, be known to DataStar as key field

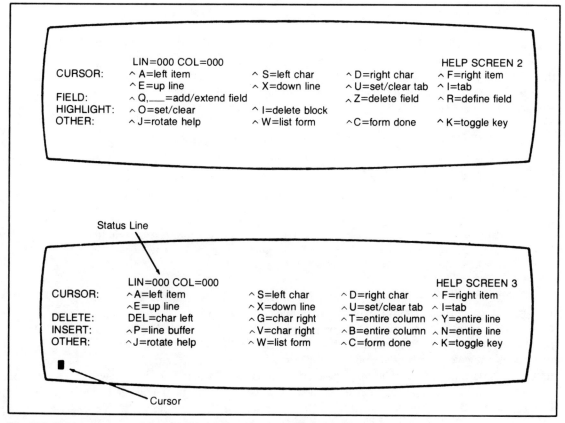

Fig. 13-3. Help screens 2 and 3, as shown in MicroPro's User Manual.

number 2 and key order number 2. Any further data fields you make key fields from that point on will be known one number down (3, 4, 5, etc.) from then on. You may change this order later on if you wish.

26) Install key field.

Move cursor to first underline character and press ∧K.

27) Notice that the underline symbols have turned into asterisks. This tells you on the screen that this is your key field. It will be known as Key Field Number 001.

This routine will continue after more discussion.

Russ now needs to set some *attributes* for his blank form. Attributes are always optional, but they are what make DataStar a very powerful program. Attributes can help you in the following ways:

● They can protect against incorrect data entry, i.e., if you want only numbers entered into the "ACCOUNT #: " data field, then you specify this. In this way, if someone tries to enter a letter or anything other than a number, DataStar will reject the erroneous data and not record it.

● DataStar will look into another file (such as an inventory file) to assist you in filling in some of the data fields. It can also use over again data that appears elsewhere in the form.

● Attributes will make automatic format conditions possible, i.e., you can add $ or # signs where needed.

So, with all of these important features in mind, Russ begins to assign attributes to some of his data fields. For instance, in the "ACCOUNT #: " data field, he will want only numbes, no letters or other symbols to be entered. This is how he assigned his attributes;

28) Assign attributes to the "ACCOUNT #: " data field.

Move the cursor into the data field, placing the cursor over the first * in the data field.

Note: if you look at the top of the screen, just to the right of the LIN=xxx COL=xxx and the Help Screen 1, you'll notice some new information. These four lines appear any time the cursor is placed in a completed data field. They are NUM=001 (this means the cursor is in the first data field you created), LEN=008 (which is the number of underlines you gave the data field, and POS=001 (which tells you that the cursor is in the first of the spaces provided, eight in this case). The cursor should be in POS=001 now.

You can use this guide later when entering information or looking for a field number that is, number 1 data field is "ACCOUNT #; " and number 2 data field is "DATE (M/D/Y): ". The last one is EDC= . This stands for *Entry Data Code(s)*. This will tell you at a glance just what attributes you have assigned the data field where the cursor is currently located. To use it, though, you have to remember what the abbreviated codes mean (i.e., a 9 means numbers only, while G means letters, numbers, and spaces may be entered). We'll look at these later. Let's continue with setting our attributes.

29) Invoke attribute commands.

With the cursor over the first * in the data field, press ^R. The screen will go blank and rewrite the top quarter of screen. At the top will be Help Screen R.

30) See the cursor after the field name at the first attribute assignment question.

Note: This portion of assigning attributes is usually confusing, but only if you use the DataStar training manual! It's actually very simple. One thing to remember is that you don't have to assign attributes to *all* of the data fields. If the possibility of entering erroneous data could be harmful, or if the data field *must* be filled in, you might consider assigning attributes to all the data fields. But if the field will contain only supplemental information or little-used information, don't waste your time giving it an attribute. Use the ^F command to jump from data field to data field in this mode.

Also, most of these attribute questions already have a *default*, a preset condition, such as Y or N. If you wish to use this default just press Return; otherwise, you'll have to enter the condition you want, and the next attribute question will appear. Other questions do not have a default. If you want these, press Y for Yes. If you do not want to invoke this particular attribute, press N for No. One last note: if you see an error message, just press the ESC key. It will cancel the last entry and let you restart the entry. If you need an on-the-spot definition of what a particular attribute is for, use the ^J command. A brief description of what the attribute can do will be given. This is a great help, no matter how often you use DataStar.

31) Assigning attributes.
32) Field Name is used when you wish to give a data field a name as well as an order number.

Press ⟨Return⟩ to skip this attribute.

33) Field Order 001 allows you to change the order in which data will be entered, i.e., Field Order 001 will be the first data field to accept data when entering data, 002 the second, and so on. We wish to keep this as the first data field, so we invoke its default by pressing ⟨Return⟩.

34) Refuse Duplicate Keys? (Y/N)

Pressing Y means that this data field will have some special symbol that no other record will have. It is not needed here, so we invoke the default N by pressing ⟨Return⟩.

Note: even though it looks like we would have to type N to choose No, pressing Return really does the same thing (meaning skip this attribute). The program is looking for a Y answer for it to activate a particular attribute. We will maintain our interactive number sequence here, but we will give you fuller definitions of the attributes.

35) Copy Attributes of Field 001. By pressing Y we would be telling DataStar it may copy whatever we enter into this data field onto another data field, i.e., if "AC-COUNT #: " is really the same thing as "CUSTOMER ID #: " and its Field Order number is 005, then upon entering the "ACCOUNT #: " data, DataStar would automatically enter the same information in the "CUSTOMER ID #: " data field. To invoke this attribute, you need only to input the Field Order Number of the item DataStar is to send to another data field (i.e., Field Order 005 in the above example). We have no need to change this, so we press Return.

36) Field Derived? (Y/N). To invoke this command means that the operator will not be entering any data here. The data will come from either calculating the data in another field, or from a list made especially for this purpose. That is, using a client's name entered elsewhere in the form. DataStar could pull the client's address into this data field from a file of constants, to create a value for this field. An example of this calculation is #005=#1+#2, which means that field 5 is calculated as the sums of fields 1 and 2. We do not need this attribute, so we press Return.

37) Required? (Y/N). We want this data field to be a mandatory entry, because we could not otherwise find this record (remember, it's our only Key Field). Type Y.

38) Right Justify? (Y/N). Right/left justify determines on which side of the data field data will be placed when it does not fill the entire field. Also, if the field is padded, it will determine which side it will be padded from. We will use this attribute, for it keeps all numeric data perfectly aligned to the right for easy viewing. So type Y.

39) Pad View? (Y/N). This attribute will not affect the data you enter; its only purpose is for display. It is used with the Right Justify attribute. We can pad the data field with any number we choose, or with spaces; zeros are perferred. We will use it, so type Y.

40) Enter Pad Character: Type 0.

41) Floating Character? (Y/N). This would insert any symbol either before or after our data. Commonly used symbols are $ and #, or + and −. We will not need this attribute, so we press Return for the default No.

42) Verify Field? (Y/N). After all your data have been entered on the blank form, the next mode would be Verify, if we choose this option. We will, so press Y for Yes.

43) Sight/Retype/List? (S/R/L). These are the verification choices we have. We can either verify what we have entered by sight, verify by having to retype the data, or verify by means of a pre-prepared list file. This list could contain addresses, Zip codes, or account numbers. The list would be stored in another file on your disk. It may be prepared by any means (WordStar would be excellent for this task). The easiest method for now is to sight verify. This means you will simply look at the data again while in the verify mode. If it is correctly entered, just press Return.

44) Batch Verify? (Y/N). This attribute delays executing the verification mode until a later time, when you wish to verify a *batch* of records, all at once. This can be particularly useful when many records are made at once. After entering your data, you would not enter the verify mode. You would simply be asked if you would like to store it

102

now. The same occurs if you just press Return, the default for No. Press Return.

45) Verify Calculate Order: When you have finished entering your data, Data-Star will usually carry out any calculations you have prescribed after allowing you to verify the data. If you wish the verify mode to come after any calculations, press the letter C. We do not want this order; we want to verify mode first. Because we have no calculations on this form, we press Return.

46) Check Digit?(Y/N). To use this attribute, any numeric data must be divisible by 11. We can see little use for this attribute. Press Return to bypass it.

47) Range Check? (Y/N). Allows you to set minimums and maximums of numeric data entered. If the range is under- or overshot, the operator is shown the correct ranges, and must re-enter the dial until it conforms. We will not need this, so press Return.

48) Edit Mask? (Y/N). This is the attribute that allows you to control just what is acceptable data and what isn't. It also works with copying data from another field or record. The Edit Mask consists of two steps. The first is entry control and content control; type Y to invoke this.

49) Examine Entry Control Character Codes: Here is a complete description of the Entry Control Character Codes.

!	Required entry for this data field.
−	Optional entry for this data field.
X	Copies a character from the previous record (i.e., relieves you from having to enter today's date on every record).
Y	Automatic copy that permits operator changes after copy.
"	Inserts the corresponding Content Control Character (next attribute list).
~	Same as above, but permits operator changes.
'	Inserts the Content Control Character only if the character positions on both sides are filled (i.e., they would allow commas to be added into a 7-digit number _'_ _ _'_ _ _).
/	Inserts the Content Control Character only if the character position on one side or the other is filled.

50) Choose the Entry Control Character Code(s). We will chose the ! only, making this data field require data be entered. Press the ! symbol. Notice above, on the status line, that the EDC now reads " =!". Each Entry/Content Character code you enter will show here for quick reference.

51) Choose a Content Character Control Code: The listing on your screen is self-explanatory. We want only numbers in this "ACCOUNT #: " field. Press the number 9. Now press Return

52) Record Edit Characters? (Y/N). Edit Characters are the pad/float characters and constants from the Edit Mask. They are usually removed from all data fields before recording your data entries. We wish to keep the pad option with whatever we enter, so type Y.

You have just finished assigning all the attributes to the "ACCOUNT #: " data field. We know you think it takes too much time, and you're right! That's why you only want to invoke, or use it on data fields that *absolutely need it*. But, once you have done it to a data field, you can really forget all about it.

We suggest that you assign some attributes to just one more data field on this form, i.e., the "P.O.#:", or purchase order number field data. We'll just list what you should enter, without any explanations as to why. If you don't know why or can't remember what the attribute is for, just type ^J and youwill get a short description of its use. So keep moving the cursor (by using the ^F and ^D commands) to the "P.O.#:" data field. Press ^R and let's set these attributes in record time.

1) Field Name	Press ⟨Return⟩.
2) Field Order = 015	Press ⟨Return⟩.
3) Copy Attributes of Field 015?	Press ⟨Return⟩.
4) Field Derived? (Y/N)	Press ⟨Return⟩.
5) Required? (Y/N)	Press Y.
6) Right Justify? (Y/N)	Press Y.
7) Pad Field? (Y/N)	Press Y.
8) Enter Pad Character:	Press 0 (zero).
9) Floating Character? (Y/N)	Press ⟨Return⟩.
10) Verify Field? (Y/N)	Press Y
11) Sight/Retype/List? (S/R/L)	Press ⟨Return⟩.
12) Batch Verify? (Y/N)	Press ⟨Return⟩.
13) Verify/Calculate Order:	Press ⟨Return⟩.
14) Check Digit? (Y/N)	Press ⟨Return⟩.
15) Range Check? (Y/N)	Press ⟨Return⟩.
16) Edit Mask? (Y/N)	Press Y.
17) Entry Control Codes:	Press ⟨Return⟩.
18) Content Control Codes:	Press uppercase H ⟨Return⟩.
19) Record Edit Characters? (Y/N)	Press Y.

As you can see, you can fly through the attribute section pretty fast, once you get the hang of it. Experiment with the other data fields: require letters only: no numbers: add different pad characters: have one data field write to another automatically. Remember, if you have a question about what an attribute can do or is intended to do, press ^J. If you wish to cancel the attribute list once you're into it, press the ESC key. Now let's enter some data and print it out. We'll also see just how well our attributes are working.

1) Save blank form and assigned attri-butes.	Press ^CC.
2) Invoke DataStar.	Press ^CD.
3) See "Enter disk drive to use for the data file (ACCOUNTS.DTA) (A/B)."	Enter B: or A:
4) See "Enter disk drive to use for the index file (ACCOUNTS.NDX) (A/B)."	Enter B: or A:
5)	You are now in DataStar.

At the top of the screen is the [Add Mode] and the [Current Form =]. The Current

Form should say [ACCOUNTS]. The cursor should be flashing at the far right side of the "ACCOUNT #: " data field. Why? Because it is going to right-justify everything we enter, that is, it will enter our data right to left, erasing the zeros we added as padding. Let's try entering some data;

6) Enter Account Number   Type 85274196.

The cursor will automatically jump to the next data field, but only if you completely fill the previous data field. If you do not fill the data field, you will have to press Return to make it jump, or use the ∧F commands.

7) Enter Date.	Type today's date.
8) Enter BILL TO data.	Type Springs Etc. ⟨Return⟩.
9) Enter SHIP TO data.	Type SAME ⟨Return⟩.
10) Enter Address.	Type 222 E. Main St. ⟨Return⟩.
11) Enter Address.	Press ⟨Return⟩.
12) Enter City.	Type Santa Barbara, ⟨Return⟩.
13) Enter City.	Press ⟨Return⟩.
14) Enter State.	Type C∧.
15) Enter State.	Press ⟨Return⟩.
16) Enter Zip.	Type 93101.
17) Enter Zip.	Press ⟨Return⟩.
18) Enter P.O. #.	Type J00819.
19) Enter SHIP VIA data.	Type Ground ⟨Return⟩.
20) Enter TERMS data.	Type Net/Net ⟨Return⟩.
21) Enter DESCRIPTION data.	Type 1 lot. 500 units TX-219/Coils (1200 lbs). Press ⟨Return⟩.
22) Enter UNIT COST data.	Type 2.00 ⟨Return⟩.
23) Enter TOTAL COST data.	Type 1000.00 ⟨Return⟩.
24) Enter SALES TAX data.	Type 0.0 ⟨Return⟩.
25) Enter TOTAL DUE data.	Type 1000.00 ⟨Return⟩.

After entering your data, you immediately go into the verify mode. The cursor should be at the end of the "ACCOUNT #: " data field. You are to sight-verify it. If the entry is correct (it should be 85274196) then press Return. If it is not, you may now re-enter it. If you have pressed Return, then you should go right to the "P.O. #: " data field. If it, too, is correctly entered (J00819), then press Return.

You are now asked at the top of the screen if you wish to save the data (after you have verified its accuracy and completeness), to erase all data, or to use ∧E to exit the current mode. If you press Y you will save the data, but if you press any other key, you will return to the top of the form and be allowed to add data to the next blank form. The data are correct (we hope), so press Return. The data should now be saved. It is here we want to stop. Here is how you leave the ADD Mode;

1) Exit current form and bring up main
    menu.   Press ∧E.

2) Proceed into SCAN MODE.   Press D.
3) Print Form and Data.   Press ^U.
4) Print Data Only.   Press ^O.

Make sure your printer is on and has paper in it before printing. A 132-character printer will be very handy, but you can get by with an 80-character one.

You can scan all of your records (although you only have one so far) by using the Scan Mode commands.

Press ^N to see the Next file.
Press ^P to see the Previous file.
Press ^E E ^C To leave DataStar and return to the system prompt.

These are the basics of DataStar. You should practice using all of its various commands and features before deciding to switch over yourself. You should *never* just drop the system you are currently using. You should use DataStar *and* your current system together for at least a year. It usually takes about this long to fine-tune the system. When you do at last switch over, like Russ Tiernan (now District Manager), you too will wonder why it took you so long to modernize your office. DataStar can be both fun and profitable!

REPORTSTAR

ReportStar, with DataStar and CalcStar, is part of the group that prints and helps you format your data into reports. Our man, Russ Tiernan, would use this one when he was preparing his quarterly report for the home office.

As is the case with the other two programs, owners of the 10 will have no problems using this program with the other two. Purchasers of the 2 do not get this program, while owners of the 4 are still faced with a file distribution problem. In the CalcStar and DataStar chapters we have provided you with a routine to PIP all the files on one disk, and, by now you are aware that you may have a space problem on your disk with that arrangement. Your alternative is to make a separate copy disk, PIPing the ReportStar files from the master distribution disk.

Making a Separate ReportStar Disk

As you probably remember, you need to put a formatted disk with PIP and D on it in Drive A, and the master distribution disk in Drive B. Type PIP and Return, and you will see an asterisk. From that point, type A:=B:filename.etx[VO] for each of the following files. Every time you get an asterisk in column 01 you can PIP another file. Here's the list:

CHAPTER1.RPT	2K	FORMSORT.COM	18K
CLIENTSR.DEF	2K	FORMSORT.OVR	14K
CLIENTSR.DTA	2K	INVCE.DEF	4K
CLIENTSR.NDX	2K	INVCE.DTA	4K
D.COM	4K	INVCE.NDX	2K

ORDER.DEF	4K	REDIT.COM	28K
PAYMENTS.DEF	2K	RSMSGS.OVR	40K
PAYMENTS.DTA	2K	REPORT.COM	32K
PAYMENTS.NDX	2K	RGEN.COM	18K
PIP.COM	8K	RINSTALL.COM	30K
PRODUCTR.DEF	2K	RSMSGS.OVR	8K
PRODUCTR.DTA	2K	STAFF.DEF	2K
PRODUCTR.NDX	2K	STAFF.DTA	2K
PUTEOF.COM	4K	STAFF.NDX	2K
		TERMCAP.SYS	2K

Generating a Report with ReportStar

ReportStar has three primary files, RGEN, REDIT, and REPORT; it accesses DataStar and CalcStar files through them. To generate a report, put your ReportStar disk in Drive A and a data disk in Drive B. If you don't have a data disk yet, you can use a formatted blank in B and follow MicroPro's *training guide*. PRODUCTS.DTA and PRODUCTR.DEF must be on Drive A, and they are part of the list we have just given you.

1) To run ReportStar	Insert your ReportStar disk in A.
2)	Insert a data disk or a formatted blank disk in B.
3) To run the Quick Report Program	Type RGEN ⟨Return⟩.
4) See the RGEN release number and a prompt to enter the name of a file that will hold all the directions you specify for creating your report.	Type B:filename (B:TEST1, for instance) ⟨Return⟩.
5) See the name you have just typed and the cursor flashing at "filename"	

The current screen shows the name for the specified report file, and it allows you to specify which data file you want to use for this report. The screen also shows you Help, instructions for selecting a data file, and the list of the form definition files for the data files that are on the disk in Drive A. The form definition files were created with DataStar, and they have the suffix .DEF. The data file counterpart to a form definition file has the suffix .DTA. Both files in such a pair have the same root file name. Your choices of files on the logged drive are the root file names. To be safe, make sure that you have a backup copy of each data file.

Selecting a Form Definition File

6) To select a form definition file	Press CTRL F to advance the cursor to the file you want, or type in the name of the file you want.

7) See the cursor on the file you want, PRODUCTR in this example.

Press ⟨Return⟩.

8) See all the field names from the form definition file displayed in the order of the numbers assigned to them in the form definition file.

Selecting Field Names

The field names listed on the current screen can be chosen for the columns of data to be printed on the report. This screen also repeats the report name (B:TEST1), the form definition file name (PRODUCTR), and the Help screen.

9) See the cursor flashing between the first field name and the blank line after "You have selected." To select a field

Press CTRL F to select the field you want or type the name of the field ⟨Return⟩.

10) See the field name you have selected appear under "You have selected."

Keep selecting field names in the order you want them on your report, or press ⟨Return⟩ to move the field names into your selection.

11) See all the field names in your report listed. See also the number of columns you have used at the top right of your screen. This tells you how wide your report will be. (Eighty columns will fit on 8½ inch paper.) To go to the next screen

Press CTRL C.

12) See the Quick Report Exit Screen.

The Quick Report Exit screen tells you "The report specificaton is now complete," and it lists the following choices for your next move.

A

Abandon Form lets you abandon the report file you have just created. ReportStar will ask for a confirming prompt. A yes (Y) answer will take you back to the beginning, which reads "Please enter your report name." If you go this way you can enter a report filename or use CTRL C to leave ReportStar. A no (N) answer will take you to the Quick Report Summary Selection Screen, which we will discuss soon.

S	Save This Report File lets you save the report file you just created and takes you back to the "Please enter your report name" screen.
L	Advance to REDIT takes you to the REDIT portion of ReportStar, which we will discuss soon.
F	Advance to REDIT
SPACE	Go Back to Field Name Selection. This command lets you return to the Field Selection Screen in the Quick Report Program without saving your current report file.
R	Save and Run lets you save the current report specification file on the disk in Drive B under the filename you entered as the report name with the extender .RPT. That would be TEST1.RPT in our example, and it automatically calls up the REPORT program and prints the report.
+ N or Space Bar	lets you continue to create or change the current Quick Report.
+ Y	allows you to start using the same report specification filename again.

Printing the Report

We will continue our interactive routine for printing the report.

13) To save the report specification file and print the report

Press ⟨Return⟩.

14) See "Do you want standard error reporting? (Y/N)"

Type Y if you want error reporting, N if you don't.

15) See "Do you want output to go to a disk file instead of the printer? (Y/N)."

Type N to go to the printer, Y to go to a disk file.

16) See a new screen for entering the date of the report.

Check that your printer is on and loaded, then type the date as MM/DD/YY.

17) See the report printed. Warning errors or fatal errors will be displayed on your screen.
18) See the system prompt for the logged disk and your printed report.

That, briefly, is all you—or Russ Tiernan—needs to do the crank out printed reports from your DataStar and CalcStar files. Please consult the MicroPro manuals for further details about this complex system.

Chapter 14

The Champ—dBASE II

People who purchased a KAYPRO 4 or 10 in mid-1984 got at least one terrific break: dBASE II by Ashton-Tate. We will go out on what we think is a strong limb to say that dBASE II is superior to any of the other database management or file handler packages bundled with your KAYPRO. Running it is like flying your own personal jet, while operating the other ones is like driving a truck. dBASE II is probably no harder to learn than the others, because there are two excellent and one good learning systems packaged with the program. Try one of the others first, and then give yourself a break with dBASE II. You won't look back.

The package includes three double-sided double-density disks (the program is stored on the hard disk in the 10) and two manuals: *dBASE II for the First-Time User,* by Alan Freedman, and a collection of Ashton-Tate user manuals that begins with a general treatment of the system by Wayne Ratliff. That volume is bound with the familar KAYPRO cover and logo, and it also contains a summary of the changes for version 2.41 (which is what you are getting in mid-1984), a ZIP manual, and an earlier manual dated 1982.

WAYS INTO dBASE II

Freedman's book, in our opinion, is a first-class introduction to a very complex and powerful system. We recommend it highly, and we feel that Freedman makes such a good introduction to the system that we would be reinventing the wheel to do it again. He uses a method that is similar in intent to our interactive method, in that he shows you a screen with a black background and green lettering to display the messages from dBASE

II. Within the screen, white lettering shows you what you need to enter at any given time. That graphic presentation—in addition to clear, short, and accurate descriptions—makes the book very easy to use.

In addition, Ashton-Tate has provided an introduction and ten interactive lessons on two disks that will walk you through the basics of dBASE II. The lesson titles (as Ashton-Tate prints them) follow.

I) Introduction, definitions of basic computer terms (reference, not interactive).

1) Create files, generate reports, and correct syntax errors.
2) Add, change, and delete in files, and record positioning.
3) Selecting subsets of data on files, and computations.
4) Record keys, indexing, random processing, and Boolean operators.
5) File and system utilities, and introduction to command procedures.
6) Sorting, updating, and use of memory.
7) Relational database construction.
8) Other forms of accepting and displaying data, dBASE II functions, and SET options.
9) Building custom reports and screens.
10) Command procedures (programming features in dBASE II).

This tutorial program is linked to a printing program that allows you to turn on your printer at the beginning of a lesson and to print out all the lessons. Depending on mistakes you might make in learning the system, this material occupies about 60 pages of printout. The tutorial program is also first-rate material, and, in some respects, it is an ideal way to learn the system. Finally, there are the combined user manuals. Among user manuals, they are written well and for the most part clear.

So, where do you start? Everyone's learning path, or curve, is different, and we can testify most accurately about our own. We started with Freedman's book, and it took about half a day of concentrated work to go through it. Some people may take longer, or they might divide it up into smaller sessions over longer periods of time. The tutorials on disk took a bit longer, and we did them after the book. Both methods are different paths to the same end, introducing the first-timer to a relational database management system. You could safely and comfortably start with either one; the choice is yours. The user's manual is drier, and it does not take you by the hand in the same way. We recommend that you consider it a reference volume and use it after your introduction through the on-disk tutorial or through *dBASE II for the First-Time User*.

dBASE II IS DIFFERENT

dBASE II is a *relational database management system*. That's a mouthful, and it indicates a system that is very different from the file handlers and spreadsheets that are also packaged with your KAYPRO.

To begin, *relational* is the operative term to distinguish dBASE II from the file handlers we have discussed earlier in this book. dBASE II is able to merge different file structures without destroying the information contained in any of the files being combined. For instance, you can merge a name and address file with a payroll file or a payment record file, or put all three together if you like. You are also able to SORT and to

INDEX (those are dBASE commands) individual records in a file at any time in any order that you want to define—alphabetical, tenure on a job, ZIP code, area code, and so on. While it is true that file handlers are good at doing just that, they do not approach dBASE II for flexibility and speed of response. Because dBASE II is relational it allows you to restructure any particular file at any time without ruining the data or changing the relationship of one file to another. All those functions (and more) can be performed with dBASE II as it is presented on your disk.

There is a further level of flexibility with this program that allows you to design your own program so data can be validated as it is entered. You can also set the program so that you can perform *audit trails* on your data. This function is very handy when you are trying to identify an accounting problem.

Further, you can design your own customized billing and accounting forms with the @ SAY commands and with the ZIP programs. Ashton-Tate claims that dBASE II is a separate programming language that is far easier to learn than COBOL and other traditional languages. In any case, it is at this second level of working with the program that you have complete control over what you want it to do for you. It is a true measure of the advance of the software business that you can run a program as sophisticated as this on your KAYPRO. As few as five years ago you would have needed a mini or a mainframe to have enough power to operate it.

Freedman's book and the on-disk tutorials will get you up and running on Level 1, and Lessons 5-10 on the disk will introduce you to some of the programming features. If you want to use all these programming features at Level 2, you will need to consult the user manuals in the KAYPRO cover.

PRELIMINARY MOVES

As is true with all master software disks that come with your KAYPRO, the dBASE II disks are designed only to be read by your KAYPRO. They cannot be written to. You need to copy them onto working disks. Owners of the 10 need to PIP the program onto disks to make backup copies.

The dBASE II system disk is marked "dBASE II, KAYPRO 4/10/Robie, CP/M dBASE II." The files on this disk occupy 388K of the available 390K, and we advise PIPing all the files *except* the ZIP files (ZIP.COM, 14K; ZIPIN.COM, 30K; and ZSCRN.COM, 20K) onto a single disk that has PIP and D (or STAT) on it. ZIP is the screen- and form-designing program that you may get to if you move into Level 2 and programming. Otherwise you won't use it, and there is plenty of room on the second disk for these files. By that time you may want to rearrange all the files in the combination that works best for you. The second disk is labeled "dBASE II, Lessons 1-4, and Start Up;" those files occupy only 206K, leaving plenty of room for ZIP. The third disk contains Lessons 5-10, and they require only 162K.

We trust you remember the routine to PIP files from one disk to another; in case you don't, here it is in a shortened form. Put a formatted disk with PIP and D (or STAT) in Drive A and a master disk in Drive B. Type PIP A: =B:*.*[VO] ⟨Return⟩. The disk in Drive A will eventually tell you that you have run out of space, and that is OK. That will happen in the middle of ZSCRN.COM, and all the ZIP files are going to the second disk anyway. You can erase ZIP and ZIPIN from the first copy disk when the PIP operation is finished. Then put a second formatted disk with PIP in A, and PIP the ZIP files onto the second copy disk. When they have copied, remove the master from Drive B and replace it with the second master disk. Type PIP A: =B:*.*[VO] ⟨RETURN⟩ again. Repeat this procedure with a third copy disk and the third master disk. Then store the master disks (or the copies if you are working with a 10) in some safe place.

INSTALLATION

We did not find a file named STARTUP on any of our disks; we assumed that file was not necessary, even though it was advertised as being there. We did follow the INSTALL instructions on the disk packet, however. Briefly, what you need to do (and this may be a redundant procedure) is the following. At the A0> prompt put the dBASE II system copy disk (disk 1 in the copying procedure) in Drive A and the second copy disk with dBASE and Lessons 1-4 in Drive B. Type INSTALL ⟨RETURN⟩. See the question, "Full Screen Operations Wanted? (Y/N)." Type Y. Then you will see a list of terminal types. You have two possible choices here, "C ADM-3A," or "Q KAYPRO II." Both will work, and we assume that the reference to "KAYPRO II" is a generic reference to the KAYPRO. We chose Q. Then, you will be asked, "CHANGE MACRO, DATE, DE-LIMITER, ETC. (Y/N)?" Choose N. You can change those parameters later when you are more familiar with the program. Finally, you will be asked to confirm and save your choices by typing Y, and you will be returned to the AO> prompt. You are ready to go with dBASE II and you will have a great time with a great program.

Chapter 15

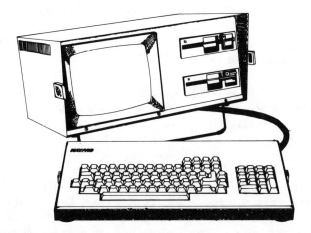

Profitplan and Microplan—
The Mathematical Spreadsheets

Profitplan and Microplan are virtually identical financial spreadsheets. They are both very useful for financial planning for a family, or a small- or medium-size business. They will give you a running breakdown of your profit and loss figures, your expenses, and they will allow you to use current data to perform financial and statistical analyses. These forecasts can be expressed in percentages and actual dollar amounts that need to be earned or spent to maintain a certain profit line. This discussion will use Version 4.04 of these plans, and (for the sake of accuracy) you should check to see which version you are using.

GENERAL CHARACTERISTICS

At the simplest level both spreadsheets may be used to generate charts and tables, even if you don't want to crunch the numbers or get into financial and statistical evaluations.

They are both extremely useful for arranging large amounts of data. Each table can handle 50 rows of information and each row can be 20 columns wide. With that spread you could handle the sales figures for 50 salespeople for 20 weeks, months, quarters, or years, or whatever time interval you happened to select. Both sheets, with their abilities to calculate, can work with more complex sets of data. You could, for instance, set up fewer time periods and build in expense columns, salary columns, expenditure columns of every sort, and then run calculations to see where the bulk of your money was being spent in your sales force, who was the most productive against which expenses, and so on.

PRODUCING A TABLE

The first steps in producing a table are to name the rows and columns and the sheet itself. When you name the particular table you can save it on a separate data disk, which you can plug into either plan. Beyond that, there are several menus of mathematical, statistical, and financial computations that you can make with the data you have entered. This potential means that you can analyze past performance, and you can also project what you would like to see for future profit/cost breakdowns.

Menus. Profitplan has six submenus and Microplan has three more, for a total of nine menus. Each of these menus has a number of selections that allow you to tailor a plan to your needs. This selection of options and actions by menu is known in the computer trade as a *menu-driven* program, and our discussion of both plans will also be driven by these menus.

Errors. Profitplan and Microplan are fairly forgiving when you make a mistake. Overall, it is worth remembering that instructions and data are not entered until you press Return. That means that you can back up over a mistake with either the delete key or the backspace key, and type over the incorrect information. Once the correct information has been entered on the screen, you may press Return and go on to the next item.

If you have entered the wrong column heading or incorrect data and you have pressed Return, it's easy enough to fix. Enter the command you want to repair (you may have to move the cursor back to the right row or column) and then enter the corrected information. The Plans will simply write over the incorrect data. Make sure that the cursor is in the right place when you do this. In general, to work the Plans successfully you have to pay attention to the location of the cursor.

The Bundled Manuals. The manuals provided with your KAYPRO give you extended examples of how to set up, run, and maintain either of the two plans, however, we will discuss the major differences between the two plans first by showing you the extra capabilities of Microplan and then by showing you the contents of the common menus.

TIPS FOR USING EITHER PLAN

- Both plans are entered by typing PLAN and Return.
- Both plans run their extensive menus (choices of which actions to take) down the right side of the screen. Commands 1-6 and 10-12 are followed by colons (:) and the colon is a signal that a submenu is hiding behind that command. Commands 4:, 11:, and 12: are restricted to Microplan, and Commands 13: and 14: are not available in the program which have been bundled with your KAYPRO.
- The first three lines on the top of your screen make up the command and status lines of your plan, and they serve as a constant reminder of where you are and what you are doing. The top line tells you the MODE. There are three modes in Profitplan, Normal, Compute, and Protect; there are two more modes in Microplan, Program and Run Program. You will see how to use them soon, but at the beginning stay with the default mode, which is Normal. The next item on the top line is ORDER=R/C. That means that you will enter information on the rows first and then in the columns. You may change that order, but you must always be aware of the order you specify for any

computation. Both plans give you a potential of 50 rows and 20 columns to work with. In general, data will be listed in the rows and types or classifications of these data will be listed in the columns. Line 2 contains the *Data Pointer*, and both plans give you the option of moving the pointer around with your four cursor keys. The Data Pointer will always tell you which row or column you are in. Line 3 says ENTER COMMAND: and the flashing cursor prompts you to the next action.

● When the manual tells you to type CANCEL they mean press the ESC (escape) key. If you find yourself in the wrong place in the program, or in trouble, hitting ESC is often a good way out.

● Your normal way to leave either plan after having saved your table is to type 9. The screen will ask you if it is all right to ERASE CURRENT DATA? (Y OR N). Don't panic. What they are trying to ask you is if it's OK to clear the data on the screen. If you don't want that data, or if you have already saved it on a disk with the SAVE TABLE command, then type Y, and you will return to CP/M with a warm boot.

CHOOSING BETWEEN MICROPLAN AND PROFITPLAN

Generally speaking, Profitplan is the simpler of the two spreadsheets, and your choice between the two will depend on how complex your financial analysis needs to be. To help you make that decision a list of the extra options available in Microplan follows.

Microplan Options: Finance Commands

To see a display of the commands available in the finance category, type 4 ⟨Return⟩ and you will see the submenu replace the main menu on the right of your screen.

61 and 62 Depreciation. Command 61 allows you to set up a depreciation schedule according to four different methods of depreciation: straight line, sum of years, double declining balance, and a double declining balance that switches to straight line. Command 62 allows you to view your depreciation schedule by the time period of your choice—quarter, year, etc.—and to store that data in a separate column.

63 and 64 Loan Payments and Interest Schedules. Command 63 will calculate the amount of an annual payment on a loan, and 64 will project the interest schedule across a number of years.

65 and 66 Cash Flow Computations. Command 65 allows you to calculate discount cash flows by a given rate, and to store those values in a new column. Command 66 calculates internal rates of return for a row or a column that holds cash flow figures. These rates may also be stored in a different column.

67, 68, 70, and 71 Percentages. Command 67 calculates percentage ratios by dividing values from one row or column by values from another row or column, while command 68 will calculate a row or column as a percentage of a total value. Command 69 is blank, or a *null value.* Command 70 calculates percentages using rates stored in another row or column of the same table. Finally, command 71 calculates a constant percentage of values in a particular row or column.

72 and 73 Lag and Lead Time Factors. Command 72 calculates lag times when you are working cash flow computations. Command 73 computes lead time figures for cash flows.

74 and 75 Growth and Savings Rates. Command 74 allows you to enter growth rates as whole numbers, and it calculates them as percentages. Command 75 calculates savings balances and stores them.

76 and 77 Taxes. Command 76 prompts you to type in tax rates and upper limits, whereas command 77 calculates taxes using the tax schedule and the pre-tax earnings already entered.

Microplan Program Commands

Program commands give you the ability to tailor Microplan to the particular needs of your family or business. Commands 121 to 127 will perform the following functions for you: save, load, and clear programs, delete steps, and print, list, and run programs. You may also list a program directory and erase programs from a disk if you wish. Note: "program" is directly related to the MODE commands (95-102), which are accessed from the STATUS: menu, command 90.

121 Load Program. This command allows you to load a program from disk into the KAYPRO's memory (a.k.a. RAM) and, by pressing Return, it will allow you to review all existing programs. You may also list a program directory or erase programs from a disk if you wish.

122 Save Program. This command allows you to save a program on your disk once it has been created. It also lets you see (by pressing Return) what other programs are stored on the disk. Caution: if a new program has the same name as an old one, the new one will replace and erase the old one. You will have to decide if that is the best course for you.

123 Print Program. If your printer is on and your paper is set, this command will print your program. This function is handy to remind you of the content and structure of your programs.

124 Clear Program. This command allows you to clear a program that you have created on your screen and that still shows there. It does *not* clear programs that have been saved on your disk.

125 Show Program. This command will display steps in a program. It is handy if you are entering data, or you want to change data and cannot remember the order of the steps in the program you are running. Press any cursor key to return to your display.

126 List Programs. This command sends the list of programs on your disk to the printer.

127 Erase Program. This command deletes a saved program from your disk. It is handy when you want to get rid of an unused program, and you want to clear space on your disk for current information.

Statistical Commands

Statistical commands allow you to analyze trends in your business using data and programs that have already been entered. Commands 131 to 144 give you the ability to calculate changes in value between periods, percent rates of growth between periods, moving averages over a variable number of periods, exponential smoothing of averages, mean values, standard deviations, standard variances, natural logarithms, exponential values, raise values by powers, find the largest and smallest values, count the number of values included in the mean, standard deviation, and standard variance calculations, and (finally!) the total values.

Commands 13: and 14:, Tables and Link, are part of Microplan's "Add-On Consolidation Module," and they are not included on the disk bundled with your KAYPRO.

We hope this brief review of the additional capabilities of Microplan will allow you to choose which of the two plans you want to start working with. If you should choose Profitplan and you store your table or tables on a separate disk, you can reload those tables from your data disk onto the Microplan disk to perform any of these advanced functions we have just described. The real question for you thus becomes how quickly you think you will need to enter the world of statistical analysis and financial modeling.

Before we discuss the options available to you in the shared Profitplan and Microplan menus, we suggest that you start either of the two Plans in your KAYPRO by inserting the disk. Remember to use your copy disk. That way, nothing can be permanently lost if you have serious trouble. At this stage of learning a new program it is good to be as playful as possible. You have nothing to lose but time. The sample data we will give you are worthless and your disk is a duplicate, which you can make again when you need to. So feel free.

A SAMPLE SPREADSHEET

This example will give you some data to experiment with at the same time it walks you through your first spreadsheet. For the sake of consistency we will follow the example given in the manuals written by Chang Labs and included with your KAYPRO; our format, however, will be different.

The left column on the following pages will give you the screen prompt, or an "if" proposition, while the right column will show you what to enter. What you should see on the screen will appear on the next line down in the left column. Instructions that run across the entire page, as this line does, will fill you in on background, or offer you choices, or explain something that is absolutely necessary.

When you create a *real* spreadsheet you will need a fair amount of data on hand that you can enter. A family would start with the last few years' tax returns and other household expense records; a small business would work with a combination of tax returns and other records of income and expense. For the sake of simplicity in learning how to enter data in either of the Plans, we will work with the following categories: Sales, Cost of Goods, (a constant 45 percent of Sales), Administration, Research and Development, Total Costs, and Gross Profit.

1) To see the FORMAT: menu   Type 1 or 16 ⟨Return⟩.
2) See items 17-28. You need to enter row titles first.   Type 20 ⟨Return⟩.
3) Data Pointer at row 1.   Type SALES ⟨Return⟩.
4) See SALES at row 1, Data Pointer at row 2.   Type COST OF GOODS ⟨Return⟩.
5) See COST OF GOODS at row 2, Data Pointer at row 3.   Type ADMIN ⟨Return⟩
6) See ADMIN at row 3, Data Pointer at row 4.   Type R & D ⟨Return⟩.

7) See R & D at row 4, Data Pointer at row 5.

Type TOTAL COSTS ⟨Return⟩.

8) See TOTAL COSTS at row 5, Data Pointer at row 6.

Type GROSS PROFITS ⟨Return⟩.

9) See GROSS PROFITS at row 6. This is the last row title.

Type ⟨ESC⟩ ⟨Return⟩ to leave this command, and to begin entering data in the columns.

10) See Data Pointer at row 1, prompt for a new command.

Type 31 ⟨Return⟩.

11) See CHOOSE (VALUE=0, CONSTANT=1, GROW=2, INCR=3):

Type 2 ⟨Return⟩.

(Here you would enter 0 when each item of the data on your line was going to vary unpredictably from the others. You would enter 1 when you could predict a constant increase. You would enter 2 when you started with a base value that would grow by a certain percentage. You would enter 3 when you had a base value that would grow by a constant amount.)

12) See prompt ask for BASE VALUE.

Type 1000 ⟨Return⟩.

13) See 1000 in column 1, prompt asks for RATE (which equals percentage of growth).

Type 10 ⟨Return⟩

14) See a progression of figures run across the SALES row. Press the RIGHT arrow to see those figures extend over all 20 columns. Then, press the LEFT arrow to get back to column 1. Press the DOWN arrow to get to row 2, COST OF GOODS. Type 3 to see the Math Menu. See the Math Menu on the right of your screen. Type 53 ⟨Return ⟩.

MULT K indicates that you are multiplying row 1 by a constant amount. Here, GOODS cost 45 percent of SALES.

15) See the prompt ask VALUE:

TYPE .45, RETURN

16) See the prompt ask row(1-50).

TYPE 1, RETURN

17) See 45 percent of each column appear in row 2. The prompt asks for the next command, and the Data Pointer is at row 3, ADMIN. Since administration costs 20 percent of SALES, you want a constant percentage of row 1 again.

Type 53 ⟨Return⟩.

18) See the prompt ask VALUE:	Type 20 ⟨Return⟩.
19) See VALUE: .20, prompt asks for ROW	Type 1, RETURN
20) See row 3 extend values across 20 columns. Again, you may move the cursor across the rows as you did in step 14. To see the Data Menu	Type 2 ⟨Return⟩.
21) See the Data Pointer at row 4, R & D, which will be a constant figure of $300.	Type 31 ⟨Return⟩
22) See the screen ask CHOOSE (VALUE=0, CONSTANT=1, GROW=2, INCR=3) as it did for row 1.	Type 1 ⟨Return⟩ for a constant whole number
23) See prompt ask for BASE VALUE:	Type 300 ⟨Return⟩
24) See Data Pointer at row 5, TOTAL COSTS (which equals the sum of rows 2, 3, and 4).	Type 3 ⟨Return⟩. Type 55 ⟨Return⟩.
25) See the Math Menu.	
26) To SUM rows 2, 3, and 4 see the prompt ask ROW BEGIN (1-50) to ask for the starting row.	Type 2 ⟨Return⟩.
27) See the prompt ask for the last row to be added: END (2-50).	Type 4 ⟨Return⟩.
28) See the screen add rows 2, 3, and 4 across all 20 columns. Now, to calculate row 6, GROSS PROFITS, you want to SUBTRACT row 1 (SALES) from row 5 (TOTAL COSTS).	Type 42 ⟨Return⟩.
29) See prompt ask ROW (to subtract from).	Type 1 ⟨Return⟩.
30) See prompt ask for ROW (to be subtracted).	Type 5, RETURN
31) See GROSS PROFITS in row 6.	Done. (Whew!)

You have now created a simple table. If you hold down the RIGHT arrow you will see the figures in your table project across the 20 columns. Then hold down the LEFT arrow to return to column 1.

CHECKING YOUR COMMAND LOGIC

When you move into the different kinds of computing that both Plans will do, you will need to remind yourself of the command logic that you have built into each row—because later computations will depend on knowing that information. You can check out any table you have entered with the following process.

1) Have your table on the screen.   Type 1 ⟨Return⟩.

2) SEE the FORMAT:Menu   Type 22 ⟨Return⟩.

3) For FORECAST see MULT K=0.45 ROW=1 (Steps 14 and 15), and MULT K=0.2 ROW= (steps 17 and 18). (Row 4 is a constant value and does not appear.) Also see SUM ROWS 2-4 (steps 24-27) and SUB ROW=1 ROW=5, which means subtract row 5 (the sum of all your expenses) from your SALES (steps 28-30).

4) To Return to your table   Type any cursor key.

CHANGING DATA

Let's try changing one set of figures so that you can see how the program will take care of what would otherwise be a long and boring clerical task. Let's say you decide that $300 per year for research and development is too paltry, and you want to bump it to $500. You can easily imagine situations in your family spending plans or in your business where you might wonder, "What if I put more money into equipment, or add another salesperson, or put more money into R & D?" Here's how the two Plans can turn that guesswork into concrete figures.

1) Table on screen, Data Pointer at row 1.   Press the DOWN arrow until the pointer is at row 4, R & D.

2) Data Pointer at row 4   Type 2 ⟨Return⟩.

3) See the Data Menu   Type 32 ⟨Return⟩.

4) See prompt ask for a ROW that needs changing.   Type 4 ⟨Return⟩.

5) See prompt ask for a COL number. Start with 1.   Type 1 ⟨Return⟩.

6) Now, you need to repeat Steps 21-23 of the entering process.

7) See 500 in column 1.   Done.

SAVING YOUR TABLE

At this point your sample table, FORECAST, exists in the KAYPRO's main memory, or RAM. A power failure could send it to Gumby Land, or *you* could if you exit the Plan with

9 ⟨Return⟩. You need to save it on your disk, which means to send it from RAM to the disk.

1) To save your table — Type 10 ⟨Return⟩.
2) See the Utility Menu. — Type 112 ⟨Return⟩.
3) The prompt asks for a name for your table. That name will go into its directory, and it will be your way to call it up again. — Type FORECAST ⟨Return⟩.
4) In later saves you will see this message; "Your file already exists. Continue with save? VERIFY (Y OR N):" If you enter a Y then the data on the screen will write over the data that has been recorded on the disk. Normally, you would type Y, and erase the old data. However, if you want to keep both the old and the new data, you have to rename the table on the screen. Let's say we don't want the old data. — Type Y ⟨Return⟩.
5) See "SAVED" in the upper left corner of your screen. — Done.

EXITING THE PROGRAM

1) If you want to leave the program before printing your report — Type 9 ⟨Return⟩.
2) See "OK to erase current data? VERIFY (Y OR N):"

This means that you are being asked if it's OK to erase the data on the screen, and that's fine because you have saved the table and its data on the disk. — Type Y ⟨Return⟩.

3) See Micro (or Profit) Plan
   Warm Boot
   A> (or B>)

The last prompt means that you are back to CP/M, and you may remove your disk from the drive.

PRINTING THE REPORT

Printing a report is easy with either of the Plans. Make sure that your printer is connected, turned on, and that your paper is set.

1) To print your report	Type 82 ⟨Return⟩.
2) Prompt asks for PAGE NUMBER (How many pages?)	Type 1 ⟨Return⟩ for this report.
3) Prompt wants a DATE (in two numbers).	Type 84 ⟨Return⟩.
4) Prompt wants the month.	Type 1 ⟨Return⟩ (for January, 2 for February, etc.).
5) Prompt wants a day.	Type 9 ⟨Return⟩ (or a number for the date you want).
6) Prompt wants the number of the row to start with.	Type 1 ⟨Return⟩.
7) Prompt wants the number of the row to end with.	Type 6 ⟨Return⟩. (You only have six rows in FORECAST.)
8) Prompt wants the number of the first column.	Type 1 ⟨Return⟩.
9) Prompt now wants the number of the last column to be printed.	Type 5 ⟨Return⟩ (You could type any number up to 20.)
10) Prompt now wants the TITLE.	Type SAMPLE 5 YEAR FORECAST ⟨Return⟩.
11) Prompt asks for more titles.	Type ⟨Return⟩ for titles 2 and 3.
12) Prompt asks you to SET PAPER. You should have set it already.	Type ⟨Return⟩ and watch it print.

If you have not already saved your program, you may do it now. In general, it is a good idea to save programs *before* you print, so that you can avoid any problems like power outages, or the dog sitting on the cord and pulling it from the wall, or any number of other awful possibilities. See the five steps to SAVE your program that we describe earlier in this book.

MENUS

As we mentioned earlier, both Plans are menu-driven. Now we're going to tackle the practical implications of that idea. The overall concept is one of *levels*. Each of the main menus in the Plans—numbers 1 through 12 with the titles followed by colons— leads to another menu, or level. Some of those, particularly Program:, lead you into a process which takes a special exit; ESCape won't get you out. We will note these different menus. Otherwise, you can count on the fact that typing PLAN will get you in and pressing ESC will get you back to the main menu, from which you can get back to CP/M with command number 9. Remember, that old number 9 will erase the data on the screen. If you have not already saved it and you want to keep it, type 112 ⟨Return⟩.

Now you have the ins and the outs of the Plans, and you have entered a sample spreadsheet. We will now discuss the different menus or sublevels of the program, so that you can see how to get around in them. Note: this section covers only the commands shared by both Plans. Commands limited to the Microplan will not be discussed.

Utility

The Utility: commands help you load tables, save tables, list tables, print tables, erase tables, clear and reset tables, and redisplay the screen. These commands are essential to working with either Plan. To see the UTILITY: menu, type 10 ⟨Return⟩. You will see commands 106-118, of which 106 and 107 are limited to Microplan.

108 SET DRIVE. This command allows you to save tables and programs on a storage disk, which is useful when you have a lot of data or a number of programs. To set (or change) drives, type 108 ⟨Return⟩. You will see, prompt ask "DRIVE(A-P):". Type A through P, depending on which drive you want to use. (Typically, your Plan disk will be in A drive and your data disk will be in B drive.

109 SET UP. If you want to change the number of rows or columns, type 109 ⟨Return⟩. You will "see OK to erase current data? VERIFY (Y OR N):". Don't be alarmed. They only want to know if you want to change the number of columns and rows that you currently have. Type Y ⟨Return⟩. The number of columns (1-94) will then be displayed.

You have the default value of 20 columns, but your KAYPRO will allow you to create a report as wide as 94 columns, or as narrow as 2. You probably won't want either extreme, but our sample, FORECAST, was only 5 columns wide. Type 5 ⟨Return⟩.

Next, you will see "ROWS (17-204):"Again you have the default value of 50 rows; the KAYPRO will permit as few as 17 rows, or as many as 204. Let's say you need a 100 rows for FORECAST, so type 100 ⟨RETURN⟩. At the prompt "VERIFY (Y OR N):" type Y ⟨RETURN⟩. The message "ROW=1−100 COL=1-5 "tells you that your table has been reformed. (If you want to save these dimensions use command 112.)

111 LOAD TABLE. If you want to see a table that you have saved, type 111 ⟨Return⟩. When the prompt asks for the name of the table you want to work with, if you can't remember all the names on the disk, type ⟨Return⟩. after seeing the table names, type FORECAST ⟨Return⟩ or any other table name on your disk.

112 SAVE TABLE. If you want to save a table, its program, and its printing instructions, type 112 ⟨Return⟩. When you see "TABLE NAME:" type FORECAST ⟨Return⟩ or the name of the table you want to save. When you see "SAVED" the job is DONE.

113 CLEAR DATA. If you want to clear the data from the screen, but save the row and column titles, print options, and the table logic, type 113 ⟨Return⟩. When the Plan asks, "OK to erase current data? VERIFY (Y OR N):" type Y ⟨Return⟩. When you see the data replaced by 0s, you are done.

114 RESET. If you want to erase all row and column titles, print options, and the table logic, type 114 ⟨Return⟩. You'll see "OK to erase current data? VERIFY (Y OR N):". Type Y ⟨Return⟩. A blank table indicates that the job is done.

115 REDISPLAY. If you want to see your table, menu, and program information after a SAVE or a number 9, type 115 ⟨Return⟩.

116 LIST TABLES. If you want a printed list of the tables on your disk, type 116 ⟨Return⟩. You will see "SET PAPER; HIT RETURN." Turn on your printer and set your paper. Type ⟨Return⟩. Settle back and watch your printer work.

117 ERASE TABLE. If you want to remove a table, its logic, and its data from your disk, type 117 ⟨Return⟩; the Plan responds with "HIT RETURN TO SEE AVAILABLE TABLES." Type ⟨Return⟩ to review table titles. Type FORECAST ⟨Return⟩ or the name of the table you want to remove.

118 PRINT TBL. If you want to print a description of your current table, its commands, logic, options, and titles, so that you can check them or have a record, type 118 ⟨Return⟩. You will see "SET PAPER, HIT RETURN." Turn your printer on and set your paper, and then ∧ press ⟨Return ⟩.

1 or 16 Format Commands

This menu of commands allows you to set up, insert and delete, reorder, and set type for the rows and columns in any table. In general, these commands are useful for setting up your table.

17 INSERT. If you want to clear a row or column and move the current row/column to the right or down, use a cursor key to aim the data pointer at the destination row/column. (This maneuver will erase the last row or column.) When the data pointer is aimed, type 17 ⟨Return⟩. The prompt asks for "ROW/COLUMN #," so type that number ⟨Return⟩. The row/column will fill with 0s, your data moves, and you are done.

18 DELETE. If you want to delete (remove) a row or column and clear the last filled row or column, aim the data pointer at the row/column to be deleted and type 18 ⟨Return⟩. (Contrary to the Chang manuals, your deleted row or column does *not* reappear in the last row or column.) The prompt asks "VERIFY (Y OR N)," so type Y ⟨Return⟩ to delete. Here again, the row or column will fill with 0s.

20 ROW TITLE. If you want to add or change a row title, type 20 ⟨Return⟩. When the prompt says "USE CURSOR KEYS TO SELECT A ROW," select the row. Type the title you want ⟨Return⟩. The program will print as many as 40 characters. The cursor moves to the next row. To leave this command, press ⟨ESC⟩.

21 SET TYPE. If you want to set type (caps, $, %, etc.) for your table, type 21 ⟨Return⟩. The prompt will ask for row number. Type the number of the row you want to work with, and you'll see your options for printing that row. Choose the option that fits the purpose of the row. If it's data use 2, if a heading use 3, and so on. Type your option ⟨Return⟩.

Next, you are asked to choose whether to underline, or not. Type 0 for no underline, type 1 to underline with dashes, type 2 to underline with equal signs, and type 3 for a normal underline. The prompt then asks if you want "trailing blank lines," which in English means how many blank lines you want under this line of data. Type ⟨Return⟩ for none, or any other number for the number of lines you want. Next, the prompt wants to know how many decimal places to use in numbers in the row; type 0 to 3, depending on what you want.

The next prompt asks "FORMAT," and in English it wants to know if you want % signs, $ signs, no commas, or other signs on your figures. Type the number that matches your choice ⟨Return⟩. The prompt asks you for the row, and you need to repeat this procedure for each row. When you finish, type ⟨ESC⟩ to leave this command.

22 SHOW ROWS. If you want to review the command logic of your different rows, type 22 ⟨Return⟩. To leave this command, press any cursor key.

23 REORDER. If you want to move rows, type 23 ⟨Return⟩. The prompt asks for the OLD NUMBER, so type the number of the row you want to move and ⟨Return⟩. The prompt then asks for the NEW NUMBER; that means where you want to put the row you just called out. Type the destination ROW number ⟨Return⟩. The ROW moves, and we're done.

25 COL TITLE. If you want to change or add column titles, move the cursor to the desired column. and type 25 ⟨RETURN⟩. When the data pointer is at the correct column, type your column title (1 stands for line 1 of the title, 2 for line 2 of the title, etc.) If you have only one line in your title, press Return. If you want to title other columns, press Return until you reach the column you want. To leave this command, press ⟨ESC⟩.

26 SET TYPE. This command follows the procedures for command 21, SET TYPE; this one sets type for the columns, while 21 does it for the rows. The format and procedures are identical, and you can return to the instructions for command 21 to track this one.

27 SHOW COLS. This command shows you the current print options and commands for your columns. If you type 27 ⟨Return⟩ you'll see your columns displayed with the command logic showing. To return to your table, press any cursor key.

28 REORDER. This command follows the procedures you saw in command 23, and it reorders the columns instead of the rows. Follow the procedure for command 23.

2 or 29 Data Menu

This menu, or level, of commands allows you to enter data, message the data, and enter formulas to work your data. Here are brief descriptions of the commands on this menu, again presented in a modified version of our interactive format.

30 ENTRY. If you want to enter data one item at a time, use ENTRY, to do so, type 30 ⟨Return⟩. The prompt asks you to move the cursor to the cell you want to work in. A *cell* is one position defined by a row and a column. For instance, for 1, column 1 in FORECAST is 1000, or row 6, column 19 is 1646; each of these numbers, or positions, in the table is a cell. Move the cursor to the cell you want to change, type the value you want to enter ⟨Return⟩. You'll see the value appear in the cell, and the cursor moves to the next column, same ROW. Type ⟨ESC⟩ to leave this command.

31 ENTER. If you want to enter data, move the cursor to the row you want to work in. Type 31 ⟨Return⟩. There are four ways to enter data in a row. To enter individual data across a row, type 0 ⟨Return⟩. When the prompt asks "VALUE," type the numerical value. Pressing Return will allow you to enter new values in succeeding columns. When you want to leave this command, type ⟨ESC⟩.

If you want the same value in each column, type 1 ⟨Return⟩. The prompt asks for BASE VALUE, so type the value you want to see ⟨Return⟩. The value moves across your table, the cursor moves down a row, and you are back to command level.

If your value will grow by a definite percentage, type 2 ⟨Return⟩. The prompt asks for BASE VALUE, so type that value ⟨Return⟩. The prompt asks for RATE, which means the percentage by which your value will grow. Type that percentage, press Return, and see the values roll across the table.

If your value will grow by a fixed amount, type 3 ⟨Return⟩. Enter your base value as before, and when the prompt asks for RATE they really mean the fixed amount that will be added to the base value for each column. Type that value ⟨Return⟩. See it march across the columns.

32 CHANGE. If you want to change a single cell in your table, type 32 and press

Return. The prompt asks for row and then for column; enter them now, following each by ⟨Return⟩. The prompt asks for VALUE, so type your new value ⟨Return⟩. It appears, and you're done.

33 SELECT ROW AND 34 SELECT COLUMN. These two commands are alternate ways to move your cursor to a different position. Using these commands may move the cursor more quickly in a very large table, but the cursor arrow keys are pretty handy.

35 FORMULA. If you want to enter a formula to change your data or do a "what if" analysis, type 35 ⟨Return⟩. The colon (:) that appears is the invitation to enter a formula. You now have several options. If your formula applies to a whole row or column, move the Data Pointer to that row or column, type L and the number of that row or column. Or, if you want to change a single cell, move the Data Pointer to that cell. Type V, the row number, a comma, and the column number.

Now, you have to build your formula. Here are the possibilities.

- + means ADD two values.
- − means subtract two values.
- * means multiply two values.
- / means divide two values.

The Plans will calculate multiplication and division *before* addition and subtraction, so you have to design your formula with that in mind. For example, L3+2*L1 would multiply line 1 by line 2 before adding it to line 3, whereas [L3+L2]*L1 would add line 2 to line 3 *before* multiplying by line 1.

For a simple example, let's assume that you have FORECAST on your screen. Line 2, COST OF GOODS, was set at 45 percent of SALES, and you have added a fixed cost of $300. To build that change into your table, move the cursor to a blank row and type .45*L1+300 ⟨Return⟩. Watch Line 2 + 300 move across your blank row.

36 GOTO. This is not Japanese chess. If you want to see a part of your table that is not on the screen, without using the cursor, type 36 ⟨Return⟩. The prompt asks for a row number and then a column number. Enter the desired coordinates, following each with ⟨Return⟩. When you see the cell you called for, use any cursor key to return to your display.

37 PLUG. If you want to recalculate a cell, type 37 ⟨Return⟩. Enter the row and then the column number. The next prompt you see is a colon (:), which tells you to type a formula. Type your formula ⟨Return⟩. See the cell change.

38 FIX R/C. If you want to recompute a row or column (to remove a PLUG or other computing command, for example), move the cursor to the row or column you want to change and type 38 ⟨Return⟩. See the row or column change.

39 NULLIFY. If you want to erase the command logic from a row or column, but you want to keep the data, move the cursor to the row or column, and type 39 ⟨Return⟩. Use command 22 to check the effect of this command.

3 or 40 Math Menu

The commands in the Math Menu from number 41 through number 50 follow the same format. First we will list the command options open to both Plans, and then we will show you the format to enter any of them. All of these commands can be stored in the computing logic of your table.

41 ADD. Command 41 allows you to add one row to another, or one column to another, and to store the results in a blank row or column—but you cannot add a column to a row.

42 SUB. This allows you to subtract one row from another, or one column from another, and to store the results in a blank row or column.

43 MULT. Command 43 allows you to multiply one row by another, or one column by another, and to store the results in a blank row or column.

44 DIV. This command allows you to divide one row by another, or one column by another, and to store the results in a blank row or column.

45 NEGATE. You can reverse negative or positive values in a row or column, and store the results in a blank row or column, by using this command.

46 INVERSE. This function computes the *inverse* or *reciprocal* (i.e., one divided by column, and stores the results in a blank row or column. If your numbers are greater than 30, then you will need to use command 86, SET CRT, to adjust your table to see the results.

47 INTEGER. Command 47 eliminates the decimal parts of your numbers, and it leaves the whole numbers in a blank row or column. For instance, 29.9 will become 29. The effect is to round the number *down*.

48 ROUND. This is a command that turns your numbers to the nearest whole number and stores the results in a blank row or column. For instance, 29.4 becomes 29, while 29.5 becomes 30.

49 CUMULATE. Command 49 totals a row or a column and stores the results in a blank row or column. This command asks for a beginning value—even if the R/C begins with 0—as a second prompt.

50 ABSOLUTE. The absolute value function turns negative numbers into positive ones for a row or column and stores the results in a blank row or column. Postive numbers remain positive.

All of these commands are entered with the same pattern, and here it is.

1) Decide which math command you need.

Move the data pointer to the destination row or column.

2)

Type the command number ⟨RETURN⟩.

3) For commands 41-44 there will be two prompts for row or column numbers to be computed. Commands 42 and 44 require the R/C to be subtracted or divided *from* to be entered first.

Type the number of the first R/C, ⟨Return⟩. Then type the second R/C, ⟨Return⟩.

4) For commands 45-48 you will enter only the number of the R/C to be worked.

Type that number ⟨Return⟩.

5) See your computation march across the blank row or column.

Constant Value Commands. Commands 51-54 allow you to add (51), subtract (52), multiply (53), and divide (54) any row or column by a constant amount. These commands will also be stored in your table logic. They are all entered with the same format, and here it is.

1) Decide which math function you want to use.	Type the number for that function, ⟨Return⟩.
2) Prompt asks for VALUE:, which means the constant amount that you want to add.	Type that number ⟨Return⟩.
3) Next, the prompt wants the number of the row/column where you want the constant applied.	Type that number ⟨Return⟩.
4) See that row/column change.	

55 SUM. If you want to total a number of rows or columns, move the data pointer to a destination row/column. Type 55 ⟨Return⟩. The prompt asks ROW BEGIN or COLUMN BEGIN, so type the number of the first row/column. The prompt then asks for END, which is the last row/column to be calculated. Type the number of that row/column, ⟨Return⟩. Your new calculations will appear in the designated row/column.

56, 57, 58 GET, FLOOR, CEILING. These three commands have the same format, but different functions, Command 56, GET, will move values from a row or column and store them in a row or column indicated by your data pointer. FLOOR will recompute a row or column and zero out any value below a floor you designate. CEILING, command 58, will remove values above a value you set. Moved and recomputed values will be moved to a free row or column. Here is the format:

1) Decide which command you want to use.	Move the data pointer to a free row or column. Type the number of the command you want ⟨Return⟩.
2) For Command 56	Type the number of the row/column to be moved ⟨Return⟩.
3) For Commands 57 and 58	Type the floor or ceiling value ⟨Return⟩.
4) The prompt asks for row/column.	Type the number of that row/column ⟨Return⟩.
5) See your row or column moved or recomputed.	

5 or 80 Print Commands

Commands 81 through 86 allow you to set all the dimensions for a particular table. This means that you can tailor each table in your files for different printing formats. These options will not show on your screen, instead they will show up when you print the report.

81 OPTIONS. If you want to format your report, type 81 ⟨Return⟩. The first two options apply to printers with automatic paper feeding capacities only. TOP MARGIN refers to how much blank space you want on the top of the page. Typically, you would set between 5 and 10 spaces for headroom. The default is 0 spaces, or no headroom. To set headroom of 7 lines, for example, type 7 ⟨Return⟩. The second option refers to your left margin. People often want a lot of space there so that they can make notes; the default is 0, or no margin. To set a left margin of 7 spaces, for example, type 7 ⟨Return⟩.

ENHANCEMENT refers to different printer features such as bold type, expanded and compressed print, etc. Check your printer manual to see what you can do with your printer.

ROW TITLE WIDTH asks you if you want to change the width of your row titles. The default is 20 characters. It can be only 4 spaces, or as many as 40, for the truly long-winded. Keep the average 20, or type the number you need.

COLUMN WIDTH asks you the same question, but about your columns. The default is 10 characters. Your column can be as narrow as 4 spaces, or as wide as 20 for those big numbers. Keep the average 20, or type the number you need.

COLUMNS PER PAGE lets you choose how many columns you want to print on a page. Note: if you have more than ten columns in a report, 11-20 will print on a second page. The default is 10 columns. Type the number of columns you need.

DECIMAL PLACES lets you choose how many places you want for your numbers. The default is one place, as in 13.2. Keep the default, or type the number you want.

OMIT ZERO ROWS asks you if you want to print or skip rows that contain only zeros. The default prints them.

SUPPRESS ZERO VALUES gives you the choice of printing your zeros (the default value), printing them as a dash (type 1), or not printing them (type 2).

PRINT ROW TITLE AFTER WHICH COLUMN asks you if you want to put any row titles between columns 1 and 9. The default is 0, which leaves the title on the far left of your printed report.

NEGATIVE NUMBERS gives you a choice of having the minus sign appear to the left of the number (the default value), to the right of the number for the accountants, or in parentheses.

PAGE CONTROL refers to printers with automatic paper feed options. The default sets the printer for continuous printing with three lines between pages. The feed option puts each page on a separate sheet of form-feed paper, while the pause option allows you to print on separate sheets of paper that you put in your printer one at a time.

OMIT COMMAS gives you the choice of omitting commas between groups of three numbers in large figures. This option could be handy if you need to save space, but commas make large numbers easier to read. The default leaves the commas in.

DOUBLE SPACE lets you double space between data rows if you want to. The default is single space.

OMIT LINE NUMBERS lets you leave out line numbers, or build them in. They can be a handy reference. The default leaves them out.

After you have gone through all these options, you can go to command 112, SAVE TABLE, to save the format you have just created.

82 TITLES. This command gives you a number of choices. You can choose to number the pages of your report, or not. The default does not number the pages. You can also choose to date the report, or not. The default is no date. If you do date it, the order is year (YY means two digits), month, day.

Next, you can choose to print a limited number of rows. The default is to print all 50 of them. You probably will want fewer than that; you have the same kind of choice with your columns. Finally, you have a choice of one to three-line title for your report, which will be centered on the top of the page. Each title can be as long as 40 characters.

As was true with the OPTIONS command, you can save all this good stuff with command 112, SAVE TABLE. If you have shortened your rows or columns, and you want to go back to work with a full range, use commands 92 and 93 after you bring the table back to the screen. That way, you could print different stages of your report, (monthly, for example) and expand the printout as the report grew.

83 REPORT. This command sends your report to the printer. Make sure it is on and the paper is set before you hit Return.

84 SHOW OPTS. This command will display all your print and title options. You might want to use this command before you print the report, just to check that you have what you want.

85 SAVE REP. This command will save your report to a different disk, or *spool* the report to the printer. If you are saving on a file disk, remember that if you already have a table or report on the disk with the same name, the new one will erase the old one. You may want to do that, but if you want to keep the old one you must think of a new name for the new report.

86 SET CRT. This command affects your table on the screen, but it does not work for your printed report. It allows you to specify the number of decimal places you see, the row and column widths, and whether or not you get to see zeros.

90 Status Commands

92 and 93 ROW/COLUMN RANGE. These commands allow you to change the size of your rows and columns from the default values of 50 rows and 20 columns. If you change these default values, the impact of that change will be seen in your table on the screen, your printed reports, and in your computations. These commands are another opportunity to tailor a table to your particular needs.

98 COMPUTE. This command allows you to run the computations you have programmed into your table. To use this command, choose the row or column you want to change or compute with the data pointer. Build in the kind of calculation you want. Type 98 ⟨Return⟩ and the Plans will recompute your figures. The table will revert back to its standard mode after the computation is performed. (Note that command 102 allows you to set up a different order from the default structure of row/column.)

101 PROTECT. This command protects the computational logic you have built into your table, and it allows you to change data in the table. The command is useful if an inexperienced person is entering data and you are fearful that he/she might change the logic. Command 101 is a toggle. When it is on you will see a P in the upper right corner of your screen.

102 ORDER. This command allows you to choose the order in which you will compute your data. Your choices are row only, column only, (the default), and column/row. This command can be very handy for "what-if" analyses.

CONCLUSIONS

That, finally, is an overview of Chang Labs' common menu for Profitplan and Microplan. They are quite flexible as spreadsheets go, and they are straightforward. We actually like the ever-present menus in the right hand column. After a while they serve as a help function. Good luck with either Plan, and remember to keep a paper system running in parallel with it for at least six months to a year.

Chapter 16

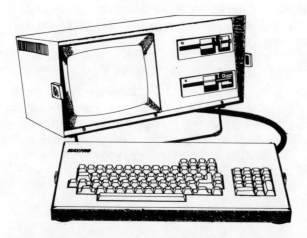

Telecommunicating
the KAYPRO Way

First, let's define telecommunicating so that its breadth of possible meanings might come more into focus for you. Charles Sippl—who is a sort of Webster of microcomputer dictionaries—has this to say about telecommunications (first as noun, then as verb):

> **telecommunications**—1. Any communication of information in verbal, written, coded, or pictorial form by electric means, whether by wire or by radio; 2. Refers to processes for conveying from one location to another, by electrical means, information that originates or is recorded in alphabetic, numeric, or pictorial form, or as a signal that represents a measurement. This includes telemetering, telegraphy, and facsimile as well as voice and television. (Also known as data transmission.) (Quoted from Charles Sippl's *Microcomputer Dictionary*, Second Edition, Howard W. Sams, Inc., 1983, p. 469).

There, that is Sippl's rather elegant—because technically precise and to the point—definition. Have you done any of the above lately? Sure you have, both as "transmitter and receiver," we'll bet. How so? Well, when talking on the phone you have been telecommunicating. The same goes for listening to the radio, watching television, picking up Morse code on your crystal set (as in —·· ——·—), or as in talking via walkie-talkies with your kids. All are forms of telecommunicating, according to Sippl's view of the science, although in some cases you are actively participating in the telecommunicating process, whereas in others—like listening to Bob and Ray on NPR—you are the passive recipient of what they are sending by radio signal to your kitchen, bedroom, car, or space shuttle.

So, what about the KAYPRO in this connection? Is it passive or active? The answer is that it can be either. What else? It is very powerful when put to use as a telecommunicating device, of that there is no question. Want a few examples? Consider these, although hundreds come to mind just as readily:

● The attorney who accesses West Law (a law database) from her sloop moored in Marina del Rey, and does so via her KAYPRO 10.

● The young structural engineer who uses his KAYPRO to find out what his boss needs to know about the latest construction specifications established by the U.S. Army Corps of Engineers.

● The retired scholar who searches psychology bibliography databases to see what has been written about Frankenstein as a symbol of the human quest for self-knowledge. (Heavy!)

● The mother at home with three preschoolers who uses her KAYPRO to earn money by doing text processing for a publisher, who records the edited text she telecommunicates each day.

● The disabled vet who uses the KAYPRO to talk with others via an electronic bulletin board.

You get the idea. Intelligent people can use their KAYPROs as intelligent telecommunicating devices for hundreds of different applications, and they do so successfully and easily every day of the week. And now to find out how they do it.

BASIC HARDWARE AND OTHER REQUIREMENTS

To use your KAYPRO to telecommunicate with anyone (or with almost any computer) anywhere, you must have the following equipment on hand:

1) A KAYPRO 2, 4, or 10.
2) Telecommunications system software package.
3) A 300 or 1200 baud modem.
4) An RS-232C serial modem cable.
5) A Bell-system standard push-button or standard rotary dial phone.
6) A communications carrier's phone number, such as, TELENET, TYMNET, or UNINET; these give you access to major computer databases such as Dow-Jones News Service, Lexis, Medline, The SOURCE, DIALOG, etc.
7) A phone number to call to reach another computer, e.g., your friend's number in Boston or Seattle.
8) A desire to tap into your infosphere.

Now, of the eight items listed, you have at this time items 1 and 2, and most likely 8, too. And the KAYPRO 2, 4, and 10 telecommunicate like champs at various baud rates, but at either 300 or 1200 if you are using the phone system. If you merely wire your KAYPRO to your friend's machine next door or down the hall or across the room, they can communicate at 19,200 baud, which is indeed speedy. (See our earlier chapter "Meet the KAYPRO Family" for a few words about baud rates, cables, serial ports, etc., if all this is foreign to you.)

And, as for software, the KAYPRO 4 and 10 come with a fine telecommunications program called Suprterm (not our spelling). At any rate, you also get with your KAYPRO 4 and 10 a close variation known as Suprterm Dow-Jones, which is used exclusively for tapping into the Dow's news service out of New York.

Well and good for those who buy the KAYPRO 4 and 10, but Suprterm is an option for most KAYPRO 2 owners. That is, KAYPRO 2 owners will have to buy the software from their KAYPRO dealer. (Since mid-1984, however, Suprterm has been bundled with the KAYPRO 4. The 4 as of early 1984 came with a built-in modem; the software to operate this modem, however, is still under development by KAYPRO. Look for a notice of its release from your dealer or in *ProFiles*.) Even so, the instructions we give you in this chapter apply to all three models when running Suprterm with an outboard modem.

Let's regroup right away. In terms of the above list of things to take care of, we count five items for you to handle before you can get online: numbers 3, 4, 5, 6, and 7. Once you have done so, you, too, will be able to get in on the telecommunicating act. And to help you get online as painlessly as possible, here is a bit of advice intended to assist you in nailing down the loose ends.

THINGS TO NAIL DOWN

Item 3: Modem. What is a modem? Well, the word means *modulate-demodulate*, which is merely another way of saying that computer language is modulated into Bell system lingo (tones) and then, at the other end, returned to computer language so the computers can talk at either end of the phone connection. Put simply, the modem is a translator that enables computers to communicate by way of positive and negative electrical charges, which are first converted into sound and then back into computerese.

Modems come in two basic configurations. The first, older type has two rubber cups which hold the receiver and transmitter on either end of the phone handset proper. The newer modems accept direct coupling to your KAYPRO and phone by means of a wire. This direct hookup is definitely the preferred method, and is the one seen more and more in use today. This modem setup accepts your KAYPRO's digital signals directly, and then modulates them into the sounds the phone can transmit over the lines to the modem and computer waiting at the other end.

Which kind of modem setup should you get? Obviously, the direct hookup type is the way to go, especially where accuracy of data transmission/reception is of major importance—which it should be at all times, in our opinion. At today's prices you can pick up a quite affordable 300 or 1200 baud modem offering the direct-connection features we've just described.

We recommend no one manufacturer's model over another's, but you should know that Suprterm was configured to work at its automatic best with the Hayes Smart Modem at either the 300 or 1200 baud rating. The difference between 300 and 1200 baud is 30 vs. 120 bits per second transmitted and received. That differential factor of four can mean substantial savings when you are online for lengthy periods of time.

We will say this, however: the Hayes Smart Modem is very good in all respects, as is the user's manual that comes with it. In fact, the Hayes modem is fast becoming the benchmark in telecommunications devices used for transmission and reception of microcomputer signals.

We also were able to use Suprterm with a much less expensive modem, the manually operated, battery-powered, 300 baud Signalman Mark I modem, produced by Anchor Automation, Inc. Although such a modem requires that you manually dial the phone, it works just fine when trying to get online with DIALOG or another of the major database service centers. Obviously, such a manual modem does not offer all the features and conveniences that the more expensive Hayes offers, but such low-priced modems are adequate nonetheless. You'll have to weigh the advantages against the disadvantages and make your own choice.

The point is merely that there is a wide variety of acceptable modems on the market today which will work quite well with your KAYPRO and its telecommunications software, Suprterm. We would recommend you check with your dealer on the matter of modem selection, and perhaps do a little inquiring in the local KAYPRO user's group. See what other KAYPRO users have found out about modem selection and satisfactory use for the dollars spent. Doing so will help you make the best choice possible for the bucks.

Item 4: Modem Cables. Here the task is much easier. All you have to do is remember that the modem I/O port is a *serial* port, and therefore needs a standard serial modem cable. Most modem manufacturers supply a cable with their modem, but if you need to get one made, go to your KAYPRO dealer and have one made for you. Why? Because they are not as easy to fashion as you might think, and your main goal now should be to get the system working with as little trouble as possible. There are enough things to become familiar with when telecommunicating for the first time—without having to solder wires to arrange the correct "handshake" pin arrangement needed to hook the modem up to the KAYPRO.

Item 5: The Phone. Here you may run into some difficulty, especially if you have the wrong kind of dial phone or push-button (touch-tone) phone in your house or office. Most modems on the market today work with either the touch-tone or rotary dial variety of phone, but not with the kind whose buttons or dial feature is an integral part of the handset itself.

Consequently, you should stay away from the "Princess," "Slimline," and "Trimline" style of push-button or dial phones. A rule of thumb is this: use no phone whose pushbuttons or dial are integrated into the handset. Why? Because such phone handsets connect directly to the telephone line, instead of to the base first and then to the phone line via a second cord. That is, such "Trimline" phones lack the base jack I/O ports needed to hook up your modem without a lot of fooling around with Bell-compatible phone adapters.

Stick, then, to the standard office type dial or touch-tone phone—you know, the one that sits on the desk, has a square base, and has a separate port at its base for the handset wire and one wire connecting the rear of the base to the receptacle at the baseboard. (Similar wall phones will also work.) Such phones permit successful installation of most modems available today.

Another thing to know here is that you must have a private line to operate your KAYPRO as a telecommunications device. Any party who picks up the phone while you are connected to another computer over that same party line can disrupt the data transmission flow, thereby ruining your session and costing you money, with nothing to show for the time you've spent online. The same principle of having a dedicated line applies to extension phones in your house. Make sure they are not going to be used when you crank up Suprterm and get into the stock market figures via The SOURCE. Such an unwanted interruption could force you to lose more than your portfolio.

You will be glad to know, on the other hand, that once you have a working modem, the right cable, the correct phone configuration, and Suprterm up and running, you should be able to access databases around the world without a great deal of trouble. For example, we know that Battelle's computer bank in Columbus, Ohio, is accessed by clients who reside in London, Paris, and other cities a bit more famous than the one where Woody Hayes telecommunicated at "close range" his instructions to his players.

Item 6: Common Carriers. There are three "common" carriers who offer you their services for a price: TYMNET, TELENET, and UNINET. What are they and how to use them? These outfits rent *signal carrier* space from various phone companies, and, in turn, they offer you an exclusive network through which you can access databases across the country. DIALOG, already mentioned, is one example. DIALOG's computers are located in Palo Alto, California, and you can tap into them only by going through one of the common carriers mentioned above. In brief, that is what such carriers do: they offer a telecommunications network for your personal use at a price.

Beyond knowing that they offer you a pipeline to mainframe computers holding vast amounts of information of all types, you need to know how to access a common carrier such as TELENET. To do so is really quite easy. You need their phone number, which is available via Bell information, or your dealer, or the database people (i.e., The SOURCE, DIALOG, West Law, etc.), or your KUG contacts, or from several readable books on the subject of going online via a microcomputer. They will be of help to you as you go about getting signed-up so you can go online. Oh yes, you'll even get your very own *password*, so you can access the computers you wish, and so that they can bill you for your time online.

Of course, as with Sprint, MCI, and other special service networks, you pay for the service as a function of the time you are in their network system. Say you access TELENET and want to tap into a particular database at DIALOG in California. DIALOG will also, of course, charge you for the privilege of tapping into their computer bank of knowledge and other good data. DIALOG then bills you for the total service charge: the TELENET fee and their own, combined into one. You can appreciate, we are sure, the necessity of knowing what you are about when going online; otherwise, several sawbucks too many will be the price you'll have to pay for your inefficient online searching, electronic bulletin board use, or whatever.

SUPRTERM

Now let's get into Suprterm, the telecommunications software that came bundled with your KAYPRO 4 and 10. Suprterm is a very easy program to use, and we think it nicely rounds out the package of applications software that you get with the KAYPRO. Suprterm offers you the following features:

- COMMAND MODE/COMMUNICATIONS MODE

- ESCAPE ⟨ESC ⟩
- BREAK
- COMMAND FILE
- DIAL
- LIST
- PRINT
- RECEIVE
- SEND
- TERMINAL
- QUIT

Main Menu

To Main Menu for Suprterm is shown in Fig. 16-1. To leave any one of the submenus for the Main Menu, merely press Return. Let's look first at what each of the Command/Communications options does for you.

ESC. Press the ⟨ESC⟩ key once. This command function takes you out of the

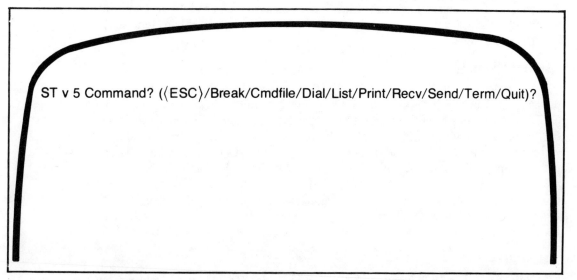

ST v 5 Command? (⟨ESC⟩/Break/Cmdfile/Dial/List/Print/Recv/Send/Term/Quit)?

Fig. 16-1. Suprterm main menu.

command mode and puts you into the communications mode. To exercise this option, merely press the Escape key.

BREAK. Here, you press B when the Main Menu is on the console. Doing so permits you to tell the computer on the other end of the line that you want to interrupt the transmission of data from a computer out there to your KAYPRO.

CMDFILE. Here you would press C twice to enter the Command File Menu; once in that, you select the CREATE option to set up a command file, or a CP/M file text that contains a number of Suprterm commands that you specify.

DIAL. Press D to have the Hayes Smart Modem automatically dial the phone number which you enter on the keyboard or via the numeric keypad, or which you have previously stored in the Smart Modem's memory.

LIST. Press L when the Main Menu is on the console. This option gets you a list, naturally, of a sorted file directory. This is an extremely useful option because it shows you what you have on a given disk, such as files, the size of each, etc. LIST is akin to D.COM, which is available only on the 10.

PRINT. This option is not currently available.

RECV. Here, entering an R from the Main Menu will put you in the Receive Menu. This menu permits you to store (in a CP/M file) data text received from another computer.

SEND. This command is activated by pressing S. The command gets you into the Send Menu, from which you select the options needed to send a file from your KAYPRO's disk memory storage to the computer on the other end of the line.

TERM. Pressing a T permits you to access the Terminal Characteristics Menu, out of which you can specify your operating baud rate, parity settings, and so forth.

QUIT. Pressing Q closes all open data files created while using Suprterm; this command then gets you out of Suprterm and back into CP/M.

So much for an ultra-quick look at the main command menu and its ten command functions. Let's look in turn at each of the submenus accessed from the Main Menu, again in quick-step fashion.

Command File Menu

You reach the submenu shown in Fig 16-2 from the Main Menu by pressing C; pressing ESC puts you back in the Main Menu. Pressing C again puts you in the CREATE A COMMAND FILE mode. Pressing an E tells Suprterm to run the command file *created and given a specific, descriptive filename,* which you must enter. For example, you might create a command file that consists of your friend's phone number, thereby making it possible for Suprterm to have the Hayes Smart Modem dial the number automatically for you. Let's call the file A:JOHN. After creating it, you must *close* it before you can run it. To do this, enter a CTRL-hyphen combination, followed by a CTRL Z command, which closes the command file named A:JOHN. This is an important step because you cannot run a command file until it has been created and closed via a CTRL Z.

Dialing Menu

Referring to Fig. 16-3, first note the ESC option which, if selected, will take you out of the command mode and put you into the communications mode. The ANSWER option tells your Hayes Smart Modem to answer automatically any incoming calls. Naturally, you would have to be in the receive mode, which also means that your KAYPRO and Hayes modem would be on and running properly. The HANGUP option permits you to break the connection between your KAYPRO and the computer on the other end of the communications network. ONLINE is a command option that puts your KAYPRO and Smart Modem in a "listening posture." By that we mean that Suprterm tells the modem to wait patiently online until it detects an incoming signal from another computer. When the signal is detected, the Hayes modem puts you online. RETRY is a handy option permitting you to redial a phone number previously entered into the command file.

Receive Menu

This menu (Fig. 16-4) is identical for both functions, the obvious difference being in the direction of data transmission. When in the Receive File mode, all incoming data characters are stored inside the KAYPRO's memory system as regular CP/M files. On the other hand, the Send File mode sends pre-existing CP/M files out the serial port, through the modem, and over the lines to the computer in the Receive mode at the other end. These pre-existing files must have been created with WordStar, PerfectWriter, or

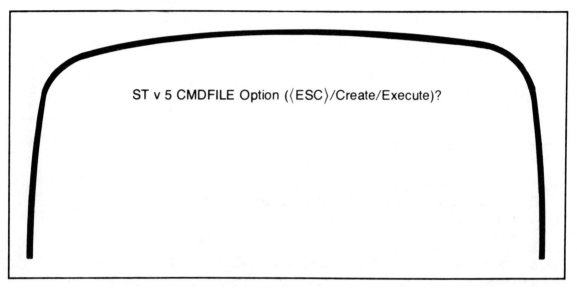

ST v 5 CMDFILE Option ($\langle$ESC$\rangle$/Create/Execute)?

Fig. 16-2. Suprterm command file menu.

some other CP/M-80 compatible text processor.

The XON/XOFF are elements of Suprterm's protocol, which tells the sending computer when the receiving computer's buffer (RAM) memory is capable of receiving more data (XON). Similarly, when the KAYPRO's RAM memory is full, Suprterm sends the XOFF signal to the sending computer, telling it to stop transmitting until the KAYPRO has stored on disk what is then in RAM. This on/off relationship is what is known as *handshaking*, and the Suprterm's protocol is extremely effective in this regard.

ADDLF is a toggle that tells SUPRTERM to add a line feed to carriage returns. When toggled on, the display is ADLFF, and when off, the toggle display is Addlf. ONOFF is another toggle which does the following: when toggled to the on position (ONoff), file transfers can commence. When toggled off (onOFF), they stop. The default mode is onOFF.

Terminal Menu

The menu shown in Fig. 16-5 is one you may well have to know your way around in, because it is your mechanism for setting baud rate and other important telecommunicating parameters. For instance, all of these fundamental operating features are set or

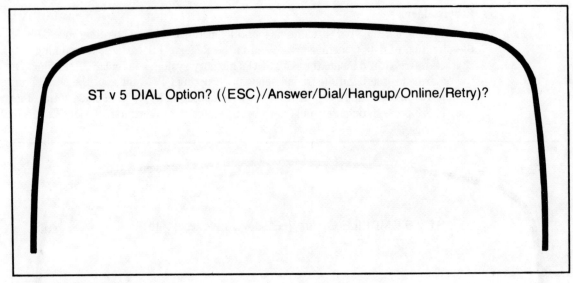

ST v 5 DIAL Option? (⟨ESC⟩/Answer/Dial/Hangup/Online/Retry)?

Fig. 16-3. Suprterm dialing menu.

changed via the Terminal Menu:

Baud Rate. You have eight optional data transmission rates available to you, coded A through H.

A=10
B=300   (This is one of two you'll want to select.)
C=600
D=1200   (This is the other rate used most frequently.)
E=2400
F=4800
G=9600
H=19,200   (This is the rate used when going from one KAYPRO directly to another CP/M-80 computer, with no phone system being used.)

Duplex. The setting is by default *full-duplex*. This means that your modem serial I/O channel is configured to simultaneously send and receive data or text. By contrast, *half-duplex* indicates that the serial modem port will enable data transmission in both directions but not simultaneously.

Echo. The *echo* mode is a method used to verify the accuracy of data transmission and reception. When selected, the *send echo* mode means that any characters entered at your keyboard are shown on your console while simultaneously being transmitted to the receiving computer on the other end of the line. Conversely, *receive echo* means that any data received by your KAYPRO is echoed back to the sender's console while being sent to you. In short, echo is a data send/receive check mechanism. Any garbage going in/out will be visually evident as such on your console; if that happens, a quick Break in the command mode will put an end to a wasteful online session.

Format. This option is used to establish the correct number of data bits that make up a character, or a unit of information. The character can be five, six, seven, or eight data bits in length. Parity (a standard bit-checking scheme) is set in terms of *even, odd,* or *none*; and the number of stop bits per character is set at either 1, 1.5, or 2.

Nulls. This option is used to insert an ASCII character whose sole purpose for being transmitted is to give the receiving computer time to process any accumulated data

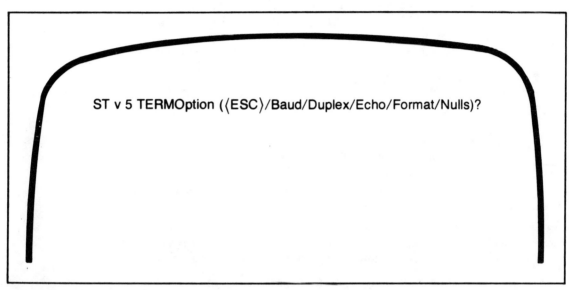

ST v 5 TERMOption (⟨ESC⟩/Baud/Duplex/Echo/Format/Nulls)?

Fig. 16-4. Suprterm receive menu.

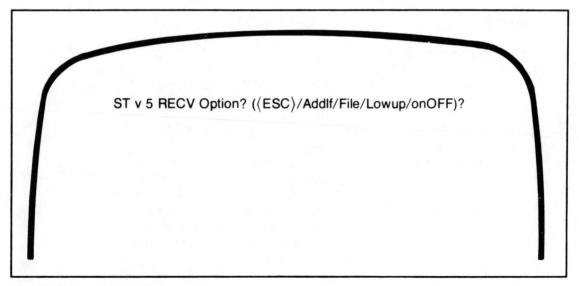

ST v 5 RECV Option? (⟨ESC⟩/Addlf/File/Lowup/onOFF)?

Fig. 16-5. Suprterm terminal menu.

in its RAM and other data processing subcomponents. Nulls, say, in effect, "This data is meaningless but I send it to let you know that I am still here and to give you the breathing room you need to process the real stuff that I have already sent your way." So much for null-speak.

GETTING ONLINE

Here is a routine to help you get online. This generic session takes you from a cold boot on the KAYPRO to a connection between your KAYPRO and the computer system selected. The program we are presenting below was successfully run on a KAYPRO 4, but the same procedures apply to the 2 and 10 as well.

Here is the equipment and information we used to get the KAYPRO 4 online:

- One KAYPRO 4.
- Suprterm ST.COM.
- One Signalman Mark I, 300 baud manual modem.
- A serial modem cable.
- A pushbutton office phone.
- The local access number for TELENET, the carrier we used. (You can also use TYMNET and UNINET.)
- A DIALOG account number and password. (This information is obtainable from DIALOG.)

Here is the procedure you should follow once you have the above hardware properly connected and backup copies of the software. (If you have not yet backed up your Suprterm software, do so now, following the procedures outlined in Chapter Six.)

ACCESSING DIALOG USING A MANUAL MODEM

CONDITION/GOAL	ACTION
1) To run Suprterm	Turn on your KAYPRO 4, getting the A> prompt.
2) to set up the proper disk relationship for running the program and for opening up a file on the disk in Drive B.	Insert the backup copy of Superterm in Drive A and a blank, formatted disk in Drive B.
3) To see the MAIN Menu on the console	Enter ST and press <RETURN>.
4) To start the Dial Process	Press D once.
5) When the Dial Menu is on the screen	Press D, then use the phone to dial the local TELENET access number. This gets you connected to the TELENET network. Leave the phone off the hook for now. If you have a Hayes Smart Modem, it will dial the number for you after you key it in on your keyboard or keypad.
6) When you hear the high-pitched steady tone in the receiver.	Switch the modem from MANUAL to DATA mode.

7) To get ONLINE	Hang up the phone and enter two carriage returns (or CTRL-hyphen). This connects your KAYPRO to the TELENET access network.
8) See the DIALOG network welcome you and ask for your DIALOG user's password.	Enter your password and press RETURN.
9) See your password accepted and the DIALOG prompt "?"	Press CTRL and the hyphen key together.
10) See Main Command Menu.	Press R for Receive Menu.
11) See the Receive Menu.	Press F to open up a file to save in ASCII the data sent to you from DIALOG.
12) See a prompt for FILE TYPE.	Press T for Terminal.
13) See a prompt for protocol.	Type Y.
14) See "Receive File Name:"	Enter B:DIALOG1.FIL and press ⟨Return⟩.
15) To return to the console and resume DIALOG accessing.	Press ⟨ESC⟩ once.
16) Use the DIALOG search function to browse and pick the file you want to save on the disk in Drive B.	
17) To exit DIALOG, return to the MAIN COMMAND MENU.	Press the CTRL and hyphen keys together once.
18) See the Main Command Menu.	Type Q once and Suprterm will automatically disconnect you from TELENET/ DIALOG and will close the file B:DIALOG.FIL.
19) To print file on Drive B.	Invoke WordStar's normal print command procedure.

There is one example of how to go on- and offline with DIALOG via Suprterm. There are, of course many other databases you can access, and many other combinations of kinds of modems you can use to get online. We recommend that you check out your Suprterm documentation carefully, explore modem prices and features, and then proceed carefully into the vast world of information that your KAYPRO makes available to you via telecommunications.

Chapter 17

co-POWER 88/Ramdisk/MS-DOS

The co-POWER 88 is an optional 16-bit co-processor that may be added to your KAYPRO 2 or 4. It is a board that can be bolted to the back of the drives in those machines to give them a 16-bit co-processor that will enable them to run MS-DOS software. The board and its accompanying software also provide a "Ramdisk," which gives you a "virtual" third drive when you are operating in CP/M. You should note that when you are running in the MS-DOS mode you will have only two drives, because the additional memory provided by the board must be used either for MS-DOS or for Ramdisk in CP/M. (We're getting a bit technical here; we'll explain some of this as we go along, although we aren't going into theory any further than is operationally necessary.)

The standard KAYPRO has an 8-bit board and a Z80A processor. That's an opening definition. This 16-bit add-on should theoretically double the speed at which your KAYPRO processes information when you are in CP/M. Notice, we say *theoretically*.

At present the board is undergoing *beta testing*—that means consumer, or field testing—by a Boston KAYPRO Users' Group, and the last word is not in. SWP, the manufacturer, is developing a co-POWER 88 for the KAYPRO 10, and at this writing we were unable to get one to test in our 10. Consequently, we will not discuss its operation. Look for more information from *ProFiles*, or from your dealer.

Back to the bits. An 8-bit board means that the central processor in your KAYPRO, or any other 8-bit machine, can process eight bits of information at once. A 16-bit board can theoretically process twice as much information in the same time. Its other feature is that it can run MS-DOS, and that means that you can run *some* IBM software on your KAYPRO. The emphasis here is on *some*. SWP has issued Versions 1.25 and 2.11 of

MS-DOS configured to work with their hardware. Version 1.25 has a limited number of applications programs that it can run; specifically, WordStar and dBASE II are known to be successful. Version 2.11 can run a much wider range of software, and you should check with your dealer to see exactly which programs will run.

The manufacturer, SWP, of Arlington, Texas, can also inform you about what programs will run. Their products are under development, and they have an interesting idea. We hope that they press on. They also offer a version of CP/M-86 that gives you access to a varied group of software. We were not able to obtain CP/M-86 from the manufacturer at this writing.

INSTALLING THE co-POWER 88

There are three ways to obtain and install the co-POWER 88. You can get it installed on your KAYPRO from the factory as a special-order option. You can also purchase it from your dealer, and have it installed at the dealership. Or, you can purchase it and install it yourself. This last method is advisable only for people who are experienced with electronic hardware.

BACKING UP THE MASTER SOFTWARE

You should back up the master software, which comes "write-protected" from SWP. Currently there is a CP/M to MS-DOS Adapter Disk that has these files: MS-DOS.COM, RAMDISK.COM, and RAMDISK.DOC. An MS-DOS operating disk that has the following files: COMMAND.COM, EDLIN.COM, CHKDSK.COM, FIND.EXE, FC.EXE, SYS.COM, DISKCOPY.COM, RECOVER.COM, MORE.COM, DEBUG.COM, FORMAT.COM, Z80.EXE, EXE2BIN.EXE, and SORT.EXE.
The CP/M to MS-DOS Adapter Disk can be copied to a formatted CP/M disk using the familiar PIP A:=B:*.*[VO] ⟨Return⟩ command format. The MS-DOS disk, however, requires you to copy it in MS-DOS. Here's how.

1) To copy your MS-DOS disc,	Reset your KAYPRO to clear the Ramdisk. Then, insert the CP/M to MS-DOS disk in Drive A.
2) See the A0 prompt.	Type MS-DOS ⟨Return⟩.
3) See a prompt.	Remove the CP/M to MS-DOS disk and insert the MS-DOS master in Drive A.
4)	Press Return
5) See MS-DOS sign on.	Enter a date, or press Return.
6) See a prompt to enter the time.	Enter the time or press Return.
7) See the MS-DOS prompt A>.	For the KAYPRO 4, type FORMAT B:/D/S ⟨Return⟩.
	For the KAYPRO 2, type B:/S ⟨Return⟩.
8) See a prompt to insert an unformatted disk in Drive B and press any key.	Do so.
9) When the formatting process is complete, See:	

System transferred	
362496 bytes total disk space	
26624 bytes used by system	
335872 bytes available on disk	
Format another (Y/N)?	Type N.
10) To copy files from Drive A	Type DISKCOPY A: B: ⟨Return⟩.
11) See: Insert Source diskette in Drive A: Insert formatted target diskette in drive B: Strike any key when ready	Press any key.
12) See a prompt telling you that the copying is finished and asking if you want to make another copy	Press N if you are finished.

USING THE RAMDISK IN YOUR KAYPRO

Ramdisk provides you with another disk drive, labeled anything from C through P, and it is useful on two counts. It gives you another disk drive to work with, and it gives you greater speed for operations that depend heavily on transfer from disk to RAM and back (a.k.a. *disk I/O*). How you manage those files is up to you, but it should be remembered that any files that are transferred to the Ramdisk drive are temporary and will have to be saved back to a disk (using PIP) after you have finished working with your program. You might also want to know that if you have a program or data in the Ramdisk and you lose power you will lose *all* the information in the Ramdisk.

OK, you have had the co-POWER 88 installed in your KAYPRO, and you have backed up the master disks. Boot your KAYPRO, warm or cold, it doesn't matter.

1) To run Ramdisk,	Insert the Ramdisk in A.
2) See the A0> prompt.	Type RAMDISK * ⟨Return⟩.
3) See the M prompt.	Remove the Ramdisk, and insert your program disk.
4) You're ready to go.	

Note: this is a shorthand version that will make Drive M your third drive. The options that you have bypassed will be discussed below.

2A) See the A0 > prompt.	Type RAMDISK ⟨Return⟩.
3A) The prompt says "Drivename (A-P) to assign the ramdisk."	You have a choice here, but for openers type a ⟨Return⟩.
4A) You could assign it to any one of 16 possible drives (through P), however, it *seems* more efficient in A. At that point your old A drive becomes B and old B becomes C.	
5A) The next prompt is "Erase contents of ramdisk file directory (Y/N?)"	Type ⟨Return⟩ for the default, which is yes. You won't lose anything.

6A) Note: You would use the N response if you wanted to save data after a warm boot, but *not* after a cold boot, or running CP/M-86 or MS-DOS.

7A) The third prompt is "Ramdisk driver load address or ⟨cr⟩ to use default"

Type ⟨Return⟩, unless you want to start programming it differently.

8A) The fourth prompt is "co-POWER 88 port address or ⟨cr⟩ to use default"

Type ⟨Return⟩.

9A) OK, you're in business.

Now, you will want to load part of one of your software programs, such as WordStar, or Perfect Calc, or whatever. Please note that Ramdisk is limited to 252K (4K is needed to operate the system), which is the size of a *single*-sided double-density disk. You will need to see which files in your software package are the most essential, and which you can dispense with.

Ramdisk operates when you load a program into it and then use it to manipulate files. For example, load WordStar into the Ramdisk with PIP, and then go. We will show you the routine.

1) To load WordStar to Ramdisk

We assume that you have followed the 3 or 9 steps to load Ramdisk. Remove the Ramdisk and insert your WordStar disk in A.

It is now B if Ramdisk is A.

2) Ramdisk = Drive A.

Type PIP A:=B:WS.COM[VO] ⟨Return⟩.

3)

Type PIP A:=B:WSOVLY1.OVR ⟨Return⟩.

4)

Type PIP A:=B:WSMSGS.OVR ⟨Return⟩.

5) That takes up 94K of Ramdisk.

Remove your WordStar disk and insert in its place a data/text disk.

6)

At the A0> prompt type WS and follow your normal pattern with WordStar.

Your key problem will be figuring out which files in a large program (such as any of the spreadsheets or word processing programs) you will need to run that program. You cannot, for example, run all of WordStar and all of The WORD PLUS, which you can do on a double-sided disk. Once you have determined that, Ramdisk will speed things up somewhat. Our experience with it has been limited to WordStar and Perfect Writer, and it is faster, but not a lot faster.

Caution: When monitoring files with STAT or D.COM, it appears that the co-POWER 88 Ramdisk reports different file sizes than are reported from the floppy disk. For example, D.COM on disk takes 4K and on the Ramdisk it requires 3K. A WordStar file called WSOVLY1.OVR takes 34K on disk, but 33K on Ramdisk. We haven't lost anything—yet—and it is a perplexing characteristic of the Ramdisk.

If you run into an error message you may want to check RAMDISK.DOC, which is a file containing SWP's documentation. Normally you would get a hard copy of this material when you purchase the co-POWER 88. KAYPRO also includes documentation when you purchase the unit from their factory.

USING MS-DOS

The co-POWER 88's version of MS-DOS has several files special to their version.

FORMAT B: /S	will produce a single-sided IBM PC disk with the Plus 88 system written on it.
FORMAT B: /D/S	will produce a double-sided IBM PC format disk with the Plus 88 system on it.
FORMAT B: /S/8 or /D/S/8	will produce eight sectors per track, which is necessary for PCDOS Version 1. Under PCDOS Version 2 and MS-DOS Version 2.11 the format is nine sectors per track. This is the default if you don't specify eight sectors. That option allows you to read disks written on the older IBM PCs.
Z80.EXE	is the program used to return CP/M from MS-DOS. Z80.EXE will prompt you when it is necessary to insert a CP/M disk.

Here's how you start MS-DOS.

1) To start MS-DOS	Boot your KAYPRO and insert the CP/M to MS-DOS Adapter disk in Drive A.
2)	Type MSDOS ⟨Return⟩.
3) See a prompt	Remove the Adapter insert the MS-DOS 2.11 disk in Drive A and press Return.
4) See a prompt for a date.	Type the date or ⟨Return⟩.
5) See a prompt for the time	Type the time or ⟨Return⟩.
6) See A:,	You are ready to work in MS-DOS. You may remove the system disk, because it has been loaded to the co-POWER 88.

Now, 17 chapters later, we have come almost to the end of what has still been a brief overview of the KAYPROs and their bundled software. We say *almost* because what follows is "The Perfect Appendix," a look at four programs from Perfect Software that were bundled with earlier models of the KAYPRO 2, 4, and 10.

Appendix A

Perfect Writer—
Another Text Processor

U nlike WordStar, Perfect Writer comes with a complete tutorial program on disk. The program consists of eight lessons:

Lesson 0: Introduction to the self-teaching program.
Lesson 1: Basic cursor control and text entering.
Lesson 2: More advanced cursor movement commands.
Lesson 3: How to read, write, and print text files.
Lesson 4: How to use the search and replace functions.
Lesson 5: How to copy and move text from file to file.
Lesson 6: How to fill, or reformat, paragraphs.
Lesson 7: Editing multiple files and dual window usage.

Perfect Writer's "dual window" feature enables you to view on your console two document files at once. You can scroll forward and backward in, edit, and add to or delete from either or both documents.

You can also move text from one document to another. Your text will shuttle from one document to another, reappearing where you want it to. If you decide you want the text back in its original spot in the first document, it can be pulled back with no trouble at all. Perfect Writer can also be used in conjunction with a spelling program called Perfect Speller.

COMMAND STRUCTURE

Your Perfect Writer text processing program consists of two broad categories of commands: editing commands and document design commands. Within the first category there are 81 commands which are spread across these fifteen editing functions:

- Cursor Movement
- Screen Display
- Split Screen Display
- Scroll Other Window
- Delete and Insert
- Insert
- Copy and Move

- Searching
- Utilities
- Setup Utilities
- Transpose
- Capitalization
- File Commands
- Mode Selection

The second major category, document design commands, covers such text design functions as these:

- Environment Commands
- Typeface Commands
- Sectioning Commands
- General Commands
- Variable Manipulation Commands
- Style Parameter Options

Finally, there are the seven commands for Perfect Speller, the bundled spelling program that came with early model KAYPROs.

USING THE LESSONS TO GET STARTED

Follow the steps given below to get into and through all of the lessons. Do so until you are comfortable with the program, its commands, and routines.

First, get the A>on the console, put the Perfect Writer Disk in Drive A and the Lessons disk in Drive B. Next, log on to Drive B by entering this command at the A> prompt:

B: ⟨Return⟩.

Next, enter this command to bring up the menu on the Perfect Writer disk in Drive A:

A:MENU ⟨Return⟩.

The menu will appear on your console, and it will look like Fig. A-1. Look at the menu's selection options. Here is what each means:

E   enables you to edit a file via Perfect Writer.
F   enables you to format your text to look as you want.
P   allows you to print a file, *after* it has been formatted.
S   allows you to use Perfect Speller to check your text.
D   shows you which files are on a given logged disk.
Z   permits you to erase or delete a file.

```
Perfect Writer Version 1.xx Main Selection Menu
(C) 1982 Perfect Software, Inc.

Selections:
 E - Edit a file                                        <pw>
 F - Format a file                                      <pf>
 P - Print a formatted file                             <pp>
 S - Check the spelling of a file                       <ps>

 D - Look at the directory on a disk
 Z - Delete (erase) a file
 R - Rename a file

 C - Send a command line to CP/M
 X - Exit from this menu to CP/M



Type one character to indicate your selection now
Your pleasure (E,F,P,S,D,Z,R,C,X): _
```

Fig. A-1. Perfect Writer main selection menu.

R enables you to rename a file.
C allows you to send a command to the operating system.
X permits you to leave Perfect Writer for the CP/M system.

Now select option E and then indicate that you want to edit something on the logged disk in Drive B, which contains the seven lessons. After you have selected option E, respond by telling Perfect Writer that you wish to look at the introductory lesson first. In response to the question

What is the name of the file you wish to edit?
>-

you reply by telling Perfect Writer you wish to edit Lesson 0:

>_ LESSON0 ⟨Return⟩

After you enter the carriage return, Perfect Writer will read Lesson 0 from the lessons disk in Drive B, and it will display the opening paragraphs of that lesson on the console. When you are finished reading Lesson 0, enter CTRL X CTRL C, answer Y (for yes) to abandon the modified buffers (do not worry—you are not erasing the lessons), and you will find yourself looking at Perfect Writer's main menu once again.

You should work your way through all seven lessons *before* you do anything else with Perfect Writer. Why? Because by working through them first, you will have gained the confidence you need to use Perfect Writer well. Also, you will have a better sense of what Perfect Writer offers that WordStar does not. Finally, the lessons force you to interact with the software, which is the fastest way for you to learn about its features and benefits.

Now that you are anxious to look at Lesson 1, merely select from the main menu option E once again. When asked which file you wish to edit, answer by indicating its name and that it resides on the disk in drive B.

What is the name of the file you wish to edit?
>_B:LESSON1 ⟨Return⟩

Follow this procedure, moving from the lessons on Drive B, abandoning altered buffers, selecting option E, returning to the main menu, and then telling Perfect Writer that you want to edit another lesson on the disk in Drive B (B:LESSON2, B:LESSON6, etc.).

PRINTING THE LESSONS

A good way to examine the Print Menu in Perfect Writer is to use it to print yourself a copy of the lesson material, so you can look it over when you're away from your KAYPRO.

Put Perfect Writer in Drive A and the lessons disk in Drive B. Enter CTRL C to warm boot the computer. At the A> enter B: to log off Drive A and on to Drive B. When you get the B> be sure to re-boot the computer (CTRL X CTRL C). You will then get the B>. When you do, enter this: B> A:MENU ⟨Return⟩.

After doing this, you will get Perfect Writer's main menu. When you do, choose option F to format a file. You will then be asked for the name of the file you wish to format. You should respond as follows:

>_ LESSON0 ⟨Return⟩.

KAYPRO 10 owners should be sure to put the period after the 0, which indicates that there is no suffix to the name of the file they want to format. KAYPRO 2 and 4 owners should add MSS after the period, as in LESSON0.MSS.

You will then see the Perfect Formatter Selection Menu, which looks like the one shown in Fig. A-2. You should look over the various options available to you. Because you want to print Lesson 0, you can then select these options in this order:

V Verbatim Format	This tells Perfect Formatter to print Lesson 0 without reformatting it.
P Printer Output	This tells Perfect Formatter to send the contents of Lesson 0 to the printer.
A Pause Between Pages	Selecting this option enables you to insert a new page after one has been printed; if you have selected this option, you must press the space bar to restart the printer after inserting each fresh piece of paper. If you have a tractor feed and continuous form paper, then ignore this option, for the paper

G Go
will be advanced automatically, page by page. This tells Perfect Formatter to begin sending the text to the printer.

These same steps should be repeated to print any file's text on the disk in Drive B. Go ahead and print all seven of the lessons and the advanced introductory lesson. Doing so will help familiarize you with Perfect Formatter, your printer, and will permit you to read over the lessons anywhere.

Before you try to use Perfect Writer, however, you should know what kind of help is available to you by way of the Help Directory, so let's look at it briefly. To examine the features of the Help Directory, run through these steps:

1) Put Perfect Writer in Drive A and the lessons disk in Drive B.
2) Reboot the computer.
3) At the A>, enter B: ⟨Return⟩ to log on to Drive B.
4) At the B>, enter A:MENU ⟨Return⟩.
5) When the menu appears, select E.
6) Enter LESSON0 ⟨Return⟩.
7) When Lesson 0 appears on the console, enter CTRL X question mark.

Typing CTRL X ? while editing a file gets you the DIRECTORY shown in Fig. A-3. Go ahead, view each of the Help Directory commands. Doing so demonstrates that help is merely a CTRL X ? away.

The folks at Perfect Software have anticipated the needs of those of you who are already familiar with text processing in general and who would, therefore, have a very easy time working your way through the seven lessons. To help you move along at your level of skill, they have included on the lessons disk an advanced introduction to Perfect

```
(Perfect Writer) Perfect Formatter Selection Menu
(C) 1982 Perfect Software, Inc.

Available formatter options are:
 C - Send the output to the console device
 D - Format for a different device type
 P - Send the output to the printer device
 O - Name the output file differently
 V - Make the top level environment verbatim
     (Verbatim causes the output to appear as it does on the screen)
 A - Pause for manual insertion of each sheet of paper
 G - Start the formatting now
 X - Return to the top level menu

pf b:lesson0.
Your pleasure: (C,D,P,O,V,A,G,X) _
```

Fig. A-2. Perfect Formatter selection menu.

```
HELP DIRECTORY    ESC..(number from below) then ESC..V

     1  MOVING THE CURSOR        7  UTILITIES
     3  DELETE COMMANDS          8  INDENTATION
     4  SEARCHING                9  MODE SELECTION
     5  FILE COMMANDS           10  CAPITALIZATION
     6  BUFFER COMMANDS         10  REPEAT COMMAND
     6  MULTIPLE WINDOWS        11  COPYING and MOVING
          'ESC..' indicates press and release the ESC key
           'C-'   indicates press and hold the Control key
```

Fig. A-3. Perfect Writer help directory.

Writer. You can access this lesson by telling Perfect Writer you wish to edit a file on Drive B as follows:

 B:ADVINTRO ⟨Return⟩.

This advanced lesson will get you to the level of operational efficiency you want in short order.

Appendix B

Perfect Speller

Perfect Speller, a 50,000-word dictionary, is very easy to use, but it only works with Perfect Writer files, whereas The WORD Plus's spelling program works with files generated by both Perfect Writer and WordStar. As you might have guessed, you must use Perfect Speller in conjunction with the Perfect Writer command disk. We understand that Perfect Speller can check nearly 4,000 words in a minute; that is only a bit more than 12 minutes to go through its entire dictionary. Figure B-1 shows the Perfect Speller options.

To use Perfect Speller, first turn on your KAYPRO and get the A>. Put the Utilities CP/M disk in Drive A and a blank, new disk in Drive B. Then, using PIP, copy PIP to the disk in Drive B. Remove the Utilities CP/M disk from Drive A and insert the master disk for Perfect Speller. Re-boot the KAYPRO, getting an A>.

With the master Perfect Speller disk in Drive A and the newly formatted disk in Drive B (which at this time contains PIP and D only), PIP all the files from the disk in Drive A to the one in Drive B. You have now copied all the Perfect Speller and all the necessary Perfect Writer files to the working disk, since the master Perfect Speller disk contains both program files. Besides, you can only use Perfect Speller by way of Perfect Writer. Remove the master from Drive A and insert in its place the working copy from Drive B. Store the master in a safe place.

Re-boot the KAYPRO (CTRL X CTRL C), getting the A>. At the A>, enter B: and press Return; at the B>, enter A:MENU and press Return again. When the main menu appears, create a letter and save it when you're done.

With a letter stored on the disk in Drive B, you are now ready to bring the Perfect Speller program residing on A to bear upon the designated file (or files) stored on the file

```
+----------------------------------------------------+
| Answer with:                                       |
|   a - Add word to dictionary                       |
|   i - Ignore word                                  |
|   c - mark word to be Changed                      |      Fig. B-1. Perfect Speller options.
|   r - enter word's Root in dictionary              |
|   e - mark remaining words and Edit text           |
|                                                    |
+----------------------------------------------------+
```

disk in Drive B. This is the procedure you run through to check the spelling of a disk file in Drive B.

At the menu select the S option, the command to run Perfect Speller. Next, you will be asked for the name of the file to be checked by Perfect Speller. You should enter the name of the file residing on the disk in Drive B.

You will then be presented with a list of options. For now, select option G only, which tells Perfect Speller to check the spelling in the letter in question.

(By the way, Perfect Speller knows nothing of grammar or the misuse of language; for example using *to* instead of *too*, when you mean to indicate degree or intensity will not faze Perfect Speller at all. The same conditions apply, of course, to The WORD Plus's spelling program, and to all other spelling and text processing software available today. Sorry!)

After the letter's contents have been checked for spelling mistakes, the words in the file that have no precise equivalent in the 50,000-word main dictionary will be identified. Then you will be offered another choice: to correct the words right away, or to have them marked with the ^ sign so you can correct them later via the FIND function of Perfect Writer's Edit File mode.

Let's correct the misspellings right now. At the question, "Scan the list of unrecognizable words now?" you should enter a Y and then Return. You will then be presented with the following options:

a   Add the unrecognized words to the dictionary *after* they have been corrected. This permits you to get your pet lingo into the dictionary, which precludes having to constantly correct words that Perfect Speller does not recognize but which you do.

i   Ignore the word not recognized by Perfect Speller.

c   Allows you to view the word in context to see how it is used, so you can be sure of its misspelling.

r   Enter the word's root into the dictionary. For example, selecting this option will put *profit* out of *profiting* or *misspell* out of *misspelled* into the dictionary—thereby permitting recognition by Perfect Speller of variant spellings using those root words.

e   Tells Perfect Speller to mark with a circumflex or "up arrow" (⌃) the mis-spelled words at once, and to return you to the Edit Text function. You can then isolate (by a search for ⌃) and correct all misspellings.

While Perfect Speller is a fine program, we do not think it is as powerful a program as that offered by The WORD Plus. Try them both and see if you don't agree.

Appendix C

Perfect Calc for
Imperfect Calculators

This chapter will introduce you to Perfect Calc, Version 1.10, which is one of several financial spreadsheets that have been bundled with your KAYPRO. Perfect Calc is more complex than either Profitplan or Microplan, and we will make no recommendations about which may be better. The issue for you is which one will suit your needs best.

OVERVIEW

"Perfect" is the name of the software company that wrote the program, and everyone would not apply that adjective to their products. This spreadsheet is very complex, and it can do a number of things for you. To obtain your decision about using Perfect Calc, we will list the kinds of options available to you in the program.

General Options. Perfect Calc can manipulate as many as seven spreadsheets at one time. It can show you two of these at once by splitting the screen horizontally or vertically, which can be very useful for analyzing data.

Family or Individual Options. The package also includes a family budget program, a financial net worth program, a check register program, and an individual tax analysis program. Note: in version 1.10 this program is keyed to the 1981 tax tables, and it needs to be updated to be used. Further, it simply spreads out Schedule A does not deal with other sometimes necessary schedules, like Schedule C. In addition, there are the bases of a stock portfolio program, a real estate analysis program, a Chi-square analysis program (for statisticians), and a professional fee analysis program for consultants and other self-employed professionals.

Small Business Options. Small business applications include an income statement program, a cost of goods statement, a sales expense statement, a general and administrative expense statement, a cashflow assessment program, an accounts receivable worksheet, an accounts payable worksheet, and a payroll analysis program.

STARTING PERFECT CALC

Perfect Calc comes with a series of lessons on a lessons disk. We are going to walk you through the lessons because we think that exercise will be the most effective way for you to teach yourself how to run the system. Not surprisingly, you will go back and forth between this book, the lessons disk, and the keyboard. We hope that you will all interact. In any case, we will provide key information where you need it—including warnings about bugs—and a running list of key commands as they accumulate. This part of the chapter will be a guide to the lessons. When you finish them, you should be in shape to start Perfect Calc, and you can then go to the manual for additional material and reference.

We assume that you have already made your backup disks and that you have stored the masters safe from harm. We also assume that you have PIP and D on your backup disks. That way, if you lose a lesson—which can happen—you can simply PIP it back on to the copy lesson disk. STAT will allow you to keep track of how much space you have left on the disk, and SYSGEN will allow you to boot up the disk without switching disks all over the place. Commands in Perfect Calc have to be entered in lowercase letters. That's unusual, but that's the way it is. Unlock your CAPS LOCK.

THE INTRODUCTORY LESSON

1)   Insert your Perfect Calc disk in Drive A.
2)   Insert your Perfect Calc lessons disk in Drive B.
3) See the A> prompt.   Type **pc b:teachme.pc** ⟨Return⟩. Remember to use lowercase letters with all PerfectCalc commands. (For some odd reason the first lesson is called **teachme. pc,** while the other lessons are **lesson1, lesson2,** etc.)
4) See the screen labeled **teachme.**

Note: from here on we will keep a running list of commands that you will need to know and give other interpretations of the lessons designed to roll you through this process. Follow the lesson on the disk and refer to this manual when you need it. Our procedures are numbered, and otherwise we follow the numbers in the lesson.

5) To scroll the screen down.   Type CTRL v ⟨Return⟩ for "page down."
6) To scroll the screen up, or back to the
   beginning   Type CTRL z ⟨Return⟩.

LineLine 89 *Entry positions* are also called *cells.*

Line 100 The *prompt line* also tells you where the cursor is. In this screen it is at cell a85, for instance. That's handy for keeping track of where you are.

Line 107 The lesson tells us there should be a ∗ on the prompt line to indicate that the current *buffer* or file has not been saved. No star appears, and we take it that means the buffer has been saved.

Line 156 You have a choice with your KAYPRO of moving the cursor wth CTRL plus a key, or with the arrow keys. Stick with the arrow keys, or GOTO. They are direct.

Line 158 Now, we're getting to the split screen feature. Terrific.

Line 159

1) To split the screen   type CTRL x 2.

2) prompt will ask "SYNCHRONIZE WINDOWS?"   Type n for no, because you want them to move independently.

3) See the screen split.

Line 165 CTRL v and CTRL z operate the window where the cursor sits.

Line 175 CTRL x CTRL v, or CTRL x CTRL z are combined commands to scroll the information in the non-cursor window. CTRL x CTRL v moves it down, while CTRL x CTRL z moves it up.

Line 194 When they say to press *Enter* they mean Return.

Line 198

To remove the help window,   Type CTRL v.

Line 204

To move the cursor to the other window,   type CTRL x 0.

Line 212

To return to one window,   Type CTRL x 1.

Line 222

To cancel a command that has not been executed—meaning you haven't pressed RETURN yet   Type CTRL 9.

Line 228

1) To quit or return to CP/M,   Type CTRL x CTRL c.

2) See the A> prompt

Note: Normally, after you have entered an entire spreadsheet or data on one of them, you would type CTRL x CTRL s to save your material before you return to CP/M. Here, it has already been saved.

LESSON 1: MOVING AROUND THE SPREADSHEET

The scrolling and window moving commands that you learned in the first lesson continue.

Lines 47-48.

To call up a different spreadsheet,   type CTRL x CTRL f.

Lines 63-66 These lines give you Perfect Calc's internal commands for moving the cursor. If you use KAYPRO's arrows, you don't need them.

Lines 84-87 These commands move you to the boundaries of the spreadsheet that is showing.

Type CTRL a to move to the beginning of a row,
type CTRL e to move to the end of a row.
Type ESC < to move to the top of the column.
Type ESC> to move to the bottom of the column.
Note: we recommend using GOTO (which is described soon) or the arrows.

Line 103 Use KAYPRO's arrows.
Line 117

To use the GOTO to get to any position on the sheet,	Type> coordinates like a1 or z128 and Return.

Line 131

1) To find HELP on the screen	Type a question mark.
2) See a menu of HELP submenus; pick one.	Type the number of your choice.
3) To return to a normal screen,	Type any page movement command.

Line 133 The universal repeat command is useful for data and formula entry, but stick to GOTO when you are searching. Type CTRL u and an arrow key.

Line 155

1) Clear entire emory	Type CTRL x CTRL k.
2) Find a file	Type CTRL x CTRL f.
3) Prompt asks for the name of the file	Type **b:lesson1.pc** for this lesson, or the name of any file preceded by a drive name, like b:.

Line 170

1) To quit and go to CP/M,	Type CTRL x CTRL c.
2) Prompt asks, "Ignore changes this session?"	Type y if the material has been saved, or if you want to chuck the changes made in Lesson 1.

LESSON 2: ENTERING DATA

This lesson centers on entering data, labels, and formulas, as well as changing formulas.

Lines 26-45. These lines show you how to enter numbers in a cell.
Lines 27-30

To enter any number in a table,	Type = or – or . or any digit, followed by Return.

Line 43 Numbers default to two places.
Lines 55-60. These show you the symbols for the different arithmetic functions you may enter in a formula:

$\wedge$ multiply to the power of (works only with positive integers).

163

         * multiplication
         / division
         + addition
         − subtraction

Line 85

1) Enter a formula	Type = (c6−d6)/d6 ⟨Return⟩.
2) See −0.20, which means your stock lost 20 percent.	

Line 96

To change a label	Type an equals sign, meaning Edit Entry.

Lines 103-106. These are internal commands you can ignore by using the arrow keys, with the exception of CTRL d (delete cursor character), DEL (delete characters backward), and CTRL g (cancel and return to original formula).

Line 118

To change a formula, for example, by multiplying the old formula by 100,	Use arrow key to insert needed elements: a left parenthesis before the one in the formula, and a right parenthesis after d6. Then add *100 and press Return.

Line 130 Use GOTO here by typing> e18.

Line 185

1) To use a number for a label,	Type = # " first.
2) See LABEL	Type number as a label.

Line 187 Use GOTO again.

Line 190 Use your RIGHT arrow key.

LESSON 3: STORING AND PRINTING YOUR SPREADSHEET

This lesson reviews the printing commands as well as other commands.

Line 29   SAVE with Perfect Calc is typical of a lot of software programs in that saving a file of the same name erases the old one.

Line 34   SAVE is known as *writing to a file.* It is a good idea to do it regularly to guard against power failures and General Murphy. To do so, type CTRL x CTRL s.

Line 47

1) To write a file to another filename,	Press CTRL x CTRL w to write file to another name.

Line 78

1) To print a *region*, you need to define its beginning and its end.	Move the cursor to the first cell, type ESC space bar (mark set).
2)	Move the cursor to the last cell, check your printer for paper, etc., and type CTRL x p ⟨Return⟩ to print file.

Line 101

If you want to build your sheet into a Perfect Writer file,

Use the extent **.mss**. This format will, however, take more money than a **.pc** extent.

LESSON 4: REPLICATING FORMULAS, INSERTING, DELETING AND MOVING

Replicating sounds like technobabble to us, so let's say *duplicating*, which is a legitimate word. In any case, this lesson tells you how to copy a formula, insert or delete it, and how to move around in your table. This is all very worthwhile stuff to know because it will help you to be flexible with your spreadsheets.

Lines 43-49. The Perfect Software people have entered the same formula for each column across the spreadsheet. Now, we'll see how to duplicate a formula, and some other good stuff.

Line 55: Duplicating a Formula

1) To enter a formula

Move the cursor to the starting cell and type an equals sign (=) to start a formula. Type sum(b13:b16) ⟨Return⟩.

2) See the prompt b18=.
3) To Save the formula for duplication in a different location,

Type CTRL w.

4) There will be no answering prompt.
5) To "sct mark at b18" (letting Perfect Calc know where to begin using the formula).

Type ⟨ESC⟩ space bar.

6) Move the cursor to the other boundary.

Type CTRL e.

Line 82

7) *Yankback* means to install the formula in row 18 from column a to column m.

Type ESC y.

8) Prompt asks "variable?" for the range (b13 to m16),

Type y at each prompt.

9) Move the cursor back to b18 and observe.

Line 112: Inserting a Row

1) To open a space in your rows.

Type CTRL 0.

2) See cursor at new line 16.

Press the space bar three times.

3) See it appear on the prompt line.

Type ⟨Return⟩ to enter it in the table.

4) "Total Cash Flow Out" appears at line 19 nwo, and the new formula, sum(b13:b17), is automatically building in the new line.

Line 142: Inserting a Column

1) To insert a column,

Move the cursor to the desired space. Type ESC o.

2) See a new blank column inserted.

Line 151: Deleting a Row

1) To delete a row,

Move the cursor to the entry position, and type CTRL.

2) See the row deleted.

Line 167: Deleting a Column

To delete a column,

Move the cursor to the column and Type ESC c.

Note: If you delete a row, column, or cell, you are likely to affect computations in other parts of the spreadsheet, and that could lead to error messages.

Line 181 *Yankback* now has two meanings. The first was to install a formula across a row (backwards). The second and new meaning is to restore something you have deleted.

To restore a deletion

Type CTRL y.

Line 301: Moving Data

1) If you want to move a row, you need to delete it first and then use Yankback to put it in a new place.

Move the cursor to row 15 and type CTRL c.

2) See "postage" disappear.

Move the cursor to line 15 and type CTRL y.

Line 216: Saving Data

1) To save data or changes to your spreadsheet,

Type CTRL x CTRL w (save table).

2) The prompt asks for the filename— the lesson forgets to tell you to include the drive name—so

Type **b:cash1.pc** ⟨Return⟩.

Line 222. To exit to CP/M, type CTRL x CTRL c.

Line 226. The program does *not* ask "Ignore changes this session?" It simply does a warm boot.

LESSON 5: COPYING BETWEEN SPREADSHEETS

This lesson contains useful information that will build on what you learned in Lesson 4. It will be necessary if you want to work with more than one spreadsheet.

Line 22.   Copying is different from deleting because it copies a table and its data to a *save buffer*, leaving the old table and data in place. It *will* overwrite a file of the same name when it copies to the new location. In this way it functions like PIP, although it is internal to Perfect Calc. When the operation is finished the table and its data will exist in two places.

Line 36. A long routine to copy information from one sheet to another starts here. We will continue to summarize commands in the right column of this page.

Preparing the Spreadsheet

1) To split the screen,

Move the cursor to a11. Type CTRL x 2, which means to create two windows.

2) Move the cursor to the upper window.

Type CTRL x o, which means move cursor to the *other* window.

3) To install the spreadsheet,

Type CTRL x CTRL f.

4) Prompt asks for filename

Type b;cash1.pc ⟨Return⟩.

5) See the spreadsheet in the upper window. Start a new file.

Type CTRL x CTRL f.

6) Prompt asks for filename

Type **b:cash83.pc** ⟨Return⟩. The lesson forgets to tell you to include the drive name, which you need on all Perfect Calc data files.

Note: In line 67 the indicator is in the lower right corner of the screen, not the lower left as the lesson indicates.

7) Switch buffers, or create a memory storage area.

Type CTRL x b ⟨Return⟩.

8) Name the *old* buffer.

Type **cash1** ⟨Return⟩.

9) Now we are going to copy the labels in cash1 to cash83, and we have to define the region to be copied.

Move the cursor to a1 and type ESC space bar.

10) See Mark Set at a1.

Move cursor to bottom of column and type ESC>.

11) Cursor moves to a20.

Type ESC w, which here means to copy column.

12) Switch buffers to check that everything is OK.

Type CTRL x b ⟨Return⟩.

13) Switch to Buffer means name the buffer, or if you have only one other buffer, which is the case here.

Press ⟨Return⟩.

14) See cash83 a1. To put the labels in the new buffer

Type CTRL y ⟨Return⟩.

15) Return to cash1.pc.

Type CTRL x b ⟨Return⟩.

16) Now copy the names of the months.

Type ESC space bar.

17) Use GOTO to travel to the end of the region.

Type>, n3. Note: the end is n3, not m3 as advertised.

18) Copy these labels to the new buffer.	Type ESC w.
19) Check it out.	Type CTRL x b ⟨Return⟩.
20) Add copied region to cash83.	Type CTRL y ⟨Return⟩.
21) If you want see the buffer directory,	Type CTRL x CTRL b.
22) *They* tell you not to save cash83, but you know how to do a save if you want to.	Type CTRL x CTRL c and exit to CP/M.

LESSON 6: SETTING UP THE SPREADSHEET

This lesson covers the following procedures: justifying entries within columns, changing column widths, and changing the display formats to show whole numbers, decimals, and dollars and cents.

1)	Move cursor to all.
2) Create two windows.	Type CTRL x 2.
3) Move cursor to top window.	Type CTRL x o.
4) Create a new file with Find File.	Type CTRL x CTRL f.
5) The prompt asks for a filename.	Type b:sales.pc ⟨Return⟩.
6) Change column width from 9 to 15 characters.	Type CTRL x w.
7) The prompt asks "global or column?" You are only changing the column, so	Type c.
8) Repeat the column procedure for columns b, c, and d.	Move cursor to column b. Type CTRL x w Type c Type 12.
9) Change column c.	Move cursor to column c. Type CTRL x w Type c Type 2.
10) Change Column d.	Move cursor to column d. Type CTRL x w, Type c, Type 12.
11) Enter column labels.	Move cursor to a1. Type Month ⟨Return⟩. Move cursor to b1. Type Sales ⟨Return⟩. Move cursor to d1. Type Graph ⟨Return⟩.

There is a mistake in line 66 (*bug* we call it in technobabble). CTRL x CTRL j, Justify Entry, comes back as unknown on our copy of the lessons disk. Use CTRL X J and it should work.

12) Enter dashes to separate labels from the numbers to come. (Remember, the quote makes a dash into a label for Perfect Calc.)

Move cursor to a2.
Type "———— ⟨Return⟩.
Move cursor to b2
Type "————— ⟨Return⟩.

13) Return to the original sheet to copy the data (that means go back to line 34) or follow our instruction in step 14.

14) To enter data

Move cursor to d3
Type January ⟨Return⟩.
Move cursor to a3.
Type January ⟨Return⟩.
Move cursor to b3.
Type 152000 ⟨Return⟩.
Move cursor to a4.
Type February ⟨Return⟩.
Move cursor to b4.
Type 133854 ⟨Return⟩.
Move cursor to a5.
Type March ⟨Return⟩.
Move cursor to b5.
Type 141000.59 ⟨Return⟩.
Move cursor to a6.
Type April ⟨Return⟩.
Move cursor to b6.
Type 82000 ⟨Return⟩.
Move cursor to a7.
Type May ⟨Return⟩.
Move cursor to b7.
Type 198000 ⟨Return⟩.
Move cursor to a8.
Type June ⟨Return⟩.
Move cursor to b8.
Type 305000 ⟨Return⟩.
Move cursor to a10 (leave a9 blank).
Type TOTAL SALES ⟨Return⟩.
Move cursor to b10.
Type =sum(b3:b8 ⟨Return⟩.

15) Back to line 91 in the bottom window. You have entered the start of a spreadsheet.

16) Now there are options for displaying your numbers.

Type CTRL x d to change display format.

17) The prompt then shows the options:
0-13 decimal places (default two).
Sci = two places after exponent E.
f   = display formula at entry point.
*   = graphic notation.
$ = dollars and cents. If you don't
          want cents, Perfect Calc will
          round to the nearest dollar.
⟨CR⟩ = return to default of two places.   Type $ ⟨Return⟩.

Note: use of the $ option builds in commas, but it leaves the total in scientific notation because the numbers given you are too big for the size of the column. If you want to see the entire number, you have to return and format column b so that it will be large enough to hold the numbers.

Lines 143-201. These tell you how to make a "graph" from stars. We consider the activity a waste of time because it will distort large values, and it will present a truly graphic picture. However, if you find this representation useful, please follow the instructions.

LESSON 7: USING ASSOCIATED FILES

This lesson is useful and valuable if you want to use the multiple file function of Perfect Calc. The key idea in this lesson is that files must be chained in order of dependency. If you are designing an accounting system, for example, and you intend to use this multiple file category, it would be a good idea to set up a flowchart of the relationship of the different files before you enter labels and data.

Lines 64-66. These point out that you have to "force" a calculation in one spreadsheet to make it affect another. Also, all spreadsheets that will be linked— "associated" they call it—must be in memory in order to work with one other.

One key command is CTRL x a, which means *associate files*, and you have to enter this command every time you add another spreadsheet. When you leave one sheet for another, to keep it in the buffer you must save it with CTRL x CTRLs. After you have used these commands once for each of the associated files, you may use the Find File command, CTRL x CTRL f. Please follow their example to see how this works.

Line 129 Note that **rental.pc** shows up in the top window. not **unit2.pc** as advertised.

Line 168 As it stands, the sample fails to deduct the cost of the mortgage, making it look as if you have $346.75 positive cash flow. The formula reads correctly, and it's not clear why it left out the mortgage. Too bad we all can't do that, although the banks would not like it. Re-enter the formula at b5 by typing =**unit1[b19]**, and you will see the correct negative cash flow appear at b5, −$3.25.

We advise extreme caution when using this system to make sure that it has not left out something critical, like your mortgage payment. John Bear, Ph.D. advises in his *Computer Wimp* to run a paper system in parallel with your new computer-based accounting system for at least six months to check that it is running properly. Good advice, we think.

Line 182. The same error occurs here. Re-enter **=unit2[b19]** at line b6, and the formula will compute correctly. Very odd! This is known as a *bug* in technobabble, or the work of General Murphy's troops. Or, did Perfect neglect to save the formula?

LESSON 8: CONCLUDING SUGGESTIONS

This lesson tells you that you can transfer Perfect Calc sheets data, and reports to Perfect Writer, but it doesn't tell you how to do it. Earlier, they noted that you needed to add a **.mss** extent to any file that you wanted to transfer to Perfect Writer.

Perfect Calc is a very interesting program, and it probably works as well as most other spreadsheets of its generation. With this sheet, or any other, be cautious, protect your data by running a parallel paper system for at least one year.

Appendix D
Perfect Filer

W hen Perfect Filer is used in conjuction with Perfect Writer it will give you a jazzed-up version of MailMerge used in conjunction with WordStar. But you pay a price with Perfect Filer because it takes many steps to get the form letter out. While we were able to get the routine shown below to run successfully, we do not make any other claims for Perfect Filer as a database program. You can do more with DataStar, for example—and a lot more easily at that.

INDIVIDUAL AND ORGANIZATION DATABASES

This series of *related data records* constitutes a database which you may, at will, manipulate in one of several ways: that is, you can add data to it, delete information from it, call up information for special related subgroups from the whole, move information from it to another "new" database named differently, and so forth.

The Perfect Filer INDIVIDUAL and ORGANIZATION database records are shown in Figs. D-1 and D-2.

PERFECT FILER MENU STRUCTURE

Seeing the various menus and submenus of Perfect Filer will give you some idea of the program's capabilities. Seeing how the one main and six secondary menus are interrelated gives you some idea of what Perfect Filer can and cannot do.

1st Level Main Menu:	1.0	MAIN MENU (Individual Member Database)
	1.1	Access Individual Members

```
First Name:              Middle:                 Last:
Title:          Salutation: (Dear)              Title2:

Organization:
Address1:
Address2:
City:                           State:      Zip:
Country:

Home Phone: (    )    -
Business Phone: (    )     -

Contact Person:

                                                Active:
Comment1:
Comment2:


                                        Date Entered:  /  /
```

Fig. D-1. Perfect Filer individual database record.

```
Organization:
Address1:
Address2:
City:                           State:      Zip:
Country:

Phone: (    )    -

Contact Person:

                                                Active:
Comment:
:


                                        Date Entered:  /  /
```

Fig. D-2. Perfect Filer organizational database record.

2nd Level	MAIN MENU
Submenus and	
Their Respective	
Submenus (*)	
1.6	DEFINE PRINTER FORM
1.6.1	Printer Form Definition
1.6.1.1	*Add a Printer Form
1.6.1.2	*Review/Revise a Printer Form
1.6.1.3	*Delete a Printer Form

SETTING UP YOUR DISKS

You have to run through a laborious file copying process before you can use Perfect Filer. Figure D-3 illustrates that process. With the figure in mind use the familiar PIP B:=A: format to copy the following files to create the Individual Member database:

MEMBER.H	SS.SAV
HASHTAB	LISTFORM.SAV
LABEL.TXT	SSDESC.SAV
DB.TXT	MAILFORM.SAV
DB.DEF	LFORMDSC.SAV
MAILTEST.MSS	LABEL2.TXT
SSLIST.SAV	MFORMDSC.SAV

Next, using PIP, create the Organizational Member Database disk. There is no MAILTEST.MSS file on this disk because it is not needed. You need to copy the following files:

DATABASE	DB.DEF
LABEL2.TXT	SSLIST.SAV
MFORMDSC.SAV	SS.SAV
MEMBER.H	LISTFORM.SAV
HASHTAB	SSDESC.SAV
LABEL.TXT	MAILFORM.SAV
DB.TXT	LFORMDSC.SAV

If you did the above correctly, you are now ready to use the software.

USING PERFECT FILER'S MAIL CAPABILITIES

You can use Perfect Filer to generate personalized form letters, but you must first create your letter via Perfect Writer. Here is how to go about it.

1) Set up the proper disk relationship to create via Perfect Writer a form letter, which will then be saved to Disk B

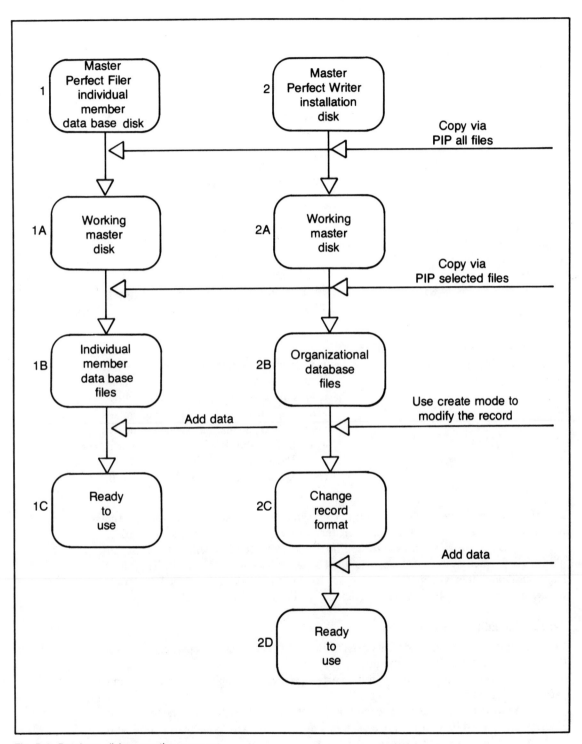

Fig. D-3. Database disk generation process.

(because ALL database files *must* reside on the database disk itself if Perfect Filer is to find and operate on them via its program routines).

Take all disks out of the KAYPRO, put the Individual Member Database disk (containing the files just transferred to it) into Drive B; put Perfect Writer into Drive A; reboot the KAYPRO.

2) Get Perfect Writer's Main Menu on the console.

At the A>, enter MENU ⟨Return⟩.

3) Give the letter a filename and tells Perfect Writer to save this file to the disk in Drive B, so Perfect Filer can find it when running the Perfect Filer program.

Select option E, to edit a file, from the Main Menu. Name this file B: FORMLTR.MSS.

4) Using the correct commands, you are able to create the letter shown below.

In creating the letter, use only the Perfect Writer and Perfect Filer formatting commands in the letter's text as shown below. Why? Because Perfect Filer recognizes only these command forms and not others available in the Perfect Writer world. Also, Perfect Filer has its own formatting commands, which are given below as well.

Here are the Perfect Filer formatting commands that you should use when putting together letters, etc., with Perfect Writer, that you wish to generate via Perfect Filer.

First, *Do not use tabs when creating the letter.* Perfect Filer will not accept tabs placed via Perfect Writer; instead, you'll get an error message (ASCII 9). Therefore, laborious though it is, you must use the space bar to create indents from the left margin. Sorry, but that is one "interactive" deficiency of Perfect Writer and Perfect Filer.

Perfect Filer Edit Commands

⟨**format**⟩. This command tells Perfect Filer to begin formatting a passage of text in the input file into paragraph structure.

⟨**unformat**⟩. This command tells Perfect Writer to stop formatting text into paragraph structure.

Vertical Bar (¦). This is the conditional hyphenation format command for Perfect Filer. When placed in a letter, for example, Perfect Filer will hyphenate a long word (e.g., accomplish¦ment) at the place the bar is positioned.

⟨**paragraph**⟩. This tells Perfect Filer to begin a new paragraph when you are using Perfect Filer's formatting command structure.

⟨**newline**⟩. This command tells Perfect Filer to start a new line of text when you are using Filer's formatting command structure.

⟨**under**⟩. Perfect Filer begins underlining at this command.

⟨**nounder**⟩. This tells Perfect Filer to stop underlining.

Backslash (/). This character tells Perfect Filer to treat the character following as it appears and not to insert two spaces following. An example might be a period occuring in the middle of a sentence.

The left and right angle bracket symbols ⟨ ⟩ also mark the spot where the "non-canned" or personalized information will be inserted into the letter once it is written via Perfect Writer, saved to disk B, and then reaccessed by its filename for use in conjunction with Perfect Filer. You *must enter in the angle brackets only the same data field names—today, name, etc.—used to identify the data fields in the individual records themselves. Otherwise, Perfect Filer will look for recognizable—because identical—field descriptors; not finding them, it will not know where to put any special or personalized information into the otherwise canned letter.*

Figure D-4 shows a sample letter formatted with the above characters and commands. Once the letter is written, there are some additional tasks to be performed.

1) Save the letter text to the Drive B disk Baxter's database disk for individuals.

Enter a CTRL X CTRL W.

2) Let Perfect Writer run the letter text through the Perfect Writer format program. (This does not mean Baxter wouldn't have Perfect Filer do its formatting to use all those ⟨ ⟩ tag commands. Filer runs them automatically when the Filer program is run, as you'll find out.)

When given the Main Menu for Perfect Writer, select F to have Perfect Writer format the letter.

3) Set the file up on disk B so Filer can format it when the program is run to generate mail.

Also from the formatter selection menu, enter D to tell Perfect Formatter to send the formatted file to a different device.

4) Run the Perfect Formatter program. When the Formatter is finished, the letter will be on the disk in Drive B, and it will appear with a new extension, i.e., FORMLTR.FIN. FIN is always given to all files that are run though Perfect Formatter's program, the only exception being the V option, or VERBATIM format.

Select Option G

```
@STYLE(topmargin 55 lines, leftmargin 0 lines, linewidth 65
chars)
@ADDRESS (BSA, Inc.,
101 Bond Market Street
New York, New York 10001)
@BEGIN (FLUSHLEFT)
<today>


<name>
<address>


<salutation(name)>:
@END (FLUSHLEFT)

<format>
<paragraph>
     Thank you so much for meeting with me so we could discuss
how your firm and mine might mutually benefit by way of doing
business together. I have great hopes that we will be able to
reach a common ground, one on which we can both <under> make more
money and have a good time to boot<nounder>!

<newline>
<paragraph>
     I was particularly impressed by what you had to say about
your current and projected needs, ones that Aggrandizement &
Associates happens to be, so I believe, well positioned to meet.
<newline>
<paragraph>
     I will contact you in a week to ten days to see what you
think of the information contained on the brief enclosed
brochure. It describes many of our client services, and also
lists a few of the hundreds of our satisfied clients.
<newline>
<paragraph>
     Again, thanks for meeting with me on my trip to Los Angeles.
It was most enjoyable spending some time with you\; and I trust
we'll be getting together again in the near future.
<unformat>

Sincerely,

Baxter $. Aggrandizement
President
```

Fig. D-4. Sample letter generated by Perfect Filer.

5) Set up disks for running the Filer program. The database is now in Drive B, and the Filer Program is in Drive A.

Exit Perfect Writer, remove the Perfect Writer disk from Drive A, put the *backup copy* of Perfect Filer Individual Member disk in Drive A.

6) Bring up the Perfect Filer Program on the console.

Drive A, reboot, at the A> enter FILER ⟨Return⟩.

7) Tell Filer that the database disk is in Drive B. This disk contains the letter, the files transferred to it earlier via PIP, and it also contains PIP and STAT.

At the prompt "Enter disk drive containing data base:" enter B: ⟨Return⟩.

8) The Date Change Menu (Fig. D-5) appears next.

Hitting your space bar or your Return key moves the X down to the "Change Date" line. Hitting the backspace key permits you to move the X up. Pressing the X once, followed by ⟨Return⟩, will allow you to enter, numerically, the correct month (e.g., 01, 06, or 12); then the same numeric format and procedure are used to enter the correct day of the month. For example, 01, 09, 84 would be January 9, 1984, and 01,01,01 would be January 1, 2001.

9) You get the Master Menu for the Individual Member database, (shown in Fig. D-6.

Enter your final carriage after the date change procedure.

Current Date = 28 February 1984

        x   Date Correct

           Change Date

Fig. D-5. Perfect Filer date change menu.

```
┌──────────────────────────────────────────────────────────────────┐
│                                                                    │
│      INDIVIDUAL MEMBER DATA BASE                                   │
│                                                                    │
│                      x      Access Individual Members              │
│                                                                    │
│                             Generate List/Report                   │
│                                                                    │
│                             Generate Mail                          │
│                                                                    │
│                             Define Subset                          │
│                                                                    │
│                             Define List Form                       │
│                                                                    │
│                             Define Printer Form                    │
│                                                                    │
└──────────────────────────────────────────────────────────────────┘
```

Fig. D-6. Individual database master menu.

10) Avoid losing any data when leaving Perfect Filer.

You must *always* enter the database via this Main Menu, and you must exit the database via this top-order Main Menu.

GENERATING THE "CANNED" MARKETING LETTER

1) When the Main Menu (for the Individual Member database) appears on the console, do the following—with respect to the logical menu heirarchy options given above:

2) Access Individual Members.

Press X.

3) Add New Members (enter the 50 individual records).

Press the Return or CTRL C keys, moving backward by pressing the CTRL P, erasing an individual data entry by entering a CTRL P and hitting the space bar. Press X.

4) Exit the individual record, bringing up the option to save or discard member's data just entered.

Press ⟨ESC⟩.

5) Select the SAVE option to preserve the member's data just entered in the record.

Press X. Do above steps until all 50 records have been entered.

6) Exit the Access Individual Members (1.1) submenu.

Press ⟨ESC⟩ until you return to the top level (1.0) of the Main Menu.

7) Load the Generate Mail Program.

Press Return to move the X down to the option Generate Mail; when the X is there, press the X key.

8) Load the canned marketing letter into Perfect Filer, which also formats the letter's text—much as Perfect Formatter would.

See the prompt "Enter Name of File:" enter FORMLTR.FIN, followed by a carriage return.

9) Tell Perfect Filer that you will use *only* single sheet stationery. You must have an adequate supply on hand, having already put one sheet in the printer, which you have also turned on.

Seeing Select Printer Form Menu (1.3.1), press Return to position the X at SINGLE SHEET LETTERS; then press X to exit this submenu.

10) Tell Perfect Filer that the output will be sent to the printer. (It will also appear on the console simultaneously, unless the X is pressed at the CRT toggle option.

Seeing the next submenu, Mail Target Selection, press Return to select the printer; press X, then hit ⟨ESC⟩.

11) Tell Perfect Filer that you wish to specify a subset of records from the total of 50 records.

Seeing the next submenu, HOW DO YOU WISH TO SPECIFY RECIPIENTS, press Return to move the X to SUBSET, then press X.

12) Tell Perfect Filer to generate the canned marketing letter (FORMLTR. FIN) for every one of the 50 individuals whose records you filled-in.

As the Subset Selection Menu, press Return to position the X by the selection ALL MEMBERS.

13) The program starts generating the 50
    form letters, stopping after each letter
    to permit you to insert a fresh sheet of
    letterhead.   Press ⟨ESC⟩.

```
First Name:              Middle:              Last:
Title:          Salutation: (Dear)           Title2:

Organization:
Address1:
Address2:
City:                   State:      Zip:
Country:

Home Phone: (    )    -
Business Phone: (    )    -

Contact Person:
                                             Active:

Comment1:
Comment2:

                                   Date Entered:  /  /
```

Fig. D-7. Unmodified organization record.

Appendix E

KAYPRO Users' Groups

KAYPRO's users' Groups have sprung up around the country, and they are very helpful to the novice and the advanced user alike. Besides offering access to a community of KAYPRO owners, they also usually are an introduction to a vast library of CP/M software that is in the public domain. That means that it is not copyrighted, and that for a couple of dollars you can obtain copies of any of this software that you want.

The groups usually have monthly meetings with presentations and discussions, and they are introduced to personal networking with your KAYPRO. These groups grow and change with amazing rapidity, and this list that follows was current in February of 1984. KAYPRO users' groups have no official relationship with the KAYPRO Corporation. Therefore, we can take no responsibility for the accuracy of the information in the list below, nor for the activities of the groups themselves. For further information you may contact the group nearest you, or you may write to KUG Manager, KAYPRO, Inc., 533 Stevens Ave., Solana Beach, CA 92075.

ALABAMA

Birmingham Area KUG
4165 Sharpsburg Dr.
Birmingham, AL 35213

ALASKA

ANKOR
1705 Bartlett Dr.
Anchorage, AK 99507

ARIZONA

AKUG
13829 N. 19th Ave.
Phoenix, AZ 85023

TUSKUG
P.O. Box 12083
Tucson, AZ 85732

CALIFORNIA

KAYPOWER
853 N. Dickel
Anaheim, CA 92805

Sacramento KUG
7001 Brookcrest Way
Citrus Heights, CA 95610

KUG—N. San Gabriel Valley
1416 N. Indian Hill Blvd.
Clairemont, CA 91711

KUG—S. Orange County
24601 Raymond Way
El Toro, CA 92630

LA-KUG
c/o Wordmovers
15818 Hawthorne Blvd.
Lawndale, CA 90260

LAKUG
3133 Corinth Ave.
Los Angeles, CA 90066

UCLA/USC KUG
Richard Baum
Political Science Dept., UCLA
Los Angeles, CA 90024

K-WEST
1924 Beryl Lane
Newport Beach, CA 92660

BAK-UP
P.O. Box 20181
Oakland, CA 94620

KSIG
N. Orange County Computer Club
P.O. Box 3616
Orange, CA 92665

KSIG
San Diego Computer Society
P.O. Box 81537
San Diego, CA 92138

San Francisco KUG
3515 Sacramento
San Francisco, CA 94118

COLAVKUG
1105 Coleman Ave.
San Jose, CA 95108

North Bay KUG
1266 Kerney St.
Santa Rosa, CA 95401

SRKUG
4772 Sunshine Ave.
Santa Rosa, CA 95405

Santa Cruz KUG
1005 Cedar St.
Santa Cruz, CA 95060

SDCSKSIG
9235 Lake Hill Rd.
Santee, CA 92071

San Fernando Valley KUG
18639 Ventura Blvd.
Tarzana, CA 91356

TUG
P.O. Box 323
Tehachapi, CA 93561

SOBOKUG
2839 Pacific Coast Hwy.
Torrance, CA 90505

N. San Diego County KUG
171 Unity Way
Vista, CA 92083

S. San Gabriel Valley KUG
P.O. Box 9253
Whittier, CA 90608

CP/M KUG
22554 Tiara St.
Woodland Hills, CA 91367

COLORADO
Aspen KUG
117 S. Spring St.
Aspen, CO 81611

Denver KAYPRO Assoc.
2153 S. Lewiston St.
Aurora, CO 80013

KAYPRO User's Association of
Fort Collins
636 S. College #152
Fort Collins, CO 80524

DENKA
P.O. Box 1507
Wheatridge, CO 80034

CONNECTICUT
CTKUG
P.O. Box 9235
New Haven, CT 06533

FLORIDA
KAPPA
P.O. Box 1563
Gulf Breeze, FL 32561

S. Florida KUG
1901 N. State RD. 7
Hollywood, FL 33021

Tamp Bay KUG
14 Cypress Dr.
Palm Harbor, FL 33563

Tallahassee KUG
3312 Lake Shore Dr. W.
Tallahasse, FL 32312

GEORGIA
KUGA
2173 W. Broad St.
Athens, GA 30606

GAKUG
742-A Lakeside Dr.
Warner-Robbins, GA 31098

HAWAII
HPCUG
578 Ala Moana Blvd.
Honolulu, HI 96813

ILLINOIS
SKyP
1701 E. 53rd St.
Chicago, IL 60637

WESKUG
320 May Ave.
Glen Ellyn, IL 60131

KOOC
433 Elder Lane
Glenview, IL 60025

Central Illinois KUG
P.O. Box 2487
Springfield, IL 62705

Champaign/Urbana KUG
602 W. Stoughton
Urbana, IL 61801

ChiKUG
605 Illinois Rd.
Wilmette, IL 60091

INDIANA
CIKUG
5230 E. 65th St.
Indianapolis, IN 46220

IOWA
Iowa KUG
Box 1250
Ames, IA 50010

KENTUCKY

KAYPRO Lexington Users' Group
Ovation Computers
140 Moore Dr.
Lexington, KY 40503

LOUISIANA

S. Louisiana KUG
3468 Drusilla Lane
Baton Rouge, LA 70809

MAINE

KUGME
RFD #2 Lincoln Rd.
Saco, ME 04072

MASSACHUSETTS

Cambridge KUG
Box 308
Prudential Center Station
Boston, MA 02199

Worcester Area KUG
8 Tanglewood Rd.
Paxton, MA 01612

Boston KUG
27 Howland Rd.
West Newton, MA 01265

BOSCOS
23 Derby Lane
Weston, MA 02193

MICHIGAN

Ann Arbor KUG
1400 Morton #2B
Ann Arbor, MI 48104

D:KUG
P.O. Box 1517 Trolley Station
Detroit, MI 48231

Detroit Metropolitan Area KUG
4900 Leafdale
Royal Oak, MI 90608

MINNESOTA

KUMIN
10338 Colorado Rd.
Bloomington, MN 55438

MISSOURI

SLKUG
Box 31126
St. Louis, MO 63131

NEVADA

Las Vegas KUG
3600 Swenson St., #331
Las Vegas, NV 89109

Three-State KAYPRO
1350 Davidson Way
Reno, NV 89509

NEW JERSEY

NJKUG
P.O. Box 326
Rockyhill, NJ 08553

KUGNJ
742 Coolidge St.
Westfield, NJ 07090

NEW MEXICO

Santa Fe KUG
836 El Caminito
Santa Fe, NM 87501

NEW YORK

Buffalo KUG
66 Russell Ave.
Buffalo, NY 14214

KUGOR
17th Fifth Ave.
Fairport, NY 14450

LATKUG
16 Maple St.
Latham/Albany, NY 12110

KUGRAM
P.O. Box 100
Malverne, NY 11565

LIKUG
20 Buckingham Place
Manhasset, NY 11030

NYKUG
300 E. 46th
New York, NY 10017

NATKUG
Box 28360
Queens Village, NY 11428

CENYKUG
1 Skadden Terrace
Tully, NY 13159

NORTH CAROLINA

Charlotte KUG
1808 E. Independence
Charlotte, NC 28205

Triad KUG
P.O. Box 8034
Greensboro, NC 27419

OHIO

Central Ohio KUG
6583 Brock St.
Dublin, OH 43017

KAYBUG
5236 Warrensville Center Rd.
Maple Heights, OH 44137

OREGON

DCUG
865 West 2nd
Eugene, OR 97402

EKUG
95 Coachman Dr.
Eugene, OR 97405

MKCUG
P.O. Box 214
Lebanon, OR 97355

NWKUG
P.O. Box 11
Portland, OR 97207

KSIG
Salem Area Computer Club
3920 Monroe Ave. N.E.
Salem, OR 97301

PENNSYLVANIA

Allentown KUG
Box 1902
Allentown, PA 18105

Delaware Valley KUG
132 S. 20th St.
Philadelphia, PA 19103

RHODE ISLAND

RHODY KUG
593 Pocasset Ct.
Warwick, RI 02886

SOUTH CAROLINA

KAYPRO Information Exchange
157 MacGregor Dr.
Summerville, SC 29483

Grand Strand Area KUG
Southeastern Computers
Lorraine Plaza
700 Highway 17 S.
Surfside Beach, SC 29577

TENNESSEE

Memphis KUG
5512 Poplar Ave.
Memphis, TN 38119

Nashville KUG
J & J Printers
1700 Hayes St.
Nashville, TN 37203

TEXAS

KAYPRO Club of Austin
1101 Cap. Texas Hwy. SE-101
Austin, TX 78746

El Paso KUG
4400 N. Mesa
El Paso, TX 79902

HKUG
16022 Lakeview
Houston, TX 77040

San Antonio KUG
2727 Woodley
San Antonio, TX 78232

WKUG
Box 6241
Waco, TX 76706

VIRGINIA

Richmond KUG
3019 Susquehanna Trail
Ashland, VA 23005

Charlottesville KUG
Box 3823
Charlottesville, VA 22903

Capitol KUG
P.O. Box 3693
McLean, VA 22103

TIDEKUG
29 Southern Shopping Ctr.
Norfolk, VA 23505

WASHINGTON

Sno-King KUG
21505 Jordan Rd.
Arlington, WA 98223

OKUG
6925 4th Way S.E.
Olympia, WA 98503

PAKUP
NW 110 Dillon
Pullman, WA 99163

Puget Sound KUG
1208 N. 32nd
Renton, WA 98056

KSIG
Spokane Microcomputer Users
Group
North 904 Dyer Rd.
Spokane, WA 99206

PUGSKUG
P.O. Box 922
Tacoma, WA 98401

TACKPUG
1201 S. 11th
Tacoma, WA 98405

Wa2-KPU
Rt. 2 Box 247
Walla Walla, WA 99362

WISCONSIN

MADKUG
1825 Monroe St.
Madison, WI 53711

WSEP
318 South K. St.
Sparta, WI 54656

WISKUG
2406 Springdale Rd., Apt. 101
Waukesha, WI 53186

WYOMING

Laramie Computer Club
P.O. Box 966
Laramie, WY 82070

CANADA

KUTE
181 University Ave., Suite 18
Toronto, ONT M5H 3M7

VIKOG
2584 Thompson Ave.
Victoria, BC V8R 3L3

Glossary

address—A number used by the computer to keep track of different memory locations.

array—A set of elements arranged in a pattern.

ASCII—Acronym for American Standard Code for Information Interchange, a 7-bit code for representing character data such as letters, punctuation, etc.

back up—To copy information or programs as a protective measure.

baud rate—The speed of serial communications; *baud* is used generally as meaning bits per second: 300 baud would be 300 bits/second or 30 characters per second.

BDOS—Acronym for Basic Disk Operating System, the section of CP/M that keeps track of disk files.

BIOS—Acronym for Basic Input/Output System; the section of CP/M that handles the hardware of the KAYPRO.

bit—A binary digit, the smallest piece of information a computer can handle. See also *byte*.

boot—Loading CP/M into the computer's memory from Drive A, *cold boot* occurs when the machine is first turned on; *warm boot* occurs when you press the CTRL and C keys simultaneously (see CP/M manual for details).

buffer—An area of memory set aside for storing and manipulating data associated with I/O devices, such as disks and keyboards.

bug—A problem or undesirable side-effect of a computer program, almost always unexpected and unwelcome (see *debug*).

byte—Eight bits, the size of a memory location in the KAYPRO; a computer "word." (A *kilobyte* or *kbyte* is one thousand bytes.)

CCP—Acronym for Console Command Processor, the section of CP/M that makes sense of what you type on the keyboard.

chip—Slang for an integrated circuit.

console—The device used for communication between the computer and you. Normally, this is the keyboard and the video display.

CP/M—Acronym for *Control Program for Microprocessors*. The most popular disk operating system for 8080 and Z-80 microcomputers, CP/M keeps track of the files and programs on the hard disk and the floppy disks and facilitates their use.

CPU—Acronym for Central Processing Unit: the microprocessor chip.

CRT—Acronym for Cathode Ray Tube: the "TV" tube used as the video display.

debug—To remove mistakes from a computer program (see *bug*).

DIR—A built-in CP/M command that lists the files of a user area diskette.

directory—The list of files in a user area or on a disk. The KAYPRO 10 allows 1000 different entries in the directory (see DIR and STAT), but on the hard disk there can be 1000 files.

file—A collection of characters, data, or what-have-you that is stored in a user area or on a disk. A file can contain a program or information to be used by other programs or manuscript, etc.

filename—The name of a file, which you see when you list the directory or use when you access a file. The general form for a filename is: B:NAME.MSS. The first part (A:, B: or C;) indicates which drive the file is in. The second part is the name, and can be up to eight characters long. The last part is called the extent, can be up to three characters long, and is separated from the name by a period.

floppy—A disk of magnetic media which is encased in a sturdy envelope. It stores data in areas called *files*.

format—The organization of data on a disk. A single-sided, double-density format on the floppy disk consists of 40 tracks per disk, with each track divided into 10 sectors.

hard disk—A fixed, durable disk for storing information magnetically. It is permanently located within the computer.

hardware—The physical parts of the computer and its peripheral equipment, as opposed to *software*.

high-level language—A computer programming language that is similar to English or mathematics. S-BASIC and Pascal, for example, are high-level languages.

input—Data put into the computer. By extension, the process or means of putting data into the computer.

load—To take information from a storage medium, such as a disk or tape and put it into the computer's memory.

machine language—A binary language that a computer can understand, as opposed to either assembly language (see the ASM section of your CP/M manual) or high-level languages like S-BASIC.

modem—Acronym for *modulator/ demodulator*, a device that connects a computer terminal to another computer terminal via a communications link such as the telephone system. With the KAYPRO, modems are connected directly to the RS-232C connector at the rear of the machine.

output—Information displayed or used

to control devices external to a computer. By extension, the process or means of getting information out of a computer.

peripheral—Any device connected to and used with your computer (e.g., a printer or modem).

pixel—An element or location on the screen for the purpose of forming characters or graphic displays.

program—A set of instructions for a computer; the *software*. When these instructions are in a high-level language like BASIC, they will always have to be converted into a set of low-level or machine language instructions by either an interpreter (M-BASIC) or a compiler (S-BASIC).

prompt—A unique character or characters displayed by a program to inform the user that the program requires some instruction or information. In CP/M, the A> is a prompt which indicates that the computer is waiting for the user to enter a command.

RAM—Acronym for *random access memory*, the memory that the computer uses for short-term storage of information and programs. Unlike ROM, the information stored in RAM is changeable and volatile, meaning it will disappear when the power to the computer is turned off.

ROM—Acronym for read-only memory, the memory that is used for unchanging information and programs. Information stored in ROM is not volatile, and will remain intact regardless of whether the power to the computer is on or off.

safety zone—a portion of a hard disk which is reserved as a space where the read-write head can move when it has nothing else to do. Also, the head must be moved to the safety zone before the computer is turned off. This is done by typing after the A> prompt; safety.

sector—A group of bytes on a disk. The standard KAYPRO double-density floppy disk has 10 sectors on each track, with each sector containing 512 bytes of information.

STAT—A CP/M program that gives the statistics of a disk's files, showing how much space (in kilobytes) each file is using and how much empty space is left on a disk.

track—A ring of information on a disk. A double-density floppy disk has 40 tracks.

user area—The 15 areas on a KAYPRO hard disk that are set up to hold files. They have no specific size, but adjust in size as necessary.

utility—A program often used, particularly by system programmers. For example, PIP is a utility program (details in the CP/M manual) that allows the transfer of files.

Index

OTHER POPULAR TAB BOOKS OF INTEREST

The Computer Era—1985 Calendar Robotics and Artificial Intelligence (No. 8031—$6.95)

Using and Programming the IBM PCjr®, including 77 Ready-to-Run Programs (No. 1830—$11.50 paper; $16.95 hard)

Word Processing with Your ADAM™ (No. 1766—$9.25 paper; $15.95 hard)

The First Book of the IBM PCjr® (No. 1760—$9.95 paper; $14.95 hard)

Going On-Line with Your Micro (No. 1746—$12.50 paper; $17.95 hard)

Mastering Multiplan™ (No. 1743—$11.50 paper; $16.95 hard)

The Master Handbook of High-Level Microcomputer Languages (No. 1733—$15.50 paper; $21.95 hard)

Apple Logo for Kids (No. 1728—$11.50 paper; $16.95 hard)

Fundamentals of TI-99/4A Assembly Language (No. 1722—$11.50 paper; $16.95 hard)

The First Book of ADAM™ the Computer (No. 1720—$9.25 paper; $14.95 hard)

BASIC Basic Programs for the ADAM™ (No. 1716—$8.25 paper; $12.95 hard)

101 Programming Surprises & Tricks for Your Apple II®/II®e Computer (No. 1711—$11.50 paper)

Personal Money Management with Your Micro (No. 1709—$13.50 paper; $18.95 hard)

Computer Programs for the Kitchen (No. 1707—$13.50 paper; $18.95 hard)

Using and Programming the VIC-20®, including Ready-to-Run Programs (No. 1702—$10.25 paper; $15.95 hard)

25 Games for Your TRS-80™ Model 100 (No. 1698—$10.25 paper; $15.95 hard)

Apple® Lisa™: A User-Friendly Handbook (No. 1691—$16.95 paper; $24.95 hard)

TRS-80 Model 100—A User's Guide (No. 1651—$15.50 paper; $21.95 hard)

How To Create Your Own Computer Bulletin Board (No. 1633—$12.95 paper; $19.95 hard)

Using and Programming the Macintosh™, with 32 Ready-to-Run Programs (No. 1840—$12.50 paper; $16.95 hard)

Programming with dBASE II® (No. 1776—$16.50 paper; $26.95 hard)

Making CP/M-80® Work for You (No. 1764—$9.25 paper; $16.95 hard)

Lotus 1-2-3™ Simplified (No. 1748—$10.25 paper; $15.95 hard)

The Last Word on the TI-99/4A (No. 1745—$11.50 paper; $16.95 hard)

101 Programming Surprises & Tricks for Your TRS-80™ Computer (No. 1741—$11.50 paper)

101 Programming Surprises & Tricks for Your ATARI® Computer (No. 1731—$11.50 paper)

How to Document Your Software (No. 1724—$13.50 paper; $19.95 hard)

101 Programming Surprises & Tricks for Your Apple II®/II®e Computer (No. 1721—$11.50 paper)

Scuttle the Computer Pirates: Software Protection Schemes (No. 1718—$15.50 paper; $21.95 hard)

Using & Programming the Commodore 64, including Ready-to-Run Programs (No. 1712—$9.25 paper; $13.95 hard)

Fundamentals of IBM PC® Assembly Language (No. 1710—$15.50 paper; $19.95 hard)

A Kid's First Book to the Timex/Sinclair 2068 (No. 1708—$9.95 paper; $15.95 hard)

Using and Programming the ADAM™, including Ready-to-Run Programs (No. 1706—$7.95 paper; $14.95 hard)

MicroProgrammer's Market 1984 (No. 1700—$13.50 paper; $18.95 hard)

Beginner's Guide to Microprocessors—2nd Edition (No. 1695—$9.95 paper; $14.95 hard)

The Complete Guide to Satellite TV (No. 1685—$11.50 paper; $17.95 hard)

Commodore 64 Graphics and Sound Programming (No. 1640—$15.50 paper; $21.95 hard)

TAB | TAB BOOKS Inc.

Blue Ridge Summit, Pa. 17214

Send for FREE TAB Catalog describing over 750 current titles in print.